The Path to the Greater, Freer, Truer World

New Perspectives on the History of the South

UNIVERSITY PRESS OF FLORIDA

Florida A&M University, Tallahassee
Florida Atlantic University, Boca Raton
Florida Gulf Coast University, Ft. Myers
Florida International University, Miami
Florida State University, Tallahassee
New College of Florida, Sarasota
University of Central Florida, Orlando
University of Florida, Gainesville
University of North Florida, Jacksonville
University of South Florida, Tampa
University of West Florida, Pensacola

THE PATH TO THE
Greater, Freer, Truer World

Southern Civil Rights and Anticolonialism, 1937–1955

LINDSEY R. SWINDALL

University Press of Florida

Gainesville · Tallahassee · Tampa · Boca Raton

Pensacola · Orlando · Miami · Jacksonville · Ft. Myers · Sarasota

W.E.B. Du Bois's speech "Behold the Land" was reprinted with permission from the David Graham Du Bois Trust, Odell Murry, Trustee, 10061 River Side Drive, Suite 747, Toluca Lake, CA 91602-2560.

This book may be available in an electronic edition.

First cloth printing, 2014
First paperback printing, 2019

24 23 22 21 20 19   6 5 4 3 2 1

Library of Congress Cataloging-in-Publication Data
Swindall, Lindsey R., 1977– author.
The path to the greater, freer, truer world : southern civil rights and anticolonialism, 1937–1955 / Lindsey R. Swindall.
pages cm
Includes bibliographical references and index.
ISBN 978-0-8130-4992-2 (cloth)
ISBN 978-0-8130-5634-0 (pbk.)
1. African Americans—History—1877–1964. 2. Council on African Affairs. 3. African American youth—Political activity. 4. Youth movements—Southern States—History. 5. Southern Negro Youth Congress. 6. Southern States—Race relations. 7. Nationalism—Southern States. 8. African Americans—Civil rights—History—20th century. I. Title.
E185.6.S95 2014
323.1196'0730904—dc23
2014003468

The University Press of Florida is the scholarly publishing agency for the State University System of Florida, comprising Florida A&M University, Florida Atlantic University, Florida Gulf Coast University, Florida International University, Florida State University, New College of Florida, University of Central Florida, University of Florida, University of North Florida, University of South Florida, and University of West Florida.

University Press of Florida
2046 NE Waldo Road
Suite 2100
Gainesville, FL 32609
http://upress.ufl.edu

For Winfield

Contents

Figures

Acknowledgments

Many deeply felt thanks to John David Smith, an unswerving supporter from day one, as well as Meredith Morris-Babb and Sian Hunter, who all patiently shepherded this project from inception to publication. I am also grateful to the readers for the University Press of Florida whose insights were thoughtful and detail-oriented while still keeping the scope of the overall narrative in mind. It is toward this kind of careful balance that all historical writing should strive. I feel fortunate to have had guidance from experienced editors and conscientious readers.

I would also like to thank the archivists and librarians who have been helpful, especially Joellen Elbashir at Moorland-Spingarn Research Center and the staff at the Tamiment Library at New York University who are always accommodating. The *Daily Worker/Daily World* newspapers have been remarkably efficient in granting permission to publish images from their vast and fascinating archive. The Estate of W.E.B. Du Bois has also been generous and obliging in granting permission to reprint his speech "Behold the Land."

I appreciate very much the feedback that I have received on pieces of the manuscript that were presented at meetings of the Houston Area Southern Historians and the Southern Labor Studies Association. The History Department at Sam Houston State University has kindly offered both financial support for research and collegial encouragement during the writing process. Many thanks especially to Brian Domitrovic, Ken Hendrickson, Terry Bilhartz, Jeffrey Littlejohn, Nancy Baker, Wesley Phelps, and Bernadette Pruitt. As always, I am thankful to have a strong network of friends and family members who have been constant champions of my work: Marshall and Lisa Swindall, Seth and Edward Foster, Liz Foster,

Jennifer Jensen Wallach, Charles Bittner, Ellen Cantwell, Philip Sinitiere. My life has changed tremendously while writing this book, and I am thankful to say that it is has been a positive journey overall.

Lastly, I hope that this book helps contribute to the important dialogue on the long civil rights movement as scholars and activists continue to uncover new paths for thought and action.

*   *   *

I would like to reaffirm my gratitude to the University Press of Florida as this book transitions from hardcover to paperback. I would also like to offer my humble thanks to all of the activists mentioned in these pages who gave their energy and courage to the ongoing struggle. Reflecting again on W.E.B. Du Bois's insights in the speech "Behold the Land," I can only conclude that we are still finding our way on the path to the greater, freer, truer world. The lesson taught by groups like SNYC and the Council on African Affairs that we, who love truth and justice, should take a long view of the struggle is still vital. We ought to remember, as these activists demonstrated, that the movement for freedom is intergenerational. Most importantly, we have a duty to keep fighting to honor their tenacity.

Sometimes we fight recurrent battles, but we must continue, even when we grow weary, because of their sacrifices. As Du Bois reminds us, happy is the man "who fights in despair and in defeat still fights." The work of the youth congress and the council illustrate the idea that democracy is an ongoing quest, and justice is ever unfolding. There probably will never be a moment when they reach completion, but, rather, the journey is about each generation standing up for these ideals in a way that speaks to their moment in history. This is the work that we are all called to undertake because, in the words of Du Bois, "it would be shame and cowardice to surrender this glorious land and its opportunities for civilization and humanity to the thugs and lynchers, the mobs and profiteers, the monopolists and gamblers who today choke its soul and steal its resources." This land belongs to us, too.

Introduction

In the autumn of 1946, it was not yet clear that coalitions organizing for African American civil and labor rights, which had been built during the Great Depression years and flourished during the war, would soon be under attack. The year 1946 held promise. The Four Freedoms had not been forgotten nor had the Atlantic Charter or the idea of a Double Victory. The opportunity existed to defeat racism and colonialism in the manner that fascism had so recently been overpowered.

Perhaps nowhere was this promise better illustrated than at the national conference held by the Southern Negro Youth Congress (SNYC) that year. "It is written all over the horizon: now or never," Louis Burnham extolled the delegates and attendees in Columbia, South Carolina. He envisioned moving forward with a strong and "truly democratic" organization comprised of "students, labor and civic leaders" who would wage a war against inequality and injustice.[1] The local black newspaper, the *Lighthouse and Informer*, estimated that upwards of five thousand left-wing activists and sympathetic spectators had made their way to the interracial SNYC gathering.[2] The capital of South Carolina, long known as a bastion of segregationism, became for a moment a stronghold for progressivism.

One of the highlights of the three-day conference was undoubtedly the tribute to the venerable W.E.B. Du Bois on Sunday evening. The delegates to the conference, members of the youth congress, and people from the local community honored the doctor who by 1946 had been part of the "principled struggle . . . on behalf of the Negro people of the United States and the unfree peoples of all the world" for nearly a half century.[3] It was the closing session of the meeting, but the chapel at Benedict College held a capacity crowd for the presentation honoring Du Bois and for his speech that followed. Admirers stood in the aisles, and when all the standing places were taken, eager listeners assembled around loudspeakers outside the packed hall. "A hush fell over the audience as youth prepared to express their 'great obligation of reverence and respect'" for "the senior statesman of the American Negro's liberation struggle."[4]

Against the organ notes of "The Battle Hymn of the Republic," a voice artfully recounted Du Bois's birth in "frosty New England," his call to the Talented Tenth and his journey "down from the Ivory Towers" to mingle with the workers of the fields, mines, and factories whom he joined in "the great struggle for Equality."[5] The crowd's excited applause filled the hall when Du Bois received a "book of reverence" that was signed by all of the delegates to the SNYC conference. His speech that night offered an assessment of the economic and social position of black Americans in the South and challenged the youthful generation to oppose the forces of white supremacy. He did so "with the full force of his great intellectual and combative powers" in "language whose grandeur and simplicity explain why Dr. Du Bois is regarded as one of the great literary stylists of our times."[6]

Thanks to the thoughtfully detailed rendering of the ceremony for Du Bois in a pamphlet published by the Southern Negro Youth Congress, readers can envision the proceedings clearly. This was a significant moment for SNYC as a "black-labor-left" alliance that was inaugurated in the 1930s.[7] Having weathered World War II, the youth congress chose this crossroads moment to venerate Du Bois, who was an activist of the previous generation but who embodied the values of their organization. He was a leader among the agitators who founded the National Association for the Advancement of Colored People (NAACP) in the early twentieth century. He was also an esteemed scholar and not only active in the Council on African Affairs but also a father of the Pan-African Congress movement of the early 1900s that had been recently reinvigorated in 1945. Du Bois, thus, represented the activism, theorizing, and internationalism that inspired the generation that founded SNYC.

But the young people of the youth congress, while motivated by the struggles of Du Bois's generation, were also influenced by the specific circumstances of their lives. They came of age during the worst economic crisis in U.S. history, and they had just fought in a global conflagration. Du Bois's speech, then, correlated all of these interrelated elements. He demonstrated how an international worldview was crucial to understanding the economic and political realities of the South, and he bade the young people to look toward the future girded with a long view of their freedom struggle. Du Bois, standing before this body in 1946, represented the past while pointing to a way forward.

Two vital themes undergird Du Bois's vision in the speech that he titled "Behold the Land."[8] First, the idea of conceptualizing the black freedom struggle as a long-term movement formed the backbone of his argument. He emphasized the notion of embarking upon a "great and holy crusade," which did not imply a brief excursion. The speech implored the audience to maintain devotion in the "walk toward a civilization which will be free." The doctor upheld a long view in his critique of South Carolina segregationist James Byrnes, who had recently ascended to the post of Secretary of State to represent the United States on the global stage. Byrnes, Du Bois noted, came from a lengthy lineage of South Carolinians who "looked *truth* in the face and did not see it." Byrnes's intellectual forebears, men like John C. Calhoun, Wade Hampton, and Ben Tillman, had "fought against freedom and democracy in a land which was founded upon Democracy and Freedom."[9] However, Du Bois observed, "eventually this class of men must yield to the writing in the stars." By acknowledging the protracted history of white supremacist thought, and there were few better examples than the South Carolinians he cited, Du Bois elongated the scope of his message. The forces of injustice were entrenched, but they were not invincible. The "writing in the stars," like Martin Luther King Jr.'s much later metaphor of the "arc of the universe," pointed toward justice. While identifying certain victory, Du Bois did not concede that the struggle would be swift. Du Bois closed his remarks by reminding the crowd that "he who fights in despair and in defeat still fights." Perhaps this was not the reassurance that some in the crowd sought. He implied a long-fought battle that included despair and even defeat. Yet, it was the continuation of that struggle toward eventual justice that was invaluable.

Second, Du Bois positioned the South, where he delivered the speech before the youth congress meeting, as a vital gateway to the broader African diaspora. This was a theme to which Du Bois had alluded in previous writing. For example, in the novel *Dark Princess*, published in 1928, the hero Matthew's romance with an Indian princess was fulfilled in the South and the birth of their son symbolized an alliance between "black and brown and yellow" peoples who would act as "a beacon to guide manhood to health and happiness."[10] In 1935 in the pioneering book *Black Reconstruction in America*, Du Bois boldly situated black workers in the South as "the foundation stone not only of the Southern social structure, but of Northern manufacture and commerce, of the English factory system, of European commerce, of buying and selling on a world-wide scale."[11] Southern African Americans, then, were central to a reformist vision that included self-rule for all people around the world as well as the "abolition of the color line and of poverty and war."[12] In the post–World War II world, Du Bois proposed once again that the South was a crucial locus in determining the future of African Americans and colonized people.

Even as African Americans had journeyed northward during the Great Migration and later to secure wartime employment, Du Bois confidently declared in "Behold the Land" that "the future of American Negroes is in the South." He posited that it was in this region that black Americans had "suffered the damnation of slavery, the frustration of reconstruction and the lynching of emancipation." It was, therefore, in this southland that "the battle of a great crusade" would be staged. More important, this was also a "firing line" for the freedom of those across the African diaspora, including the West Indies and the African continent. Du Bois's pioneering book *The World and Africa* also came out in 1946, and in it he argued that Africa was central to any discussion of global history.[13] In a similar way, "Behold the Land" globalized the discussion of the South: as Africa had played a critical part in human history so the U.S. South was central to understanding the history and potential future course of people of African descent.

Before the audience at the SNYC conference, Du Bois ambitiously portrayed a vision of the South that could be an exemplar for the postcolonial diaspora. Out of the upheaval of the war, the land of the South could be rescued from the "fear of mobs" and crooked politicians "who build their deviltry on race prejudice." Instead, a new culture could be constructed that was based on cooperative agriculture and industry that was carried out by unionized workers who made decent wages and could build healthy home lives. The resources of the South, in his view, should not be sacrificed to "thugs and lynchers" but restored to the people. Such a vision provided a "gateway to the colored millions" and could be "the Path to the Greater, Freer, Truer World."

* * *

Taking a cue from Du Bois, as well as a line from his speech, this book will explore the work of two organizations, the Southern Negro Youth Congress (1937–1949) and the Council on African Affairs (1937–1955), which were formed during the late 1930s and were casualties of the post–World War II red scare. Both of these groups employed a global, Pan-African perspective and were created as a consequence of historical circumstances of the thirties. The youth congress was born in response to the impact that the dual crises of economic depression and racial segregation were having on the African American community in the South. The council was formed because of the dearth of current and accurate information about the continent available in the United States, especially in light of the Italian invasion of Ethiopia and the trend toward ruthless discrimination against native black South Africans.

SNYC and the Council on African Affairs were also examples of the coalition-building that took place during the period of the Popular Front, roughly 1935 to 1939, in which the Communist Party in the United States (CPUSA) sought to join forces with liberals, New Dealers and other progressives to organize for civil rights and labor reforms. Leaders in both the council and SNYC were members of or closely affiliated with the CPUSA, but neither organization was started directly by the party nor was the direction of their work dictated by any specific political entity. Though the youth congress and the council did espouse left-wing viewpoints in their publications, both groups maintained a nonpartisan policy. These organizations did critique capitalism and advocate a more equitable distribution of wealth; however, the council was primarily concerned with disseminating information on Africa and lobbying for colonial independence while SNYC focused on organizing against segregation, disfranchisement, violence, and lack of employment opportunities for African Americans.

Why study these particular organizations? The Council on African Affairs and the Southern Negro Youth Congress illustrate well the black-labor-left collaborations of the Depression era as well as the global vision that was conspicuous in the organizing of this time period. These two coalitions also demonstrate the stresses of the postwar era on left-wing groups, as both ended up being casualties of Cold War politics. In addition, while their work has been analyzed within the scope of several vital projects, both of these groups were significant enough to be the focus of more sustained discourse. For example, the Southern Negro Youth Congress has been addressed in books such as Robin Kelley's *Hammer and Hoe*, Glenda Gilmore's *Defying Dixie*, and Erik Gellman's recent *Death Blow to Jim Crow*. These works consider SNYC within the framework of investigating the broader themes of the Communist Party in Alabama, radical activism in the South, and the organizing of the National Negro Congress, which all point to the breadth of the youth congress.[14] Collections that explore the lives of individual activists, like James and Esther Jackson or Jack O'Dell, have helped reveal aspects of the SNYC's work within the context of their singular experiences.[15] Similarly, the work of the Council on African Affairs appears in a number of important historical studies and biographies; however, Hollis Lynch's excellent piece from 1978, though not monograph length, remains one of the only dedicated explorations of this crucial group.[16] These two organizations left behind rich archives that deserve to be fleshed out more completely by scholars and activists.

Though the Council on African Affairs and SNYC are both fascinating in their own right, examining these two groups side-by-side is instructive for a couple of reasons. Looking at both groups more clearly shows the cooperation that occurred between progressive activists who were involved in coalition-building. For example, Du Bois, Paul Robeson, and Max Yergan, who were all leaders in the council, could be depended upon to speak at SNYC events. The youth congress used publications from the council in their leadership training schools. As a representative of the Pan-African Congress (PAC) movement, Du Bois corresponded with SNYC and made sure they were aware of the resolutions passed at the 1945 PAC convention. Examining these two groups concurrently also more effectively demonstrates the intergenerational nature of civil rights and labor organizing from the late 1930s to the early 1950s and into the 1960s. Certainly, the tribute for Du Bois was a meaningful example of the esteem in which these young people held their predecessors. In addition, *Freedomways* journal, founded in 1961, can be viewed as progeny of both the Council on African

Affairs and SNYC because activists from both groups were involved in its inception as it chronicled a vibrant new upsurge in civil rights mobilization.

Finally, assessing the council and the youth congress within a single volume also highlights the way in which the idea of a global South was employed both in the region and in New York City, where the council was headquartered, and it complicates the definition of a southern activist or a southern organization. While SNYC concentrated its activism primarily in the southeastern United States where de jure segregation was manifested most profoundly, the group viewed the region in which they operated as part of a global praxis. Analogously, the council, while spotlighting Africa, rarely failed to include the practice of racial discrimination in the southern United States within its call for self-determination. Freedom for colonized people, in the council's view, meant full civil and economic rights for black Americans in the South as well. Moreover, the stalwarts of the Council on African Affairs, including Paul Robeson, Max Yergan, Eslanda Robeson, and W. Alphaeus Hunton, each had southern roots and/or had experienced a seminal southern encounter that motivated their progressive activism and antiracism. Though they were based in the northern region of the United States geographically, spiritually they knew the sting of southern bigotry. The grim political, economic, and social realities of the former Confederate states were never far from their minds in their work to liberate people of African descent. Without discounting the discrimination in the North, their knowledge of the southern experience connected them with that region, aroused their indignation, and influenced their advocacy.

The Council on African Affairs and the Southern Negro Youth Congress demonstrate well the scope of the theory of a long civil rights movement. The work of both of these groups contributed to the internationalism that was prominent during the phase of the movement that began during the Great Depression, and the disbanding of these organizations lays bare the cleavages that the movement suffered during the early Cold War. This book, then, aims to show that the idea of a global South was inherent to the ideologies of the Council on African Affairs and SNYC while also situating these two groups within the scope of the long civil rights movement. Du Bois, ever prescient, seemed to know in 1946 that the concepts of a global South and a long civil rights movement would be vital to understanding the past and organizing toward the future of black

Americans. Recent scholarship has only begun to parse out these significant ideas.

Positioning the Council on African Affairs and SNYC within the Long Movement Theory

The idea of a "long civil rights movement" has grown out of a body of work by scholars who questioned the adequacy of the narrow framework that limited the black freedom struggle within the parameters of roughly 1954 to 1965, from the *Brown v. Board of Education* decision to the Voting Rights Act. Quoting activist Bayard Rustin, historian Jacqueline Dowd Hall referred to this as the "classical" phase of the movement in her valuable 2005 article "The Long Civil Rights Movement and the Political Uses of the Past."[17] This phase of mass mobilization that utilized direct action nonviolence to shatter de jure segregation and demand civil rights legislation was truly exceptional. For many years, the classical period of the civil rights movement dominated the historical discourse and focused on conveying that narrative through the lens of charismatic male leaders like Martin Luther King Jr. This template has been broadened significantly in recent scholarship that, in the words of Jeanne Theoharris and Komozi Woodard, "takes a long view of the movement and its geographical, temporal, and philosophical complexities, beginning the story in the 1930s and extending well into the 1970s." Such an expanded framework, Theoharris and Woodard explain, enables scholars to "show that the Black Freedom movement was not just Southern, not led only by men, not simply a series of spontaneous urban uprisings, not started in 1955 nor ended in 1965."[18]

While many chronicles of the classical phase of the movement located the origins of that upsurge in the World War II era, researchers now are recognizing that, as Thomas Sugrue has cogently argued, "The period from the Depression through World War II, in particular, cannot be seen solely or primarily as a 'prelude' or 'foreshadowing' of what was to come later. . . . The emergence of interracial coalitions, an emphasis on the intersection of race and class, and the explosion of organized and unorganized protests give this era importance in its own right."[19] The theory of a long movement, then, opens the field for a more expansive dialogue that sheds light on the importance of civil rights mobilization that occurred in the thirties and forties as well as vital themes such as the role of women, the local nature of black freedom campaigns, and the struggles that occurred outside of the South. The long movement theory illuminates a protracted, multifaceted struggle that complicates familiar dichotomies "between North and South, nonviolence and Black power militancy, de facto and de jure segregation, and the movement before 1965 and after."[20] It coaxes the narrative to go beyond the pivotal scene of Martin Luther King Jr. speaking at the Lincoln Monument in the summer of 1963 in order to uncover lesser-known figures and campaigns that can nevertheless help shape and add depth to our common understanding of the political, economic, and social struggles that have emerged from the black experience in the United States.

Critics worry that the potentially sprawling nature of the long movement thesis is too vast in that it "collapses periodization schemas, erases conceptual differences between waves of the BLM [Black Liberation Movement], and blurs regional distinctions in the African American experience."[21] Sundiata Keita Cha-Jua and Clarence Lang also thoughtfully point out the dangers of conflating the distinguishing elements of various phases of civil rights mobilization. They maintain that "Black liberals, nationalists, and radicals have organized against the multiple forms of racial oppression and utilized similar tactics, but that does not mean that their conceptions of 'black freedom' were identical."[22] Such concerns are valid and encourage researchers to designate clear definitions and carefully stipulate ideologies, goals, and tactics within the phases of struggle that are under discussion. If invoked conscientiously, the long movement theory can reveal crucial connections by "tying together stories usually told separately in order to alter common understandings of the black freedom struggle (and how we arrived at the dilemmas of the new millennium)."[23]

This study uses nomenclature such as "civil rights struggle," "movement for black freedom," and "black freedom struggle" to connote the mobilization and lobbying efforts of SNYC and the Council on African Affairs during the 1930s, 1940s, and early 1950s (in the case of the Council on African Affairs). While this examination views SNYC and the council as part of the long movement, the narrative will make a clear distinction when referring to the exceptional period of the civil rights movement, or the classical phase, from the middle 1950s to the middle 1960s. References to the ideas of self-determination and liberation encompass the broad movement across the diaspora for colonial freedom. The ideas of full freedom or full civil rights allude to the vision that SNYC and the council had for people of African descent that included suffrage rights; equal access to housing, education, employment, and other economic opportunities; terminating all forms of segregation and racial violence; and independence for those under colonial rule.

The work of both the Southern Negro Youth Congress and the Council on African Affairs fits comfortably within the chronology of a long movement that Jacqueline Dowd Hall has delineated. With the specific purpose of countering distortions of the classical phase in the civil rights movement that have been posited by the New Right, she proposes an outline of "a more robust, more progressive, and truer story." This account "took root in the liberal and radical milieu of the late 1930s . . . accelerated during World War II, stretched far beyond the South, was continuously and ferociously contested, and in the 1960s and 1970s inspired a 'movement of movements.'"[24] Both the Council on African Affairs and SNYC were founded in 1937 as interracial coalitions that included liberals and radicals from the Communist left. These organizations seized upon Franklin Roosevelt's formulation of the Four Freedoms during World War II to argue for domestic civil rights and colonial independence. Their vocal critique of the shortcomings of American freedom was "ferociously contested" as World War II transitioned into the Cold War and the definition of freedom emphasized loyalty and conformity.

Activists in the council and SNYC were deemed subversive, which led to internal turmoil and external repression. The disbanding of both organizations in the early Cold War also illustrates Dowd Hall's theory of a "long backlash."[25] The push-back against civil rights, she proposes, did not begin with the fierce hostility toward school desegregation in the post-*Brown* years. The retraction of wartime labor gains and, especially, the anticommunist tidal wave that began in the late 1940s wrenched apart many black-labor-left alliances as illustrated by the vicious split in the Council on African Affairs and the unyielding pressure from segregationists motivated by racism and anticommunism that was brought to bear on SNYC in 1948. In severing many of the coalitions that fought for economic rights, civil rights legislation, and colonial freedom, the red scare that followed World War II "structured and limited the ways in which the [classical phase of] the movement was able to express itself and its aims."[26] The phase of the movement from the late 1950s through the 1960s, then, was forced to reframe its demands and embark upon new strategies because of the strictures of the Cold War.

Thus, the trajectories of the youth congress and the council help elucidate the complexities of a long movement that was born during the Great Depression, maintained through World War II, and was ruptured by Cold War pressure. However, SNYC and the council also clearly demonstrate some of the ways in which "pockets of resistance survived" and reconnected later with activists in the 1960s.[27] The activists involved with SNYC and the Council on African Affairs found creative ways to reorganize and conceive of new strategies. *Freedom* newspaper, for instance, was a left-wing newspaper that was a reaction against the skewed reporting of the mainstream press in the early 1950s. After both the council and the youth congress folded, activists from both organizations, along with several newcomers, founded *Freedomways* journal, which illuminated the classical phase of the movement through the pens of a previous generation of activists as well as the student activists of the 1960s and 1970s. These men and women were, to use a phrase of Dayo F. Gore's, "political long-distance runners" in the way that they "carried their ideas, strategies, and lessons from Cold War activism into a variety of political spaces in the 1960s and 1970s."[28] The Cold War had altered the terrain, but many on the left continued to seek and initiate new modes of organizing and outlets for their advocacy. Some may have been fighting in despair, as W.E.B. Du Bois had predicted back in 1946, but, as he also foretold, they were still fighting.

The Council on African Affairs, SNYC, and the Idea of a Global South

Though it was perhaps more readily apparent in the council's work, an international perspective was fundamental to the ideologies of both the Council on African Affairs and the Southern Negro Youth Congress. As historian Robin Kelley has observed, "for over two centuries, black writers and activists defined themselves as part of a larger international black community—'an African diaspora.'"[29] Kelley posits that the question of citizenship rights undermined many African Americans' sense of belonging in the United States and motivated black leaders to seek allies outside of the country.[30] Even though the Fourteenth Amendment, which protected rights of citizenship to all born in the United States, had been ratified during Reconstruction, segregation law undercut elemental freedoms, and disfranchisement obstructed basic civic engagement for African Americans. In addition to the abrogation of citizenship rights, the global vision shared by the Council on African Affairs and SNYC stemmed from three primary considerations that were grounded in the circumstances of the time period in which they functioned.

First, the worldwide turmoil caused by the economic crisis of the 1930s and the concurrent spread of fascism during that decade broadened the outlook of many black activists. Black radicals and intellectuals, especially, made vital linkages between fascism and imperialism since they were "global systems rooted both in capitalist political economy and in racist ideologies."[31] Second, the influence of the Communist Party was probably at its height in the African American community during the Great Depression and particularly during the Popular Front period. The Comintern in Moscow outspokenly indicted U.S. racism and, at their Sixth Congress in 1928, asserted that African Americans represented "an oppressed nation with the right to national self-determination and anointed them the vanguard among colonized nations."[32] Thereafter, the Communist Party in the United States worked to, for example, recruit African American workers into the labor movement and defend the rights of the Scottsboro youths who were dragged into court on rape charges because of racial bias.

The impact of Communist Party organizing in local African American communities in places like New York City and Alabama has been documented by historians, as has the impact that visiting the Soviet Union had on a number of black Americans in the 1930s.[33] Jack O'Dell, a member of SNYC and later a contributor to *Freedomways*, summarized well the appeal of the Communist Party to black activists: "I never met anyone who joined the Communist Party because of Stalin or even because of the Soviet Union. They joined because the communists had an interpretation of racism as being grounded in a system." He further clarified the relevance of contemporary conditions to the attraction of the Communist Party: "The great reality of my generation was segregation, fascism, and colonialism. The communists were on my side in all of those things."[34] Joining the

Communist Party, or participating in campaigns with the party, immediately connected African Americans to an international political network.

And third, the Italian offensive into Ethiopia in 1935 awakened many African Americans to the dangers of the spread of fascism. In recording the coverage of the invasion in African American newspapers, historian James H. Meriwether discerned that "Black Americans turned their attention to Ethiopia on a sustained level unmatched by that accorded any previous event in Africa."[35] The fall of Ethiopia, which had long been a symbol of African sovereignty, encouraged many people of African descent to propose an early critique of the international fascist movement even though isolationist attitudes were still prominent in the United States.

The escalating spread of fascism coupled with the economic crisis of the Depression and the mobilization of the Communist Party against segregation and colonialism, then, helped to expand the international awareness of many African American activists in the 1930s. The founders of the Southern Negro Youth Congress and the Council on African Affairs were certainly moved by these issues, and their work demonstrates the influence of all of these elements. For instance, Edward Strong, who helped initiate the creation of SNYC, was a Communist Party member and an adamant critic of the mushrooming fascist movement. He even traveled to the front of the Spanish Civil War and wrote about his experiences there in order to encourage more African Americans to join the International Brigade to assist the Republicans as fellow antifascists. Max Yergan and Paul and Eslanda Robeson, who were instrumental in establishing the council, traveled to the Soviet Union in the 1930s and were impressed by the country's critiques of racism and colonialism. In the case of Ethiopia versus Italy, Paul Robeson told an interviewer in 1936 that his sympathy was "all with the Ethiopians."[36]

The global perspective of the Council on African Affairs and the Southern Negro Youth Congress was influenced by the Communist Party as well as a Pan-African consciousness. The struggle against racial injustice in all of its forms, including segregation and colonialism, was top priority for black activists. The extent to which they allied with the Communist Party stemmed mainly from the party's antiracist positions and its attempts to organize in black communities and to eliminate white chauvinism in the party. As historian Nell Irvin Painter concludes, probably no one joined the party solely because of the self-determination thesis. Rather, it was the party's "more pragmatic activities that succeeded in attracting ... large numbers of southern blacks during the 1930s."[37] Still, those practical campaigns for goals like unions, jobs, and justice in the court system would probably not have been implemented in the absence of the self-determination thesis.

Asserting that the black belt states in the South, which had sizeable black populations and were epicenters of racial injustice, were the "most poised for leading revolution within the African diaspora" was a powerful rhetorical tool.[38] It positioned the U.S. South not only in a global discourse on revolutionary change but also claimed that the region could be at the vanguard of a movement to overturn colonialism throughout the diaspora. This kind of message paved the way for groups, like the Southern Negro Youth Congress and the Council on African Affairs, that viewed the South as a pivotal region of the African diaspora while also embracing left-wing politics.

While it is undoubtedly a region "born of global forces," scholars have worked to position the South during the rise of American imperialism in the late nineteenth and early twentieth centuries.[39] At that time, the absence of significant land redistribution after the Civil War left a largely agrarian landscape that was worked mainly by landless black farmers whose toil benefitted a tiny white oligarchy. In linking the rise of monopoly capitalism during the Gilded Age with the brutal conquest of the Philippines and the "forcible repression" of African Americans, historian Herbert Aptheker has provocatively argued that "American imperialism and white chauvinism are blood relations."[40] It was this fundamental relationship between imperialism and white supremacy that animated the ideology of the Council on African Affairs and the Southern Negro Youth Congress.

Their organizing and lobbying conceptualized the U.S. South as part of the global diaspora of colonized people because of the subjugation of black Americans, which they viewed as being an heir of Western empire-building. As Europe consolidated its empires across Africa and Asia in the late 1800s, the United States joined the imperial project after the Spanish American War and the acquisition of Spain's former territories. Simultaneously, black Americans in the South were wrested of rights and legally separated by the *Plessy v. Ferguson* ruling. Interestingly, new scholarship has argued that "the American discourse surrounding . . . the 'Philippines problem' encouraged some reformers, government experts, and social scientists to think about the South as a particular manifestation of a broader problem around the globe."[41] Historian Natalie J. Ring maintains that during the early twentieth century, when considering issues like economic development, public health, and agriculture, many reformers "linked the uplift of the U.S. South to the uplift of its colonial possessions abroad."[42] Thus, the idea of a global U.S. South that was conceptualized within the context of Western imperialism was not unique to the Council on African Affairs or SNYC when they appeared in 1937. These two groups drew from existing discourses to frame their international perspectives and reformist objectives.

*   *   *

This examination of the Southern Negro Youth Congress and the Council on African Affairs unfolds in the following four chapters. Chapter 1 discusses the origins of each organization separately but within the scope of contemporary issues including the Great Depression, the international spread of fascism, the organizing of the Communist Party in the United States, and the global network of people from the African diaspora located in London. The section on the Southern Negro Youth Congress considers its creation along with that of the National Negro Congress. Tracing its early conferences and campaigns, this portion of the chapter charts the activity of SNYC from its inception to 1941 while paying special attention to the strategies and political, social, and cultural goals of the group. The part of the chapter focusing on the council concentrates on the creation of the group and on assessing its earliest publications, since it was not a mass organization but rather aimed to disseminate information. The special rapport between the council and activists in South Africa is established as is the affiliation between the group's leaders and the region of the U.S. South.

Chapter 2 illuminates the trajectory of both groups through World War II. Using the framework of Franklin Roosevelt's Four Freedoms speech and the Atlantic Charter, the chapter explains how these public documents shaped the discourse on freedom during the war and shows the ways in which SNYC and the Council on African Affairs adapted these ideas as models to argue for citizenship rights and colonial independence. This chapter demonstrates the wide appeal that both groups enjoyed while antifascism was broadly embraced and the Soviet Union was a U.S. ally. The vital role that women played in both groups is also underscored in this section.

An analysis of the Freedom Train exhibit that traveled throughout the country in the immediate postwar years opens chapter 3. The documents that publicly portrayed the idea of freedom in the exhibition are explored as a metaphor for the transitioning definition of freedom after World War II as the Cold War began to grip the American political scene. While SNYC and the Council on African Affairs were still engaging the Atlantic Charter and the Four Freedoms as the basis for progressive reforms, the onset of anticommunism constricted the notion of freedom. The chapter shows how the council's efforts to lobby the United Nations for African self-determination were stalled, and a bitter internal feud ruptured the organization. Meanwhile, SNYC encountered a host of impediments from segregationist agitators. Racism camouflaged as anticommunism created a repressive climate in the South and forced SNYC to disband. The legacy of the group, however, continued through later initiatives like *Freedom* newspaper and *Freedomways* journal.

Finally, chapter 4 considers consequences of the Cold War climate while tracing the decline of the council during the early 1950s. By this time, the group had lost members, could no longer host events in public venues like Madison Square Garden, and had to defend itself against the government's subversive classification. Council leaders Paul Robeson, W.E.B. Du Bois, and Alphaeus Hunton grappled with travel restrictions, an indictment, and even a prison term because of their political activities. Even through this taxing period, the council produced its newsletter and praised the non-alignment conference in Bandung, Indonesia. Yet, court subpoenas and financial hardship eventually closed the doors of the council's offices permanently. This chapter points out that the council's work filled an important gap in the history of the Pan-African Congress movement and maintains that the group's advocacy set a vital precedent for subsequent organizations like TransAfrica.

This chapter also maintains that *Freedom* newspaper was a consequence of the Cold War. As the mainstream press adopted an anticommunist outlook, long-distance political runners from SNYC and the council formed

Freedom to advance a progressive viewpoint during some of the most suppressive years of the early Cold War. The short-lived newspaper offered an alternative vision of freedom that countered Cold War loyalty and conformity with calls for freedom from Jim Crow and freedom for colonized people. Though *Freedom* only lasted a few years, many of its contributors regrouped and founded *Freedomways* journal in 1961 to carry on their participation in the long civil rights movement and chronicle the endeavors of those new student-activists who were making the struggle their own.

1

Origins

Sometime in the early summer of 1941 a letter arrived at the headquarters of the Southern Negro Youth Congress (SNYC) in the Masonic Temple Building in Birmingham, Alabama. It was "painfully" written in pencil on a plain sheet of paper torn from a notebook by fingers "evidently unused to handling a pencil or pen." The plainspoken but heartfelt letter announced in unadorned language a mother's profound relief: "I am glad to say that my poor child is free." This simple pronouncement from the parent of Nora Wilson belied what had surely been an agonizing months-long clash with bigoted authorities in the rural southland.[1] Echoing the injustice meted out toward nine young black men in Scottsboro, Nora Wilson's ordeal illustrated well the lengths to which those enforcing racial discrimination and economic peonage were willing to go in order to maintain their white supremacist system. However, Wilson's clash with the law also exemplified unity within a small black community, due to their effort to see her freed, as well as determination among a group of young progressive activists.

Eighteen-year-old Nora Wilson lived with her family, including six younger siblings, in the small hamlet of Millbrook, Alabama. She had to leave school to help support the family when her father fell ill with malaria. Reporting in *Cavalcade*, the newspaper of the SNYC, Augusta Jackson adroitly evoked the countryside in which Wilson's sharecropping kin eked out a living. In the one-train-stop town, a couple of paved blocks, a cotton warehouse (which pointed to the primary economic endeavor of the inhabitants), and a handful of stores were the sole indications of civilization before "the red dust of the country roads begins to strangle and choke" any soul passing through the region. A visitor would undoubtedly have the unsettling feeling that this was a place "that the twentieth century had not yet reached." Virtually untouched by the postwar reforms of the Reconstruction era, Wilson, like all black sharecroppers, knew that the relationship between white landowners and black farmers in Elmore County had hardly changed since the mid-nineteenth century. Such circumstances would have been familiar to the millions of African Americans who struggled each day in the fields of the black belt, stretching from tobacco country in Virginia and the Carolinas down through the cotton lands of the deep South.

It was in this environment that Nora Wilson had the audacity to approach a white employer one day to find out why her younger sister was being accused of stealing six ears of corn. Wilson's intuition probably told her that there had been some mistake or that there was at least an explanation for the situation. Yet, her verbal protest to the wife of the property owner landed Wilson in the Wetumpka Women's Prison where she faced charges of assault with intent to kill, even though it had been the housewife who had slapped Nora. The reaction of the wife revealed with startling clarity the racist mindset of the class that owned most of the farmland and jealously guarded the political power of the region: "My husband got his gun to kill her, but I wouldn't let him, and I had her put in jail. . . . I can't imagine why she would dare to talk to me like that. Isn't it awful for a white lady to have to take that?"[2] Above and beyond the issue of the missing corn lurked Wilson's impudence in addressing this housewife on equal terms. Such behavior was rigorously outlawed in the strict segregation system that functioned in place of enslavement.

Even though the offended housewife had requested that the charges be dropped, Wilson languished in prison having been sentenced to hard labor for eight and a half months on the charge of abusive language. As a writer in *Cavalcade* keenly and heartbreakingly observed, "Nora was a poor unknown Negro girl in the heart of the Black Belt where the careless blotting out of a Negro life scarcely merits a line of print in the papers."[3] Frightened for her daughter, and not knowing where to turn for assistance, Nora Wilson's enterprising mother accosted the members of the Caravan Puppeteers who had stopped nearby on a southern tour. The puppeteers were a fledgling progressive group of entertainers who attempted to enlighten communities on political issues like voting rights. Fortunately, Mrs. Wilson had stumbled upon a group who would indeed help. Once the activists in the troupe informed the Southern Negro Youth Congress of Wilson's plight, a field representative was dispatched to investigate the situation.

Wilson's case was then publicized by SNYC. Public consciousness, along with money to help with legal services, was raised at mass meetings and through leafleting. Wilson was visited in jail, and telegrams on her behalf were dispatched to the solicitor and the governor.[4] Evoking the widespread outcry fomented by the International Labor Defense (ILD) and the National Association for the Advancement of Colored People (NAACP) against the wrongful imprisonment of the young men accused of rape, a supervisor at the women's prison concluded bluntly, "This is a nigger case and we don't like publicity on these things." He further queried the young people who came to Wilson's defense, "Have you any connection with the Scottsboro case—this case gave us a lot of bad publicity."[5] In his concern over bad press for a legal system that upheld gross injustices against black citizens, this prison authority unwittingly made a cogent connection in comparing the actions of SNYC in the Nora Wilson case to those of the ILD and the NAACP in the Scottsboro cases.

Like the ILD, SNYC had ties to the Communist Party, which partly informed the internationalist perspective of the youth congress. Like the NAACP, the young activists were an interracial group motivated to work against injustice on issues such as lynching, disfranchisement, and segregation. Despite these similarities, the SNYC had its own unique, nonpartisan character that was born out of the Depression and shaped by the energy of the young people who refused to sit by idly while their community faced daily assaults on their dignity and economic wellbeing. Perhaps the most important result of the Nora Wilson case was the establishment of a Southern Negro Youth Congress local council in the town of Millbrook. As activist Jack O'Dell has discerned, every period in which the black freedom movement made significant gains included young people as an "organized component" of the struggle.[6] In the late 1930s through the 1940s, the Southern Negro Youth Congress was a forerunner in the black freedom movement. SNYC developed an international vision that conceptualized the oppression of African Americans in the U.S. South as part of a broader struggle for liberation throughout the African diaspora. Yet, they also stood ready and willing to aid individuals like Nora Wilson when the group received a call for assistance.

"Freedom, Equality, Opportunity": The Genesis of the Southern Negro Youth Congress

Economic conditions for southern African Americans in the late 1930s were dire. Despite President Roosevelt's ardent attempts to stabilize the national economy through his New Deal programs, the lives of many black Americans remained virtually untouched by relief efforts. As groundbreaking as it was, the specific issues facing African Americans were frequently overlooked by FDR's sweeping legislation. For instance, aid to farmers tended to ameliorate the problems of landowners rather than tenants, and few blacks owned much land in the South. Neither domestic workers nor sharecroppers—occupations predominated by black and immigrant workers—were eligible for aid under the landmark Social Security Act of 1935. Job creation programs, like the Civilian Conservation Corps, were often implemented at the state level and, thus, vulnerable to the whims of segregationist bureaucrats.

An editorial from the *Southern Workman*, out of Hampton, Virginia, declared early in 1936 that "there is no problem today of graver import to the colored people than that of finding employment." During times of crisis, the black worker was the last to be hired as "hosts of colored people . . . are anxious to work . . . [but] must wait far into the period of desperation until the majority of other workers have been employed."[7] Citing causes including lack of access to quality education, lack of opportunities to purchase land, and lack of mobility, a report from the Works Progress Administration in 1937 pointed out that "the problems of the Negro cotton grower are unquestionably more vexing than those of his white neighbor."[8] A series of articles in the *Journal of Negro Education* in 1936 outlined the severity of the African American economic plight during the Great Depression. These included the discriminatory practices carried out under the National Recovery Act and the prejudice in many labor unions that problematized the organizing of black workers. All of the contributors, including intellectuals, trade union organizers, Communists, and Socialists, agreed that some kind of mobilization in the black community was essential to combat this acute situation. John P. Davis concluded, "If it be said that these are problems which time alone can solve, then our answer must be that it is time we begin to seek a solution."[9]

In fact, Davis had been at the center of a movement that sought to bring together black people around the country into a united front against racial violence, discrimination, and the current economic crisis. Davis had organized the Joint Committee on Recovery in 1933 to monitor legislation and advocate for African American rights as policy was being crafted in Washington, D.C. Frustrated that efforts had met with little success, Davis, along with Ralph Bunche, a professor in the Political Science Department at Howard University, called a group of black leaders to a conference at Howard in May 1935. At this conference it was agreed that a National Negro Congress, or a federation of black organizations, was necessary to work in the national interests of black people.[10]

The congress was convened in February 1936 in Chicago with leaders from a broad range of African American organizations including churches, fraternal societies, trade unions, and political parties. Over eight hundred delegates braved the midwestern winter to participate in the general sessions at the Eighth Regiment Armory. The discussions on the conditions and struggles facing black people produced several basic demands. These included the right to jobs, relief and security as well as aid to black farmers, an end to lynching, access to the vote, equal educational opportunities, and gender equality for black women.[11] The import of world events was not lost on the men and women at the congress who also voted to oppose war and fascism, particularly the recent Italian invasion of Ethiopia. Historian Lawrence Wittner observed that the "heterogeneity" of the resolutions passed demonstrated that "the purpose of a National Negro Congress was not to promote a specific program or ideology, but to develop a united movement for racial progress."[12]

Rousing speeches by Max Yergan, who had served the YMCA in Africa, and A. Philip Randolph, founder of the Brotherhood of Sleeping Car Porters, punctuated the proceedings. The crowd enthusiastically embraced Angelo Herndon, a young organizer for the Communist Party recently liberated from a Georgia prison sentence, and called for support for the Scottsboro youths against wrongful imprisonment. While Herndon represented a new generation of black leadership, historical precedents were not forgotten. The congress was convened on the anniversary of the birth of Frederick Douglass, and the sessions were called to order with a gavel fashioned out of the hull of the last ship that transported enslaved Africans across the Atlantic. When it was decided that a national office be established to coordinate local councils of the congress, John P. Davis was elected executive secretary and A. Philip Randolph was elected president of the newly formed coalition. In summarizing the goals of this new project, Randolph commented that the movement represented a "united front against Fascism and the repression of the rights of Negroes."[13]

The history of the National Negro Congress (NNC) from its inception in 1936 to its dissolution in 1947 reflected a complex and vacillating political climate through the Great Depression, World War II, and the early Cold War. The congress was beset at times by internal acrimony, erratic political alliances, and accusations of being merely a front for the Communist Party. Its varied legacy, however, did include a torrent of organizing in the South. A bright young activist at the initial National Negro Congress meeting named Edward E. Strong, who was originally from Texas but had lived in the North as well, agreed to serve as chairman of the youth councils of the NNC. He probably noticed that most of the delegates to the Chicago congress in 1936 represented black people in northern cities and centers of industry. Strong worked to imbue the specific needs of African Americans in the South with the energy of a youth movement in issuing a call for the establishment of a Southern Negro Youth Congress.

The idea for a southern youth congress arose naturally from the upsurge in activism by young people not only in the United States but also around the world during the 1930s. The economic crisis was not confined to the United States and concern about the worldwide spread of fascism, exemplified in the invasion of Ethiopia and the civil war in Spain as well as Hitler's rise to power, motivated young people to action. In his book *When the Old Left Was Young*, historian Robert Cohen reflects on this phenomenon when he posits that the "student rebels of the Depression era rank among the most effective radical organizers in the history of American student politics." Moreover, these students harnessed the "crisis atmosphere of their time" by "fanning their classmates' egalitarian idealism and revulsion for war and fascism."[14] Two of the largest and most influential of the student protest groups at this time were the American Student Union (ASU) and the American Youth Congress (AYC). These organizations mobilized college-aged citizens for progressive social change by pushing their largely privileged, middle-class cohort to acknowledge the plight of the working class and encouraging greater racial egalitarianism. These young people also scrutinized U.S. foreign policy and world events carefully, knowing that it would be their generation called to fight if war ensued. Several of the young people who became core leaders of SNYC, including Strong and James Jackson, were also involved with these national groups. Louis Burnham, a central figure in SNYC, helped establish chapters of the ASU on several black college campuses in the South.[15]

The student movement, then, as Cohen points out, helped serve as a training ground for leaders of the SNYC. While activists such as Strong, Burnham, and Jackson shared a commitment to social justice issues with the broader national student movement, groups like the ASU and the AYC had not enjoyed much success organizing black southern youths. It was the SNYC, with its focus on civil rights as well as economic issues plaguing both young people and the larger black community, that mobilized many young African Americans. The Southern Negro Youth Congress was unique in the history of the student campaigns of the era in another important area. While SNYC was led by young people, it organized among entire communities. This was not a group that was confined to the expected locus of youthful organizing: the college campus.[16] Thus, SNYC exemplified the spirit of the nationwide student mobilizing of the late 1930s and early 1940s but it also broadened its base of supporters in an uncommonly successful manner.

The national youth protest groups like the ASU and AYC were not the only bands of young people on the move during the Depression era. The National Association for the Advancement of Colored People (NAACP), which was founded in 1909, was a prominent voice for black civil rights by the 1930s. Several articles in the organ of the NAACP, *Crisis*, noticed that students were awakening to national and world issues. One of these pieces observed small pockets of black student protest percolating around the country throughout the decade and concluded that "a broad powerful mass student movement" was possibly on the horizon.[17] Not to be left out of this trend, the NAACP established its own youth council in the mid-1930s. The extensive influence of the nation's largest civil rights organization was demonstrated when it had established over one hundred youth councils and college chapters by 1938.[18]

The NAACP youth groups, however, were firmly molded in the image of the parent organization. NAACP leader Walter White took care in reminding members that the youth councils should work in harmony with the senior branches "as one unit in the community." Additionally, NAACP branch executive committees were encouraged to invite a representative from the youth council to their meetings.[19] The more radical SNYC, in comparison, was not confined in such a way. Though it had been initiated through the National Negro Congress coalition, SNYC was a self-governing body with its own leadership. It did have an adult advisory council that provided advice and guidance but, as Strong asserted immediately after its founding, SNYC was only "fraternally associated" with the youth councils of the NNC. He explained that SNYC was an "autonomous youth federation."[20]

A global perspective was intrinsic to SNYC's genesis. The group's solidarity with youth around the world, James Jackson recalls, was a "hallmark" of SNYC that distinguished it from other youth organizations. This was a vital connection because, he explains, the "bonds of world solidarity reinforced [the] will of youth in the South."[21] The youth congress's global outlook was informed by the magnitude of current world events as well as the internationalist worldview of many of the congress's leaders. Strong, for instance, had traveled to the World Youth Congress in Geneva in the summer of 1936. That same summer a military uprising by right-wing nationalists challenged the newly elected Republican government in Spain. The conflict in Spain was an early indicator that fascist forces were on the move in Europe. Strong was one of many concerned progressives to visit the war-torn nation. In an insightful article published in the *Crisis* magazine, he forthrightly maintained that there was, contrary to most reports, not a civil war raging in Spain. The conflagration was, in his view, "tantamount to a foreign invasion . . . under the leadership of international fascism."[22]

Strong deftly appealed to the interests of people of color in his argument. In pushing for antifascist support, he pointed out that Spanish Republicans had backed Angelo Herndon and held mass meetings for the Scottsboro youths. A victory for fascism in Spain could threaten democracy in France and advance Italy's consolidation of the Mediterranean as well as their incursion into Ethiopia. Additionally, the extension of fascist doctrines would be particularly devastating, Strong observed, to "dark people" of the colonial and semicolonial territories around the world, who would be increasingly targeted by Nazi-like race-hating ideologies. As illustrated by Strong's perceptive contextualization of the war in Spain, people from subjugated groups, such as African Americans, were some of the first to discern the potential threat of the international proliferation of fascist ideologies.

Edward Strong's analysis of world events was also partially informed by his membership in the U.S. Communist Party (CPUSA). In order to situate the founding of the Southern Negro Youth Congress both philosophically and politically, it is helpful to take a look at its relationship to the Communist Party in the United States. The origins of the CPUSA go back to 1919; however, the group of nascent radicals was forced underground almost immediately due to the antiradical purges, like the Palmer raids, that occurred in the wake of World War I. By the 1930s, the party was growing. The stock market crash and the extent of the economic crisis was convincing more people that capitalism was a deeply flawed, perhaps even broken, system. In addition to their focus on trade unionism, the Communist Party was the most mobilized political party with regard to civil rights issues in the United States during the Great Depression, especially during the Popular Front period of 1935–1939.

Though African Americans had historically been loyal to the party of Abraham Lincoln, the largely pro-business, laissez-faire outlook of the Republican Party was clearly out of touch with the severity of the economic crisis. The Democrats were managing to extricate scores of black voters from the Republicans for a variety of reasons: Franklin Roosevelt's personal charm, his wife's attention to progressive causes, the appointment of Mary McLeod Bethune to the National Youth Administration, and the promise of change through the massive legislative overhaul of the New Deal. Still, the assurance of jobs and social security had generally failed to materialize for African Americans, who were often marginalized in the reforms of the era. Roosevelt, moreover, refused to take a firm stand against lynching and racial segregation for fear of alienating the southern wing of his party, whose congressional votes he needed in support of his foreign and domestic agendas. While it was a better alternative than the Republicans, the Democratic platform was ultimately unsatisfying to Roosevelt's critics from the left.

In contrast, Communists, especially at the local level, were willing to speak out against lynching, racial segregation, and colonialism. They were also working to organize black workers into labor unions, particularly after the formation of the Congress of Industrial Organizations (CIO) in the mid-1930s.[23] The Communist Party in the United States had attempted to theorize an organizing strategy around the question of African Americans as an oppressed minority. They had also, with varying degrees of success, endeavored to ameliorate racial chauvinism within their own organization. Nonetheless, blacks were divided over the issue of allying with the CPUSA. Some were hesitant because dictates from Moscow could take precedent over attention to issues facing African Americans. But the severity of the economic downturn along with continued discrimination and racial violence aroused some, like newspaper editor Carl Murphy, to conclude that "since the abolitionists . . . no white group . . . has openly advocated the economic, political and social equality of black folks." Thus, the Communists "appear to be the only party going our way."[24]

The question of the Communist Party manipulating black citizens in exchange for their support loomed in the minds of those who were unsure whether the group was trustworthy. Historian Nell Irvin Painter acutely sums, "the CP unquestionably used Negroes, as have the Democrats and Republicans over the years. What is important here is that blacks . . . were able to use the Communist Party in their turn."[25] The Communist Party offered, for instance, education on political issues and organizing tactics, an international apparatus from which to advocate issues important to black people, the backing of local affiliates, and national publications to raise consciousness on the violence and economic distress in the South. All of these instruments were used by radical black activists and fostered the push for civil and human rights on the national and world stage. The Communist Party, for example, helped provide legal aid for the Scottsboro defendants, organized rent strikes in Harlem, and tried to unionize sharecroppers in Alabama. Whether the group was doing so with the ultimate objective of securing support for the future revolution can be debated.

However, whatever their motivations might have been, the Communist Party was mobilizing around issues that were important to black activists, and some would take advantage of this opportunity.

Because the group affiliated with members of the Communist Party, a few critics of the Southern Negro Youth Congress have discounted the organization as having mindlessly followed party dictates.[26] However, Hosea Hudson, a Communist Party leader from Birmingham, Alabama, objected to the idea that SNYC was a tool for the party, since most of the members of the youth congress were not Communists.[27] Junius Scales, a white southerner and onetime vice president of SNYC, hints at Communist dominance of the group but also asserts in his memoir that the youth congress enjoyed "a genuine mass base among Negro students and workers."[28] Glenda Gilmore notes in her recent book on white southern activists that the party took credit for the SNYC.[29] Yet, in his study of black Americans and the Communist Party, historian Wilson Record stipulates that the group was not simply a front for the party. He draws a more nuanced picture of the youth congress: while party members were in positions of leadership, they did not control the resolutions passed at the annual national conferences where SNYC members from across the ideological and religious spectrum debated issues and voted on resolutions.[30]

Additionally, in her dissertation on SNYC, Johnetta Richards finds no evidence that the SNYC received funding directly from the Communist Party.[31] According to budgets prepared in annual grant applications, the primary sources of financial support for SNYC were grants from foundations, individual contributions, union contributions, annual conferences, and membership and charter fees.[32] The Communist Party could have indirectly funded SNYC through union contributions; however, the majority of the support for SNYC seems to have come from grants. The Robert Marshall Foundation, for example, was an important source of funding from 1942 to 1948. This fund was endowed through Robert Marshall's estate with wealth he had inherited, but it was managed by his brother George Marshall, an activist who worked with left-leaning groups including the National Federation for Constitutional Liberties and the Civil Rights Congress.[33] Overall, the Southern Negro Youth Congress, like many Popular Front coalitions, had members who were affiliated with the Communist Party, but they were not the only voices who decided the group's agenda.[34]

As was the case in the national student protest movement, many of the key leaders of SNYC were members of or close to the Communist Party. But SNYC was by no means a single-minded group. Edward Strong characterized the youth congress soon after its inception as comprising "different religious opinions" as well as political viewpoints "from the conservative right to the progressive left."[35] A retrospective article in *Freedomways* similarly stressed that "SNYC was both non-partisan and non-sectarian."[36] Moreover, local councils were formed by constituents from their communities, and the programs of these councils were determined individually based on the needs and resources of those communities.[37] The self-direction of the local councils was corroborated in the range of activities reported through their correspondence to the national leadership of the SNYC.[38] Finally, article 2, section 1, of the SNYC constitution clearly stated that the object of the organization was to unite black youths regardless of religion, creed, sex, nationality, or political affiliation as well as young white people who opposed oppression and disfranchisement and adults who sympathized with the struggles of the emerging generation.[39] SNYC's founding document, then, did not discriminate on the basis of political ideology, race, or age even though it maintained an African American youth-oriented moniker.

Despite its grassroots composition, the presence of Communist Party members coupled with the progressive goals of SNYC regarding issues such as segregation, voting, and lynching ultimately made the group vulnerable to red-baiting tactics in the early Cold War. The youth congress was, therefore, born out of the predicament of the economic depression to focus on civil rights and labor rights for African Americans. The group illustrated two of the reformist phenomena of the era, including youth activism and the organizing of the Communist Party, though SNYC was not directly administered by the party. Awareness of global events fostered the group's perspective on colonial freedom and curbing the spread of fascism.

A Black-Labor-Left Coalition: SNYC, 1937–1941

Frederick Douglass, best remembered as an eloquent abolitionist and a father of the nineteenth-century black freedom movement, worked on the docks in Maryland as a young man. He knew enslavement and tasted freedom when he escaped from bondage and became a trans-Atlantic advocate of the antislavery cause. Yet, he had also been a dockworker on Baltimore's harbor in his early years. As a militant activist as well as a working man, Douglass was an excellent representative of the spirit of the first congress of black southern youth. SNYC honored Douglass by calling the congress to meet on the anniversary of his birth in February 1937. Enthusiasm flowed from the pen of journalist and activist Claudia Jones, who implored young workers who might be hoeing in the fields for no wages to heed the approaching emancipation of black youth by taking part in this conference.[40] Over five hundred delegates responded to the call from the youth council of the National Negro Congress. By all accounts, it was a diverse crowd—including students, domestic workers, sharecroppers, church representatives, writers, coal miners, and school teachers—that gathered in the former confederate capital of Richmond, Virginia. These men and women traveled from across the South, from Texas to West Virginia, represented a number of religious backgrounds, and came from a range of age groups, though most attendees were in their twenties. Significantly, the group was interracial, as reaching out to like-minded whites of the Depression generation was a core value of SNYC. This was a generation facing both economic hardship and the possibility of world war. It was, in James Jackson's words, "a generation that conceived of itself as the hope of its people."[41]

Among the lively throng was a youthful James Farmer, who later became an important leader in the Congress of Racial Equality (CORE) and organizer of the Freedom Ride campaign in 1961. In his memoir Farmer recalls borrowing his father's car for the long, dusty road trip from Texas through the Deep South with two colleagues. In a moving recollection, Farmer recounts the indignities of Jim Crow segregation they encountered on their journey. Refused lodging or restaurant service for the two-day trek, the three young men slept in the car and subsisted on hastily prepared bologna sandwiches before arriving at the conference "overcome with fatigue."[42] Many of those who responded to the call had certainly gone through similar ordeals to convene in Richmond and were hoping to curtail the daily humiliations of the segregation system.

Support for the youth congress came from many camps, which underscored the multiplicity of viewpoints held by the delegates. Greetings to the conference were sent from groups including the National Youth Administration, the NAACP youth council, and the League of Young Republicans, in addition to several trade unions and religious organizations. The speaker's list read like a broadside of noteworthy leaders in the black community: E. Franklin Frazier of the Sociology Department at Howard University, Max Yergan from the Young Men's Christian Association, A. Philip Randolph, who was founder of one of the first black trade unions in the country, John P. Davis of the NNC, and Mordecai Johnson, who was president of Howard University. Edward Strong's speech highlighted the reasons for gathering. At the forefront of the concerns cited was the right to equal employment opportunities and equal pay when employed. Another chief issue was political expression and the fact that this generation was coming of age in the South without the right to vote. Finally, he stressed the crises of mob violence and miscarriages of justice. "But we say that unity in action is the road to progress," proclaimed Strong. He closed, "We have met for freedom, equality, and opportunity."[43] Those last three concepts, taken together, became a motto of the youth congress, and Strong was elected executive secretary of SNYC by those assembled.

Mordecai Johnson's keynote address was fervently received. Johnson counseled the young generation as it took on the fight against injustice. Johnson's honed oratory had James Farmer "laughing and weeping, and determined to go out and slay whatever dragons remained alive."[44] The president of Howard cautioned the audience that "the danger to the South does not come from Socialism or Communism, but from those forces who wish to enrich the few at the expense of the many."[45] These words turned out to be rather prescient as the congress formed that weekend in February stood strong against injustice for over a decade until political freedoms were curbed by anticommunism during the Cold War, leading to the dissolution of SNYC.

Discussions at the 1937 congress on jobs, inadequate education, disfranchisement, crime, segregation, and peace led to the passing of numerous resolutions. National officers, who comprised the executive board, were elected, and a field representative set out to tour the South and encourage the establishment of local councils. It was further decided that an annual conference of delegates from local councils would act as the governing body for SNYC and an adult advisory committee would offer advice and support. Those in attendance settled on the priorities around which the group would mobilize: unionization of African Americans in the South, particularly agricultural, domestic, and industrial workers; support for the Scottsboro youths and Angelo Herndon; and condemnation of the spread of fascism coupled with maintenance of peace.[46] Thus, it was not surprising that the first major campaign of SNYC was to help unionize tobacco workers in the Richmond area. These resolutions highlighted the group's commitment to labor rights and the struggle against wrongful imprisonment. By early 1937, war still raged in Spain, Addis Ababa had fallen to the Italians, and Germany had signed a pact of cooperation with Italy. SNYC's denunciation of worldwide fascism and their continued concern for the survival of Ethiopia as an independent African state underscored their internationalist perspective.

During the congress's first year of existence, more than twenty local SNYC councils were founded. Before its dissolution in the late 1940s, over one hundred local councils had been operational. According to a SNYC manual, at least fifteen dues-paying members with elected officers must be assembled in order to apply for a charter as a local council.[47] These local groups organized around the prevailing issues in their communities as well as resolutions adopted at the national SNYC meeting with guidance from the national leadership. In tobacco country, some of the most profound issues facing the black community dealt with workers' rights. There had been few attempts to organize black tobacco workers in Virginia until 1937–1938 when the workers were assisted by two young activists affiliated with SNYC: James Jackson and Christopher Columbus Alston. Black workers there had a long, distressing relationship with the tobacco industry. In the early nineteenth century, enslaved people had worked the fields. After the Civil War higher-paying cigarette manufacturing jobs went mostly to white workers. African American workers, who were the descendants of slaves, were relegated to tobacco stemming, which was the lowest paying and most arduous labor. To add insult to injury, stemming was seasonal so many workers had to toil at multiple jobs. While independent stemmeries employed tens of thousands of workers, they were exempt from paying minimum wages.[48] That was, until the late 1930s.

The Tobacco Workers International Union (affiliated with the American Federation of Labor or AFL) had been established in the late nineteenth century but had not put much energy into recruiting black workers. The strict segregation in job assignments made interracial organizing especially difficult and the AFL, generally speaking, had not been welcoming to black workers. Historically, the AFL had concentrated on organizing skilled workers and those in craft guilds. Women, immigrant, and African American workers were largely overlooked by the union, which was mostly comprised of white male members. However, in the middle 1930s, the AFL faced competition from the CIO. The Congress of Industrial Organizations operated on a broader mandate that aimed to organize workers across racial lines. Having heard the CIO's message to organize all workers, black and white, tobacco stemmers in Virginia undertook an unprecedented and spontaneous strike. Following their walkout, the workers looked for guidance and found the SNYC activists willing to assist the movement. Jackson and Alston helped the workers proceed through negotiations with management, which led to the implementation of an eight-hour work day, increased wages, and recognition of representatives at the bargaining table.

The strike set off a wave of protest throughout the tobacco factories and ultimately led to the establishment of seven unions in the Richmond area. The strikes were the first in the local tobacco industry since 1905 and represented the first strike of any kind in Richmond for fifteen years. Where workers had been languishing for nine to fourteen hours a day, they now left the plant after working eight-hour shifts. It was estimated that around $300,000 in purchasing power was added to the stemmers' community as a result of the strikes. Just as notable was the fact that the workers were capably aided by activists not more than twenty-three years old.[49] The movement among the tobacco workers also inspired other laborers in the broader region such as teachers, fishermen, oyster harvesters, and peanut workers to begin trying to organize.[50]

The unionization of the tobacco stemmers was a victory for the black community in Richmond and an excellent example of a progressive labor coalition fostered by SNYC. The black laborers were motivated by their dreadful wages and working conditions as well as the CIO's movement to organize southern industrial workers. Whereas unionizing had previously been scant in the tobacco industry and dismissive toward African Americans, a new commitment to interracial organizing was perceived by the workers. The symbiosis of awakened black workers, a broad CIO organizing campaign, and the availability of SNYC activists to aid the workers fused beautifully in this situation. James Jackson, a member of the Communist Party, soon left behind his training as a pharmacist and took to full-time activism. His reputation grew in his hometown of Richmond, and he became a leader in SNYC. The tobacco workers' campaign also elevated the status of SNYC in the eyes of the local community. The group now had tangible evidence that it was capable of successfully acting on its resolutions.

The momentum established within its first year carried into SNYC's second conference in Chattanooga, Tennessee, in the spring of 1938. Over three hundred delegates, including fifty white delegates, represented communities from across the South. The assembled group was almost exactly half men and half women who were mostly between the ages of eighteen to twenty-five. They were sent by a variety of religious, civic, and student organizations.[51] Among those present was a young teacher who conducted classes seasonally in a one-room schoolhouse that contained precious few textbooks. Because her meager twenty-five-dollar-a-month salary was based on a quota of pupils, the young woman was compelled to walk miles from farm to farm in all kinds of weather trying to recruit students. Another young miner from Alabama had left school to help support his family at age fifteen because he felt there was no future for him on the farm. Weakened from the grueling physical labor and frightened of mining accidents, the young man later returned home only to find that his father had lost their land.[52] Many, like these young people, faced frustrating circumstances and uncertain futures but hoped to find a way to cooperate with others in their generation to confront their shared economic distress.

In addition to the issue of job opportunities, several themes resonated throughout the proceedings of the second SNYC conference. After learning about the conditions faced by their fellow delegates across the South, the group concluded that the black community needed to push for access to the ballot. Having a voice in government was essential to addressing issues such as education, lynching, ownership of rural land, access to industrial jobs, and equal pay for equal work. The importance of honoring African American cultural heritage was another major topic of conversation at the conference. President William Richardson and executive secretary Edward Strong noted in their speeches that consciousness had been raised about black culture through the establishment of the Richmond Community Theater. Performances by acclaimed artists like vocalist Roland Hayes had also been sponsored.[53] More ventures that stimulated appreciation of African American culture were encouraged for the coming year.

Events on the world stage were also assessed in the conference speeches. In the spring of 1938, Republican forces aided by international volunteers struggled to fend off Franco's forces in Spain. Japan had invaded China and Germany had annexed Austria, its neighbor to the South. As Hitler maneuvered to expand his fascist empire, the young people in SNYC continued to call for peace and solidarity with youths who were oppressed by fascism and colonialism across the globe. In the spirit of camaraderie among young people, Strong observed in his speech that Hitler had destroyed the youth movement in Germany along with the aspirations of Jewish youth. Rayford Logan, a history professor at Atlanta University, paralleled the global struggle to maintain democracy directly with conditions in the South. He boldly asserted, "In many respects the South is as fascist as is Italy or Germany."[54] In this formulation, the American South was part of a global network because of its repression of the rights of a significant portion of its citizenry. It would remain so as long as the South was ruled by a single party that barred African American citizens from participating in the democratic process and kept them socially as well as economically subjugated.

Overall, a feeling of optimistic determination prevailed among the eager yet serious-minded young people in attendance at the conference. Capturing this sentiment, Edward Strong's speech compared the SNYC activists to "the cavalcade of the first American frontiersmen" who sought freedom and economic security in the wilderness of the North American frontier. He exclaimed, "Youthful frontiersmen and Cavalcaders, we are seeking for ourselves and our people . . . the abundant life."[55] His words inspired the title of the soon-to-be-launched SNYC newspaper, *Cavalcade*, which carried a masthead proclaiming that it represented "The March of Negro Youth."

In the years before the United States officially joined the world war, two of the major campaigns of SNYC, as referenced at the second conference, were accentuating African American cultural forms and combating disfranchisement. In his seminal study *The Black Arts Movement*, James Smethurst identifies SNYC as an important promoter of African American art and literature in the South.[56] In many southern communities, black citizens were allowed little to no access to resources like libraries, art galleries, theaters, and public concerts. SNYC's focus on culture grew out of this form of discrimination. The youth congress's cultural programs also provided a forum for discussions on African American art and history as well as a social space for black citizens to consider their cultural identities.

This was a very interesting and forward-thinking aspect of SNYC. Not only did the organization seek to eradicate the most glaring manifestations of racial injustice (for example, disfranchisement, Klu Klux Klan terrorism, and discrimination in employment), but also the group ruminated upon and attempted to alleviate biases that served to reinforce on a daily basis the inferior position of black citizens in the social system. For example, SNYC groups sought to provide access to recreation facilities for children. They also worked to provide opportunities for quality home economics instruction to train young people to effectively run their households. The youth congress perceived the need for social clubs such as 4-H to be established for black youth in isolated rural areas. People in rural towns also lacked opportunities to go to concerts, view artwork, or attend theater productions. Such discrepancies might appear minor on the surface, but ameliorating them certainly helped African Americans, especially in the rural South, momentarily escape the indignities of life under segregation and enjoy moments of communion and cultural pride with each other.

In addition to the community theater in Richmond, a People's Community Theater was organized by SNYC activists in New Orleans. These were nonprofit ventures "designed to entertain" as well as "advance social ideas" and raise the audience's cultural awareness.[57] In 1941, the People's Community Theater produced a play dramatizing the lives of sharecroppers, *Land of Cotton*, written by Randolph Edmond and directed by Tommy Richardson.[58] Though short-lived, a group called the Caravan Puppeteers was cosponsored by SNYC and the American Youth Congress in 1940. The puppeteers toured farming areas in the South presenting skits on issues such as voter education and the importance of peace. Following the shows, short speeches were made highlighting the social themes in the sketches and leaflets on the right to vote were distributed.[59] This grassroots effort was an important way for young activists to connect with sharecroppers and tenant farmers in the rural communities. As previously mentioned, it was through the puppeteers that Nora Wilson's mother was able to secure assistance from SNYC for her daughter's case.

Starting with the national conference in Birmingham, Alabama, in 1939, each SNYC congress featured some kind of cultural presentation for the entire community. The theme of cultural heritage was especially prominent at the Birmingham meeting. The proceedings opened with a festival of music that included traditional songs from the black experience such as work songs and spirituals, which were sung with "fervent feeling."[60] The visual art showcase at the conference resonated strongly in the community. Prior to the congress, a black high school student had been awarded a prize in a city art show but had been banned from attending the segregated show where his piece was displayed. The SNYC art show, on the other hand, was the first in the city to highlight the works of African Americans including the talented young artist from Birmingham.[61] The 1939 conference included an address from Alain Locke, editor of *The New Negro* collection, which was one of the foundational texts that theorized the cultural movement centered in Harlem in the 1920s. During the closing night, conference attendees also had the chance to see an acting troupe from Dillard University perform works by young black playwright Randolph Edmonds. This cultural showcase was especially significant to the large number of delegates from remote areas. For these farmers, laborers, and rural townspeople, this was perhaps the first time they had ever seen art that was crafted by black hands and plays starring black actors being showcased.[62]

The SNYC commitment to culture was maintained in subsequent years when, for example, acclaimed African American vocalist and actor Paul Robeson performed at the 1942 and 1946 conferences. SNYC also sponsored a tour of the South for dancer Pearl Primus in the mid-1940s. In the late 1940s, the group inaugurated an Association of Young Writers and Artists, which hosted a contest with a cash prize to foster the work of youthful artists. While cultural needs could have easily been overlooked in a period of acute economic and political distress, SNYC, sharing some of the spirit of the Works Progress Administration's art programs, endeavored to instill cultural pride into southern African American communities. The youth congress understood that all aspects of social relations were undermined by racial subjugation. Affirming the cultural identity of southern African Americans was as valid a goal as establishing a political voice. Cultivating new artistic talent could enrich communities and foster new forms of expression against injustice.

Probably the most significant literary endeavor of SNYC was its newspaper, *Cavalcade*, which was launched in April 1941 and capably edited by Augusta Jackson (who became Augusta Strong after marrying Edward Strong). She shared the editing duties with Louis Burnham starting with the October 1941 issue. Almost every installment of the newspaper included poetry, visual art, and/or a short fiction piece. The paper provided an important medium for publication of aspiring writers and visual artists who probably had few public outlets for their work. The pieces in *Cavalcade* were all imbued with social consciousness and often addressed a historical theme or specific social issue facing African Americans in the rural South. In fact, one of the most crucial and enduring contributions of the SNYC newspaper was the vivid representation of life in farming communities as people were trying to grapple with segregation, limited economic opportunities, and the possibility of impending war. Black Americans who were toiling during the Depression and standing on the cusp of world war were brought to life in the pages of *Cavalcade* as their latent militancy, historical consciousness, and everyday struggles working the land were voiced.

For example, in "A Boy and his Mule," Albert Whitfield imagines a young farmer alone tilling the fields and pondering his place in society by conversing with his only nearby companion, a mule. The boy solemnly points out, "Mule, you ain't the only person dat looks at cotton and corn all day long with a harness round your neck." He continues, "You ain't de only person who goes home at night and dine on nothin' but corn and hay. We colored folks, we just like you."[63] This concise, unpretentious narrative probes directly at the foundation of economic life in the South by adroitly paralleling the circumstances of the sharecropper or tenant farmer with his enslaved forebears who were also "harnessed" to the land. Whitfield poignantly conveys that the feudal relationship between the landowners and those who harvested the land has evolved little since the time of chattel slavery when African Americans were bought and sold just like animals on the farms.

In a style recalling the dean of black poetry, Langston Hughes and his famous poem "Weary Blues," Waring Cuney's piece "Organize Blues" evokes both rhythm and social consciousness. The poet encourages black Americans toward activism: "Going to the meeting / Hear what I say / Going to the meeting / Hear what I say / Poor folks got to / Organize the blues away."[64] A similar spirit challenging the status quo of the South is captured by Eugene B. Williams in a brief poem. Echoing Hughes's classic "I, too, Sing America," Williams asserts that new songs will reverberate in Dixie: "songs of We Want Justice / For white and black alike / With melodies unending / Until that note we strike."[65] Cordelia P. Key effectively contrasts the inherent income discrepancies in the upbringing of two children, one white and one black. The poet takes care to point to the dignity of the black child who "had sworn / To bravely face each coming morn" despite the impoverished circumstances the child faces.[66] In a poem addressing the contemporary fear of conscription among young people, Eugene B. Williams interestingly turns to the blues to suggest not the anxiety of the new recruit but the pain for the women left behind: "Now they've got him in the army, marching with a gun / And so you see me here / this sad and lonely one."[67] These young writers represented on paper the vitality of an emerging generation in the South who simultaneously acknowledged the conditions in which they were raised while critiquing the system that enabled these conditions to persist. This cohort rejected the blatant discrimination of the society that they were to inherit and effectively encapsulated the mood of that era.

Cavalcade also carried news items covering labor campaigns and events sponsored by progressive groups such as the National Negro Congress, the League of Young Southerners, and the American Youth Congress. For instance, headlines followed an organizing victory for steelworkers as well as the struggles of Alabama coal miners in the spring and summer of 1941. An insightful article on "Culture and Labor" pointed out that industrial workers in Birmingham were only one generation removed from rural life and thus folk culture, like quilting, craft making, theater and singing, resonated deeply in the black community in that city. The League of Young Southerners utilized this knowledge in creating a skit for a coal strike called "Why Popsicles Melt." It explained the strategies of owners to destroy unionization efforts through the metaphor of popsicles, which was the nickname given by company men to members of the United Mine Workers.[68] In keeping with the internationalist perspective of SNYC, a sidebar called "Youth Around the World" regularly featured the goings-on in youth movements around the globe.[69] *Cavalcade*, then, offered an assortment of reportage, literary pieces, and news from the local SNYC councils as well as the headquarters in Birmingham—all for the price of five cents a copy, or fifty cents for a subscription. The price was kept low so as to be affordable for its constituency. Perhaps most significant were the poetry and letters, like the one from Nora Wilson's mother, which movingly depicted the circumstances of black rural life as well as the militant consciousness that was welling up within the hearts of the oppressed.

Another major campaign by SNYC in the prewar years aimed to help secure the franchise for black citizens. The local council in New Orleans, one of SNYC's largest groups, had been running a voter registration drive and raising awareness through slogans such as "A 'voteless' people is a hopeless people. Do you want to be hopeless?"[70] Following the national conference in that city in 1940, the youth congress resolved to push for access to the ballot across the South with a right to vote campaign. Though issues such as chronic unemployment were also discussed in New Orleans, the delegates felt that "the right of the Negro to vote in the South is a test and a challenge to American democracy."[71] In a pamphlet titled "Our Battle for the Ballot," James Jackson pointedly queried President Roosevelt, "You have declared, Mr. President, that you have spent many sleepless nights pondering the fate of Democracy abroad. What will you do about this blight on our Democracy here at home?"[72] The Fifteenth Amendment to the Constitution had been ratified during Reconstruction and secured the franchise for African Americans. However, voting rights had been circumscribed by various strategies in the South since the collapse of Reconstruction reformism and the rise of the so-called redeemer governments in the late nineteenth century. Along with the literacy test and the white primary, the poll tax was one of the most notorious tactics used to prevent impoverished African Americans from exercising their democratic rights.

A bill to address this injustice had been written but was languishing for

Figure 1. Southern Negro Youth Congress voting campaign, Edward Strong Papers, Manuscript Division, Moorland-Spingarn Research Center, Howard University.

lack of support. The Geyer Anti-Poll Tax Bill had been introduced by Representative Lee Geyer in committee but was facing stiff congressional opposition. SNYC decided to raise awareness around the country about the problem of poll taxing with the two-pronged strategy of rallying support for passage of this new legislation and pressuring the states that maintained a poll tax. These states included Alabama, Arkansas, Georgia, South Carolina, Virginia, Tennessee, Mississippi, and Texas. Working together with the Southern Conference for Human Welfare and the League of Young Southerners, SNYC instigated a "National Anti-Poll Tax Week" campaign for May 1941. Previous SNYC voter drives at the local level had organized around the strategy of raising money to help black citizens pay the poll tax so that they might attempt to vote. This campaign instead aimed to garner support for a national law that would eradicate the poll tax. They argued that the poll tax was blocking upwards of ten million potential voters from participating in the democratic process.

This was a high profile movement that called for as much publicity as possible, including newspaper coverage, leafleting, and the sale of stickers, buttons, and posters, which could be ordered by local councils from the SNYC headquarters. In cities like Birmingham, sympathetic citizens who purchased buttons sometimes pinned them inconspicuously under a lapel for fear of losing a job or being confronted by police.[73] Unions and groups like the American Peace Mobilization along with concerned individuals from California to Colorado and Michigan to New York wrote to SNYC requesting materials to disseminate. Edward Strong urged concerned citizens to send a "deluge of letters and telegrams" to Congress on this issue.[74] A series of articles in *Cavalcade* advertised the anti-poll tax crusade and deftly linked disfranchisement with other issues such as education.[75] Remarking that a scant 12 percent of the citizenry of South Carolina could vote, one article observed that those in political power would never make equitable appropriations for education while "their very positions are dependent upon keeping the masses in ignorance."[76] The southern oligarchy would remain safely entrenched as long as it could suppress manifestations of grassroots political power.

In June 1941, *Cavalcade* declared the Anti-Poll Tax Week to have been a success. Petitions had been sent to the House Judiciary Committee to urge passage of the Geyer Bill. Mass meetings were held and literature was distributed by SNYC locals and civic, trade union, and peace groups across the nation. Supporters as far north as Bronx, New York, sold buttons and stickers.[77] The youth congress's mobilization was recognized by Representative Geyer of California, the sponsor of the House bill, who praised the organizers of Anti-Poll Tax Week for helping to focus national attention on this important issue.[78] Though ultimately the bill did not become law, the SNYC campaign was useful because it revealed the extent to which people around the nation were disparaging of any impediment to voting. This realization, in the view of SNYC leaders, presented "widespread possibilities . . . for organizing [around] this popular sentiment."[79]

Still, obstructions such as the poll tax were not outlawed until the Voting Rights Act of 1965 was passed. President Lyndon Johnson signed this bill only after persistent campaigns led by the Student Nonviolent Coordinating Committee (SNCC) and the Mississippi Freedom Democratic Party (MFDP) had dramatically demonstrated that African Americans were being shut out of the democratic process. The struggle for the MFDP delegation to be seated at the Democratic National Convention in the summer of 1964 and activist Fannie Lou Hamer's memorable testimony before the credentials committee clearly illustrated to the nation the injustice that was rife within Johnson's own party. Thus, SNYC had correctly predicted that a mass movement, involving white and black southerners allied with northerners, would be the engine that could stimulate national legislation on voting rights. Although SNYC vowed to continue the anti-poll tax drive as part of their Right to Vote campaign, international events took center stage by the autumn of 1941.

The SNYC's global outlook can be seen in, for example, many of the speeches at the annual congresses and the articles published in *Cavalcade*. Solidarity with Spain and Ethiopia as well as people in the colonized world went hand-in-hand with a robust antifascist perspective. In 1941, the American Youth Congress sponsored a trip to Cuba for youth from the United States to form closer relationships with young people in Latin America. Edward and Augusta Strong, from SNYC, accompanied the delegation that aimed to "achieve unity through organization in the common fight against fascism and imperialism."[80] Reporting on the visit after returning to the United States, the young visitors to Cuba were impressed that "the people, in spite of the terrible treatment which they receive from the American corporations and businesses, gave the delegation the greatest hospitality, friendship and the feeling of solidarity."[81] Meanwhile, weighty events were playing out in the European theater of war. Germany had invaded Poland and occupied the Netherlands, Belguim, and part of France by the summer of 1940. Denmark and Norway had also fallen to the Nazis, and the Battle of Britain had commenced.

Angelo Herndon reported on the 1940 SNYC national conference for the *Daily Worker* newspaper. He emphasized in his article that cries against joining the imperialist war in Europe echoed throughout the meeting where all of the delegates were "definitely committed against . . . the war."[82] Calls for peace became increasingly urgent in the pages of the SNYC newspaper in the spring of 1941. For instance, in covering a national antiwar conference in New York, an article from April connected the right to vote campaign with the preservation of peace and seemed to back the American Peace Mobilization group's call for repeal of the Lend-Lease Bill and conscription. The Lend-Lease Bill, which was passed by Congress in March 1941, enabled the United States to sell military supplies directly to the Allies.

Edward Strong and Esther Cooper Jackson represented SNYC at a meeting called by the American Peace Mobilization group. The antiwar parley attracted five thousand other delegates.[83] In June 1941, an editorial titled "Keep America Out of War" prominently occupied almost half of the front page of *Cavalcade*. The piece condemned Roosevelt's issuing of a national emergency to assist the European allies while turning his back on problems on the domestic front. The war was lambasted as an imperialist fight to shore up European colonialism. No progress would be made, the editorial asserted, on the segregation, racial violence, and disfranchisement that African Americans confronted every day while the U.S. government was preoccupied with Europe's affairs.

Certainly these were relevant points; however, they stood in direct contrast to the position taken in the October 1941 issue of *Cavalcade*. The headline reading "Youth Rally to Defend U.S.A." was followed by dual front-page articles saluting black soldiers. The tone of these pieces was upbeat as the contributions by black soldiers and the training they received was detailed. SNYC leader Louis Burnham was quoted, saying, "The struggle against Fascism is a struggle which Negro youth understands and supports." The issue continued with numerous calls to beat Hitlerism abroad as well as "K-K-K-ism" at home.[84] This abrupt about-face on the war issue coincided with the signing and subsequent betrayal of the Nazi-Soviet pact that temporarily kept the Soviet Union on the fringes of Europe's war with fascism.

From August 1939 to June 1941 a tentative peace was upheld between Germany and the Soviet Union because Hitler and Stalin agreed to respect each other's sovereignty. During that period, the Communist Party in the United States took a strict position against the war even though England and France declared war on Germany in September 1939 and Roosevelt inched ever closer toward publicly siding with the Allies. As demonstrated by the five thousand in attendance at the mass rally for the American Peace Mobilization in April 1941, U.S. support for the war was far from unanimous until December 1941. Congress had declared U.S. neutrality back in

1935, and isolationist ideas persisted in America until that infamous day at Pearl Harbor.

The U.S. Communist Party, however, came out fervently in favor of the war after Hitler's invasion of the Soviet Union in the summer of 1941. *Cavalcade* did not go to press in the summer months of 1941, but the leadership's adherence to the Communist Party's position on the war was illustrated by the issues that did go to press that year. Editorials in April, May, and June clearly opposed the war, while articles in October were clearly advocating that the United States join the war. The Communist Party was derided by some on the right as well as the left of the political spectrum for so transparently following dictates from Moscow on this issue.[85] Some activists who had been sympathetic to the party and engaged in Popular Front coalitions became disillusioned. It appeared that despite their championing of labor and civil rights issues at the local level, the Communist Party was ultimately beholden to Moscow on matters of foreign policy.

This was one instance when SNYC national leadership seemed to be following the political stance of the Communist Party. Though the party itself was rarely, if ever, directly discussed in *Cavalcade*, the vacillating position on the war in its pages could have been jarring to its readership. In addition, this issue momentarily undermined the youth congress's stated declaration of nonpartisanship. *Cavalcade* called for a second European front as early as November 1941 while appealing to the Roosevelt administration to "abandon the sham of neutrality."[86] This was a far cry from the June editorial that had denounced Roosevelt's declaration of a "national emergency" for the war. However, the positions articulated in *Cavalcade* did not necessarily represent the perspective on the war held by all SNYC local councils. The newspaper was produced out of SNYC headquarters largely by the group's national leadership, several of whom were affiliated with the Communist Party.

Still, the youth congress did not overlook its constituency in favor of foreign affairs during the tumultuous summer and autumn of 1941. There was continuing coverage of rural issues in each *Cavalcade* issue and the question of the war, whether pro or con, was always framed to include an analysis of its impact on black soldiers, black communities on the home front, and people in the broader colonized world. Neither did the

SNYC leadership's position on the war seem to impact the overall popularity or effectiveness of the group. Subsequent conferences drew large crowds of hundreds and even thousands of attendees. For example, the national conference in 1942 at Tuskegee Institute was well attended and included Paul Robeson's first historic performance in the South. The 1946 national meeting in Columbia, South Carolina, was undoubtedly a tremendous success and probably represented the pinnacle of the youth congress's influence.

It was also during this period that SNYC was officially placed on the House Un-American Activities Committee's (HUAC) list of subversive organizations. The list was ostensibly to keep tabs on groups that were a threat to national security, but it also enabled the federal government to monitor just about any group of political activists with left-wing affiliations. Thus, from January 1940, when the Southern Negro Youth Congress was added to the list, until the dissolution of the organization about nine years later, SNYC was under continued surveillance by the FBI and, at times, the CIA.[87] The youth congress struck back against HUAC's assertion that SNYC was a subversive group. They declared in the *Pittsburgh Courier* that Martin Dies and his un-American committee had "nothing tangible to back up their charges."[88] At the 1940 national conference, an "uncompromising fight against the un-American Dies Committee" was included in Edward Strong's list of vital issues to be tackled in the upcoming year.[89] The consequences of government scrutiny, coupled with red-baiting tactics, eventually crippled the youth congress in the repressive atmosphere of the years following the war. Yet, the inclusion of SNYC on this list in 1940 did not seem to have much of an immediate impact on the organization. As mentioned above, some of the largest, most historic mass rallies of SNYC were in the early and middle 1940s.

It was possible that HUAC's attention to SNYC in 1940 occurred partly because of political turmoil in the National Negro Congress.[90] Tensions that had been simmering for some time exploded that year with the resignation of the organization's president, A. Philip Randolph. NNC had been actively cooperating with CIO trade union organizing drives and, as this movement grew, the composition of the group's membership was evolving. Randolph charged, upon his dramatic exit, that the NNC was no longer a coalition of African American groups as had originally been envisioned but rather a white-dominated and Communist-led group. Though it had been left-leaning since its founding, accounts differ as to what extent the NNC was directed by party members.[91] Nonetheless, it was clear that there was a vitriolic cleavage in the organization's leadership in 1940.

Some historians contend that the group was never as effective under Max Yergan's term as president following Randolph's departure.[92] The group's influence and effectiveness was arguably in decline following Randolph's departure during the complex political climate of the 1940s. This internal scuffle probably landed on the radar screen of HUAC, which was usually eager to uncover any alleged Communist conspiracy. Since SNYC had been affiliated with NNC, it stood to reason that HUAC viewed both groups through a similarly red-tinted lens. SNYC, however, never endured an internal fissure over the issue of Communist-guided leadership. It was probably the grassroots nature of its organizational structure that prevented the issue of Communist Party influence from splitting the group. The youth congress distanced itself from NNC and emphasized its independence while carrying on with its programs through the war.[93]

All in all, the period leading up to World War II was one of growth and activity for SNYC. By the time the United States, allied with the Soviet Union, was actively pursuing fascists on the battlefield in the winter of 1941, SNYC had roots in over one hundred local councils in every state in the South. Though financial constraints were a persistent difficulty, the youth congress was strong enough to continue its activism through the war despite the departure of key leaders Edward Strong and James Jackson to military service. The status of SNYC at this juncture was summarized well by Tuskegee University president, and SNYC backer, F. D. Patterson. He unequivocally stated at the 1940 convention, "The Southern Negro Youth Congress is in my opinion one of the most hopeful evidences we have had of the progress of the Negro race during the present decade."[94] While the youth congress was conducting a multifront struggle for civil rights in the South, the Council on African Affairs began forming networks between Africa and the United States to agitate against colonialism on the continent.

Working "in the Interest of African Freedom": The Founding of the Council on African Affairs

In the winter of 1946 a letter arrived at the office of the Council on African Affairs in New York City from an enthusiastic student enrolled in a college in the South. The school had engaged a white South African to deliver a lecture that portrayed native black South Africans as being "well fed, happy and content with their lot under their benevolent masters." This description was not unlike the myth espoused by the southern oligarchy that African Americans were comfortable and well treated during enslavement and, later, segregation. To bolster his case on amiable race relations, the South African speaker asserted that there had been no labor disputes in South Africa in two decades. This was a blatant lie. Black South African mine workers had been on strike that very summer against inhumane working conditions and paltry wages. The strike was violently crushed by police action in which at least nine workers were killed and hundreds injured. Indigenous South Africans had also been hit by famine that year due, in part, to the fact that the majority of the population was confined to meager portions of land that were wholly insufficient to feed their numbers. Representatives from white South Africa, like this speaker, painted an optimistic image of a "contented" black population even as the government began codifying the laws that formed the backbone of the apartheid system.

However, one student in the audience that evening was not deceived. The writer of the letter bravely stood up from the crowd and queried the South African on the recent strikes in the Transvaal and even quoted wage rates that had been published in *New Africa*, the newsletter of the Council on African Affairs. When the speaker denied this evidence, the intrepid student "dug out" his copy of *New Africa* and put it in the hand of the speaker. The student then interrogated the visitor on issues such as hunger, the pass law system, voting rights, and living conditions for black South Africans. When the speaker was at a loss for words, he was soundly booed, and many in the previously sympathetic audience got up and left. The student concluded that though he would probably have to "face the administration" for embarrassing the guest lecturer, he felt that articulating the true facts of the situation in South Africa was "well worth it."[95] Clearly the editor of *New Africa*, W. Alphaeus Hunton, was tickled to hear about this episode as he published the letter under the headline "This Makes Us Happy!"

Another letter indicative of the council's important work arrived on Hunton's desk sometime in July 1953. The writer of this letter was from Johannesburg and had recently read one of Hunton's pamphlets on South Africa. This sincere correspondent, identified only by initials, confessed to harboring a "sickening hatred" for Americans ever since the execution of the Rosenbergs, who had been accused of passing nuclear secrets to the Soviet Union, earlier that year. However, after studying Hunton's postscript to "Resistance in South Africa," the letter writer was heartened and recognized that "there are fine, generous, brave Americans who, in the midst of all their own troubles, can take to heart the sufferings of oppressed people on the other side of the world."[96]

These letters revealed that the Council on African Affairs was fulfilling its stated goals of disseminating accurate, up-to-date news from Africa and influencing public opinion about issues and events on the continent. Moreover, the organization provided a vital network between people in the Pan-African world. The plucky student from the southern United States was connected to black South Africans as well as African American activists in the North by way of *New Africa*. Imagine if he had not been an avid reader of the council's newsletter. The audience at that forum would have gone home having been exposed only to the guest lecturer's sunny, and disingenuous, depiction of South Africa. Armed with facts from the continent, the student had the courage to insist that the truth be acknowledged and, in doing so, compel the crowd to reject the fallacious perspective of the speaker.

Though based in New York, this anecdote demonstrated the impact of the council's advocacy in the South. Likewise, the letter from Johannesburg illuminated linkages between the Council on African Affairs and the continent. Hunton and the council's other leaders were in touch regularly with African intellectuals and activists, but this letter illustrated the broad reach of their writing, which touched the general public on both sides of the Atlantic. The council's publications, while aimed primarily at Americans, also kept Africans informed and swayed some of their opinions of people from the United States. In fact, *New Africa* was considered provocative enough to be banned by governments in Kenya, South Africa, and the Belgian Congo.[97]

W.E.B. Du Bois, in his 1946 speech before the Southern Negro Youth Congress, rendered an evocative parallel between the southern United States and South Africa: "That great hypocrite, Jan Smuts, who today is talking of humanity and standing beside [James] Byrnes for a United Nations, is at the same time, oppressing the black people of Africa to an extent which makes their two countries, South Africa and the Southern South, the most reactionary peoples on earth." Byrnes, a segregationist, served as President Harry S. Truman's Secretary of State and, in the eyes of progressives, symbolized the ascendancy of U.S. white supremacy to the global stage. Byrnes and Smuts collaborating as world leaders represented injustices perpetrated against dark-skinned people on two continents.

Since the black people of colonized Africa and the United States shared a common oppression, they needed to cultivate alliances that would engage activists in constructing a new, more democratic political discourse across the Pan-African world. The Council on African Affairs helped fulfill this need by, for example, lobbying for support of African freedom in the United Nations and U.S. foreign policy, sponsoring meetings that promoted dialogue, and circulating news about Africa in their publications. The Southern Negro Youth Congress and the Council on African Affairs maintained an internationalist perspective grounded in the belief that all people of African descent deserved to walk in full human dignity. However, not all black Americans were receptive to such a Pan-Africanist perspective. One concerned African American wondered in a letter to the Council "why in the world would one worry about the racial conditions in Africa when we as a minority group catch hell in this country?"

Hunton's reply eloquently connected the common derivation of racial oppression across the African diaspora. He argued that one has "to be concerned with the oppression of our Negro brothers in Africa for the very same reason that we here in New York . . . have to be concerned with the plight of our brothers in Tennessee, Mississippi or Alabama." Hunton continued, "Jim-Crowism, colonialism and imperialism are not separate enemies, but a single enemy with different faces and different forms."[98] In order to combat this single but multifaceted enemy, organizations with shared principles but specific points of focus were necessary. The Southern Negro Youth Congress, though advocating internationalism, had chosen the U.S. South as its battleground for African American rights. The Council on

African Affairs, though its leaders shared common southern roots, advocated for the liberation of Africa from a northern metropolis in the United States.

"Imperialism Is Still the Menace": The Council's Early Years, 1937–1941

It was no coincidence that the organization initially designated as the International Committee on African Affairs was created not long after the Italian invasion of Ethiopia in 1935. The fascist takeover of what was viewed by many in the diaspora as a symbol of ancient African glory as well as autonomy on a continent largely colonized by Europeans ignited indignation among black Americans. As historian James Meriwether has documented, the middle 1930s were a watershed in which the relationship between African Americans and contemporary Africa was redefined.[99] This was due in no small part to Benito Mussolini's aggressive incursion into Ethiopia. Many African Americans believed the brutal takeover of Ethiopia was somewhat overlooked in the West as the Roosevelt administration tried to hammer out an economic recovery plan and Europe kept a wary eye on Germany. Emperor Haile Selassie's impassioned plea for assistance before the League of Nations was largely unheeded.

African Americans followed global events, such as the offensive against Ethiopia, in black-owned newspapers that enjoyed their most expansive readerships in the mid-twentieth century.[100] These news sources helped inform African Americans about domestic and world events. Thus, black Americans, especially scholars and activists with a global perspective, deduced a direct connection between fascism and imperialism. They were but branches from a common trunk of political oppression. Ralph Bunche, an early supporter of the council, observed in 1936 that fascism "has given a new and greater impetus to the policy of world imperialism which has already conquered . . . virtually all of the darker populations on the earth."[101] Bunche, an African American scholar, was quick in detecting the tyrannical qualities of fascism and its potential for expansion.

The Council on African Affairs, then, originated during the troubling circumstances of domestic economic distress and the burgeoning fascist movement of the 1930s. This was coupled with a growing international awareness in the black community that stemmed from journalism that disseminated news from around the world. In addition, organizing by groups like the NNC and SNYC emphasized a global outlook that was influenced partly by the U.S. Communist Party. For example, when the party's International Labor Defense (ILD) came to the aid of the wrongfully accused Scottsboro youths in Alabama in the early thirties, their defense raised international awareness about racial injustice in the United States. Some black Americans, then, viewed the Communist Party as a vehicle for action against racism and colonialism. The council embodied all of these contemporary phenomena as its main leaders were closely affiliated with the U.S. Communist Party.

The group also drew upon the journalistic trend of the era by generating a newsletter that helped contribute to an international political discourse on anticolonialism and self-determination for the African continent. The swelling tide of fascist thinking was not lost on the founders of the Council on African Affairs, who had witnessed this expansion firsthand in their extensive international travels. In fact, the inspiration for a "radical, black-led, and interracial" activist organization dedicated to informing the public about the continent and promoting African liberation took shape not in the United States but in the United Kingdom and Africa.[102]

The cofounders of the Council on African Affairs, Paul Robeson and Max Yergan, had spent considerable time abroad by 1937 when the organization was initiated. Yergan had been raised in the southern United States and was deeply influenced by his grandfather's Christian worldview, which was grounded in the late nineteenth-century conviction of uplifting the race, including those brothers in Africa. Yergan recalled that his grandfather, who had been enslaved, exhorted a young Max from his deathbed that he wished one of his progeny would undertake missionary work on the continent.[103] Following his education at Shaw University in his home state of North Carolina, Yergan built a promising career in the Young Men's Christian Association (YMCA), which he served in India and South Africa. Yet, after working more than a decade in South Africa, Yergan felt restrained by the YMCA's focus on redeeming Africa by saving individual souls. He had been radicalized by observing the oppression of black South Africans. He had also been drawn to Marxist theory and had cultivated an acquaintance with Pan-African activists on trips to London and the Soviet Union. As a result of his ideological shift toward Marxism and

Pan-Africanism, Yergan definitively broke with the YMCA on the grounds that their work "did not meet the urgent demands of the social and political situation" in South Africa. He believed that the government of South Africa was "quite definitely committed to a policy which is destructive of any real growth among Africans of that country."[104]

Upon returning to the United States in the late 1930s, Yergan's left-wing political perspective was demonstrated in his work with the Council on African Affairs and the National Negro Congress as well as his relationships with leaders in the Communist Party and his teaching at the City College of New York. His progressive politics might also have contributed to CCNY's decision not to reappoint Yergan to teach a course on black history in 1941.[105] Thus, Yergan's radicalizing southern experience occurred in southern Africa. His southern U.S. roots had laid the foundation for Yergan's early views on ameliorating race relations through Christian outreach; however, this program seemed inadequate in the face of the brutal oppression against indigenous black Africans that he observed for many years in South Africa.

Paul Robeson revealingly mused in his 1958 memoir that he had "discovered" Africa while living in London in the 1930s.[106] He had grown up in New Jersey firmly rooted in the segregated African American community where his father, who had escaped enslavement in North Carolina, preached in the AME Zion church. Robeson reflected later that he grew up in a very southern atmosphere in Princeton because the town was full of students from that region. The southern university of the North, as Robeson described it, was run by Virginian segregationist Woodrow Wilson in the early years of the twentieth century during Robeson's boyhood.[107] "We lived for all intents and purposes on a Southern plantation," he observed in hindsight.[108]

After completing degrees at Rutgers University and Columbia Law School, Robeson pursued a career in the arts in Harlem in the 1920s where he was celebrated as an actor and vocalist of African American spirituals. In New York, he married Eslanda Cardozo Goode, whose southern heritage included the distinguished South Carolina Reconstruction politician Francis Lewis Cardozo. An invitation to portray Othello in 1930 brought Paul and Eslanda to England, where they ended up living for much of the decade. Between Paul's concert tours and acting engagements, the couple mingled with West Indian and African students and intellectuals from throughout the British Empire. These colonial transplants came to the metropolis for work and networked in groups such as the West African Students' Union, the League of Coloured Peoples, and the International African Service Bureau.

In London, Paul studied African languages and took advantage of a rare opportunity to play a black revolutionary hero as penned by a black author in C.L.R. James's *Toussaint Louverture*. Eslanda studied anthropology and journeyed to Africa in 1936 to undertake field research for her doctorate. While there, she spent time with Max Yergan and his family in South Africa and learned about the history and political circumstances of the native people. The political awareness of both Robesons grew during their various travels through the United Kingdom, Europe, and Africa, and, like Yergan, they were moved when they visited the Soviet Union in the early 1930s. The anti-imperialist position advocated by the Comintern as well as the outlawing of racial discrimination in the Soviet constitution appealed to them as it did to an array of African American visitors during that era.[109] Eslanda lamented in the memoir of her 1936 trek across the African continent that "in America one heard little or nothing about Africa."[110] The Robesons and Yergan sought to change that. Through a dialogue carried on, at times, in the Robesons' London flat, they agreed to establish the group that became known as the Council on African Affairs.[111]

Back in the United States, the Popular Front against fascism, in which progressive activists, liberal New Dealers, and Communist Party organizers formed coalitions to tackle civil rights and other issues, informed the political climate of the early years of the council. Based in New York, the Council on African Affairs never employed the grassroots-style mobilization adopted by the Southern Negro Youth Congress, with its numerous, self-governing local councils. The council, in contrast, consisted primarily of a core of activists who worked to raise public consciousness about events in Africa. The group's public ideological stance and organizational direction was generated largely by Yergan, Robeson, Hunton (when he joined the group in 1943) and, to some extent, by W.E.B. Du Bois, who was active in the group's later years.

Though Robeson was not directly involved in much of the day-to-day functioning of the Council on African Affairs in its early years, he did adopt a more hands-on leadership role in the late 1940s. The group pursued an array of strategies, including sponsoring lectures from African visitors, delivering speeches, holding conferences and rallies, circulating petitions, and lobbying political leaders. Yet it was probably through their writing that the council made its case for African self-determination most success-fully. Max Yergan and W. Alphaeus Hunton produced a steady stream of cogent, fact-based pamphlets and press releases on conditions in Africa. Especially under Hunton's astute editorship, the group's newsletter *New Africa*, later renamed *Spotlight on Africa*, contained voluminous, perhaps unprecedented, documentation of African issues. Eslanda Robeson also contributed her book *African Journey* as well as numerous pamphlets and articles. Paul Robeson, an inimitable celebrity but not a prolific writer, shined as an eloquent speaker and charismatic fundraiser for the organiza-tion. Members of the Council on African Affairs in its early years included an impressive range of scholars and activists such as Channing Tobias, Mary van Kleeck, Mordecai Johnson, Hubert Delany, Ralph Bunche, and Rene Maran.[112]

*   *   *

Recent scholarship on black American activism during the late 1930s through the early Cold War has effectively fleshed out a nuanced frame-work of left-wing, internationalist advocacy that conjoined civil rights and labor issues that Martha Biondi described as a "black-labor-left nexus."[113] Plainly, the contributions of groups like the council that fit into this dis-course cannot be simply boiled down to being fronts for the U.S. Com-munist Party, as the federal government charged during the antiradical purges of the early 1950s.[114] The distinguished sociologist St. Clair Drake posits that examining the Council on African Affairs reveals the tension between two preeminent left-wing ideologies of the time: Soviet-based Communism and Pan-Africanism.[115] James Meriwether has also noted that the council's proponents illustrate how "radical internationalism could be blended with a black nationalism, with its emphasis on racial conscious-ness and unity."[116]

The body of the Council on African Affair's public written record, chiefly consisting of pamphlets, press releases, issues of the newsletter, petitions, and conference proceedings, shows that the fundamental message conveyed was of solidarity between oppressed peoples, especially those of African descent. The group also called for self-determination for European colonies and full freedom for African Americans. Practically all of the other major issues addressed in the council's work can fit into the themes of unity and liberation. For example, cooperation with the exiled leaders of the African National Congress for the emancipation of South Africa's black population from the increasingly repressive system of racial discrimination was a continuous theme that resonated in the council's pamphlets and at the famine relief rallies in 1946. This support for the indigenous black population of South Africa encompassed both unity and liberation. These two concepts also formed the bedrock of the Pan-African movement, which reemerged after World War II and undergirded many of the independence campaigns that took shape on the continent in the 1950s and 1960s.

The body of written work produced by council leaders, coupled with the meetings sponsored by the group, illustrates that the Council on African Affairs was at the vanguard of a political dialogue on Pan-Africanism in the United States at an important historical juncture. Because the group's leaders were associated with the Communist Party, the council was treated as a Communist organization by the government and the mainstream press. Yet, as Meriwether implies, the politics of the organization were more complex and embodied a critique of colonialism and capitalism that also advocated a nationalist perspective on liberation, cultivated by a Pan-Africanist vision. The nationalist strands of the group's Pan-African outlook were demonstrated in, for example, *New Africa*'s coverage of and support for the Mau Mau movement in Kenya, the articles and petitions that strongly rejected the white South African government's challenge to annex South West Africa, the support for indigenous African leaders, the call for arming Africans during World War II, and the cry for Western leaders to uphold the resolutions of the Atlantic Charter for self-determination for all colonized people after the war.

In addition, Drake is astute in discerning the tension between Pan-Africanism and Communism apparent when analyzing the Council on African Affair's activism. For instance, there was coverage of the Soviet Union, in particular for its anticolonial stance, in the council's newsletters, and labor organizing was emphasized as an important tactic in campaigns for African liberation. Most glaringly, the council was not represented at the significant

Pan-African Congress in Manchester, England, in 1945. This was due partially to the friction between the council and the organizer and theorist George Padmore, who convened the conference and who had broken with the Comintern resolutely in 1934. Nevertheless, during its existence from 1937 to 1955, the council filled an important ideological gap in the discourse on Pan-Africanism in the United States. The Council on African Affairs functioned in an era following the dissipation of the international Pan-African Congress movement of the early twentieth century and the height of the Garvey movement of the 1920s but before the militant generation of activists in the 1960s championed African liberation.[117] The literature produced by the Council on African Affairs demonstrated that African liberation and solidarity with colonized people was the first priority of the group. Soviet-style Communism was acknowledged and occasionally held up as an example of a political system that maintained tenants clearly lacking in Western-style capitalist democracy, such as a critique of imperialism and support for exploited colonial laborers. In order to contextualize the council's Pan-African ideology, a brief analysis of the early twentieth-century Pan-African movement is useful.

First, what was Pan-Africanism? In the early years of the twentieth century, Pan-Africanism was a political project with the ultimate aim of unity amongst people of African descent and self-determination, including independence and self-government, for colonies of Europe. Broadly, it highlighted themes such as racial solidarity between people in the diaspora and embraced democratic ideals of political and social equality in opposition to race discrimination.[118] By midcentury, Pan-Africanism had evolved into a more complex political ideology as it was theorized by scholar-activists like Trinidadian George Padmore. He posited that Pan-Africanism endorsed an Asian-African front against white supremacy, Gandhian-style nonviolence in the pursuit of independence, and a rejection of monopoly capitalism as well as supporting universal brotherhood, social justice, and peace for people everywhere. More specifically, Pan-Africanism sought to attain government for Africans by Africans under a form of democratic socialism with state control of the means of production and distribution. In Padmore's long-term vision, individual sovereign states would federate into a United States of Africa.[119] This conception was an inspiration for Kwame Nkrumah's idea for an Organization of African Unity in the postindependence era.

In addition, W.E.B. Du Bois and Marcus Garvey led two important Pan-African movements in the first decades of the 1900s. After Henry Sylvester-Williams, from the British West Indies, initiated the Pan-African Congress of 1900 in London, Du Bois inaugurated a series of international Pan-African congresses following the close of World War I in 1919.[120] The meetings were held in Paris in 1919; London, Brussels, then Paris in 1921; London and Lisbon in 1923; and New York in 1927. Since Europe could no longer claim to be at the vanguard of progressive civilization after instigating a war to end all wars, Du Bois and others believed it was time to begin seriously reconsidering Europe's role in Africa. These conferences facilitated consciousness-raising on the issue of colonization as well as solidarity between people from the diaspora. Though the conferees did not directly demand the liberation of Africa, as their heirs did after World War II, the forum of the early congresses nurtured the idea of a shared racial heritage. These meetings, as Du Bois later reflected, "brought face to face . . . a group of educated Negroes . . . that might lead black men to emancipation in the modern world."[121]

In the meantime, Marcus Garvey's United Negro Improvement Association (UNIA) attained a mass following in the United States as the great migration of African Americans from the rural South to northern urban centers was also gaining momentum. A Jamaican by birth, the captivating Garvey's call for race solidarity and a movement back to Africa resonated with thousands of black working people in the United States and across the diaspora. During a time characterized by lynching, racial segregation, and few economic opportunities outside of sharecropping or menial industrial jobs, Garvey's brand of race pride became "far and away the largest nationalist organization to emerge among Blacks in America" during its peak years of 1918 to 1923.[122] Garveyism demonstrated the powerful appeal of nationalism that had been latent in the working-class black population in a way that unsettled middle-class organizations such as the NAACP that did not appeal to the working masses with the same fervor of Garveyism.

The success of Garveyism caught the attention of the Communist Party as well. Though historically the Communist movement rejected appeals to racial solidarity as evidence of bourgeois nationalism, class-consciousness was not historically a strong force among African Americans. Thus, the Communists hoped to tap into the deep wells of racial consciousness as an organizing strategy. The self-determination thesis, or Black Belt thesis, that emerged in 1928 theorized that since black workers were concentrated in the South at the bottom of a hierarchical agrarian economic system, their liberation and the overturning of the southern ruling oligarchy were necessary components of a proletarian revolution. Conceptualizing black America as a distinct people, or nation, meant that the Negro Question could be formulated as a national question and, therefore, that an appeal to nationalism could be useful in the recruitment of black members. These theories were implemented by the Communist Party in the United States with fluctuating degrees of success in the late 1920s through the 1940s during their organizing among African Americans.[123] Though the CPUSA was never successful at recruiting mass numbers of black Americans, numerous bright, energetic activists were attracted to the party's international perspective and its critique of capitalist exploitation. This was especially true during the Depression when the National Negro Congress and the Southern Negro Youth Congress were founded.

On the international stage, a void was left when the Pan-African congresses faded and Garveyism lost direction after its leader was convicted of mail fraud and deported from the United States in the late 1920s. Historian Imanuel Geiss has pointed out that the Communists filled this vacuum by allying with colonized people against imperial Europe during the period of roughly 1927–1934.[124] Communism shared with Pan-Africanism an opposition to both colonialism and imperialism. However, for the Communist movement, these tenants were rooted in the ultimate goal of a worldwide revolution that could be assisted by uprisings in colonies. During this period, the global apparatus of the Communist International (Comintern) and the Communist Trade Union International (Profintern) fostered dialogue between activists in the colonized world.

As organizing activity among black people in the United States, Africa, and the West Indies was energized, an important figure emerged from the ranks of the Profintern: Malcolm Nurse, known better as George Padmore—his pen name. Padmore cut his theoretical and organizational teeth during his work as a Communist, which included making contacts across the Pan-African world and editing the *Negro Worker* newspaper. Yet, in the early 1930s when the Comintern decided to dissolve the International Trade Union Committee of Negro Workers in order to placate Western powers in the name of an alliance against fascism, Padmore resigned in indignation.[125] It seemed to him that the Comintern was willing to sacrifice a global, anticolonial black coalition for political purposes. Padmore concluded that Pan-African liberation was not the first priority of the Communist movement and that, even worse, the Comintern might have been recruiting black workers only when they served the larger purposes of Communist policy.[126]

In the middle 1930s, Padmore moved to London where he led the International African Service Bureau and interacted with Pan-African intellectuals and activists, as the Robesons did during their time in that city. While the Robesons were in conversation with Max Yergan, who wanted to create a new organization focused on Africa in the United States, Padmore continued writing and propagandizing for the Pan-African liberation movement from England. He ultimately organized the vital 1945 Manchester Congress and become an advisor to Kwame Nkrumah after he led the Gold Coast to independence from the British in 1957. In terms of the international Pan-African movement, Padmore can be thought of as connecting the early twentieth-century pioneers, like Du Bois and Garvey, to the middle twentieth-century leaders who steered independence movements on the continent, such as Nkrumah, Nnamdi Azikiwe, and Jomo Kenyatta.

The founders of the Council on African Affairs, then, were influenced by both the international Pan-African scene in London and the Communist movement. Yergan, additionally, had observed conditions on the continent firsthand through his work with the YMCA as had Eslanda Robeson on her 1936 journey. Following its founding in 1937, the council cultivated a rich discourse on Pan-Africanism through its newsletter and, importantly, provided forums for dialogue on Africa through the lectures, rallies, and conferences it hosted. Just as Geiss perceives a vacuum in the global Pan-African movement that was briefly filled by the Communist movement, the Council on African Affairs filled an ideological space in the United States left in the wake of the 1927 Pan-African Congress in New York and the dissipation of the Garvey movement. While the council's advocacy of Pan-African liberation was influenced by the Communist Party, unlike the Comintern or the U.S. Communist Party, which did not always maintain an anticolonial critique as their first priority, the Council on African Affairs' primary focus was African independence. Even when

it would have been politically expedient for the group to drop its advocacy of African self-determination in the early 1950s when Paul Robeson's
passport was revoked for speaking out on Africa, the leaders clung to their
fundamental ideology of promoting Pan-African solidarity and colonial
liberation.

In his 1955 magnum opus theorizing on the political economy for a liber-
ated Africa, Padmore presented Pan-Africanism and Communism as separate binaries.[127] In his view, these were the alternatives for the new leaders
of the emerging nation-states in the post–World War II era. Though his
contributions to African nationalist ideology were immense, perhaps Padmore's conception of Pan-Africanism *or* Communism provided too narrow a framework and fomented too rigid a fissure between two camps that
shared an important anticolonial perspective. This undoubtedly stemmed
from his acrimonious break with the Comintern in 1934. Interestingly, the
appeal of Pan-Africanism to the first generation of leaders after independence was based, in part, on Padmore's Marxist training.

W. M. Warren posits in his insightful introduction to Padmore's *Africa and World Peace* that "the appeal of Pan Africanism was its linking of
socialism with nationalism, [and] nationalism with international cooperation."[128] Padmore himself concedes in *Pan-Africanism or Communism?* that
"Pan-Africanism recognizes much that is true in the Marxist interpretation
of history," but he underscores that Pan-Africanism rejected the notion
that Communists alone held "the solution to all the . . . problems facing Africa."[129] Undergirded by a critique of exploitative Western policies toward
Africa that it coupled with a strong call for African self-determination, the
council embodied the primary tenants of Pan-Africanism championed by
Padmore. Still, the group's affiliation with the U.S. Communist left meant
that there was little or no communication with Padmore's Pan-African
Federation, which organized the 1945 Pan-African Congress. Though Padmore noted in a letter to Du Bois that the Council on African Affairs had
been invited to the 1945 congress, he was later dismissive of the council as
"never more than a sort of leftish welfare organization."[130] Sadly, because of
their differing views on the role of the international Communist apparatus,
Padmore's group and the council, who shared a vision of Pan-African liberation, did not collaborate. Nevertheless, in the United States, no group
spoke out more stridently or lobbied more vigorously for Pan-African

liberation during the years of its existence than the Council on African Affairs.

The work of the council got off the ground in the summer of 1937 when Max Yergan sent out an invitation to a lecture and discussion that included two speakers from South Africa. The meeting was in New York under the auspices of the International Committee on African Affairs.[131] The following year, a pamphlet by Yergan titled "Gold and Poverty in South Africa" was published by the International Industrial Relations Institute and included an outline of the International Committee on African Affairs' policy and program. As a group focused on studying the conditions of "life and work in Africa" and promoting "international cooperation for the welfare of the African people," the organization conducted research and published reports while facilitating the exchange of ideas and providing an organizational channel between Africans and progressive-minded people in America and Europe.[132] An invitation to join the organization emphasized the increasing importance of African affairs in light of the spread of Italian fascism in Ethiopia and Nazi ambitions to take over portions of the continent.

This pamphlet was based on a speech delivered at a conference held at The Hague in 1937 that examined global distribution of raw materials. Yergan's detailed analysis pointed to the appalling living standards endured by the laborers who helped South Africa produce one-third of the world's gold. He underscored that improving conditions for mine workers was complicated by the fact that organizing black workers was outlawed. Furthermore, black South Africans could not vote and were "victimized by every conceivable combination of political and economic hardship."[133] In order to facilitate change, Yergan suggested pushing for labor rights and active cooperation between democratic-minded white liberals and the black majority.

Drawing on similar data, Yergan delivered an address on "The Status of the Natives in South Africa" before the annual meeting of the Association for the Study of Negro Life and History in the autumn of 1938, which was published in the *Journal of Negro History*.[134] In this speech for a primarily African American audience, Yergan adroitly paralleled the political situation of black South Africans with the Dred Scott decision of 1857 when the U.S. Supreme Court ruled that black Americans had no rights that whites were bound to respect. Surely this was a correlation that pricked the hearts of many in the crowd. Again hitting close to home, Yergan told those assembled that racial segregation was practiced in South Africa "as in the United States" in order for "the dominant ruling class . . . [to] extract the maximum labor and taxes" while according the "minimum in wages and social services."[135] Yergan cautioned that the incursion of fascist forces onto the continent represented a frightful second phase of the scramble for resources that was initiated when Europe divided Africa in the late nineteenth century. The banner of imperialism was now being carried by fascists. Not surprisingly, the North Africa campaigns would play a crucial role in the next world war.

These pieces by Yergan were an early indication of the direction of the Council on African Affair's advocacy. As seen in the pamphlet "Gold and Poverty in South Africa," leaders of the group produced well-researched documentation of conditions in Africa that was disseminated as broadly as possible.[136] South Africa was also a natural focus for the council since Yergan had contacts there and was well acquainted with the country. The group utilized international and domestic gatherings, such as the Association for the Study of Negro Life and History convention, to stress the significance of events in Africa and their centrality in the global political discourse. In 1941, the group's name was changed to the Council on African Affairs, and it became increasingly active in the ensuing war years.

Both the Southern Negro Youth Congress and the Council on African Affairs were born out of the political and economic circumstances of the late 1930s. The crisis of the Great Depression coupled with racial subjugation in the southern United States motivated the young people who formed SNYC, while the oppression of colonialism and the emerging apartheid system in Africa moved the founders of the council to raise consciousness about events on the continent in the United States. Leaders of both groups also had ties to the Communist left, which they believed could be a force for progressive change because of the party's positions against colonialism and their mobilization against racial injustice in the United States. Their connections with the Communist Party, however, had consequences. The Council on African Affairs' affiliation with the Communist Party ultimately distanced the group from other Pan-African activists such as the influential George Padmore, who had broken with the Comintern. SNYC's association with the Communist Party probably helped contribute to the group being labeled as a subversive organization and most likely helped determine the group's position on the war during the period of the Hitler-Stalin pact.

Their focus on civil rights as well as labor issues illustrates well existence of a black-labor-left nexus in the late 1930s and early 1940s. Moreover, the international perspective of SNYC and the council demonstrates a strong global component to the coalition building of that time period. Leaders of these groups had traveled to places like Cuba, Spain, England, the Soviet Union, and Africa, which certainly informed their political discourse. At the same time, they had roots in the southern United States, which enabled them to conceptualize of the American South as part of the African diaspora and situate the struggle for civil rights for African Americans as part of a broad global fight against fascism and colonialism. Once the United States officially joined the war, the fight against fascism took center stage.

2

The World at War

Franklin D. Roosevelt delivered his State of the Union Address before Congress in January 1941 a few months after being elected to a third term as president. In this speech, President Roosevelt traced the isolationist tradition in U.S. foreign policy to the present day. He made the case that the United States was being threatened by forces of tyranny that were currently being fought by the Allies across several continents. It was up to Americans, in Roosevelt's view, to increase the production of arms to support the Allies. This supply of munitions would also help fulfill the future needs of the United States. However, taxes had to be raised in order to pay for the nation's increased defense program. Roosevelt knew that he was asking the American people to make significant sacrifices on behalf of the cause against fascism. He, therefore, closed his speech with a historic encapsulation of the rationale for taking up arms against the Axis powers: the Four Freedoms.[1] These four consisted of the freedom of speech, freedom of worship, freedom from want, and freedom from fear. Roosevelt brilliantly summarized the case for war in a way that would be accessible to all Americans. As an orator, he was quite skilled at deconstructing complex ideas and had been doing this with much success through his fireside chats since 1933. The man who had explicated and sought support for his legislative overhaul known as the New Deal was now presenting the foundation for war to Congress and the people.

In the address, Roosevelt emphasized that any peace secured following a fascist victory could not guarantee the liberties cherished by those living in the republic. He carefully elucidated the kind of future that could be expected following an Allied victory: "we look forward to a world founded on four essential human freedoms." After listing each freedom, he stressed that these freedoms were to be preserved "everywhere in the world." The ideas of freedom of speech and freedom of worship were very familiar to Americans as they were contained in the hallowed First Amendment rights that were added to the U.S. Constitution to protect individual liberties against the potential domination of a strong central government. Freedom from want was a slightly more abstract conception but would have resonated deeply with a populace that was still enduring the worst economic crisis in U.S. history. Roosevelt defined the idea as securing to every nation "a healthy peace time life for its inhabitants." This could be interpreted in a myriad of manners; however, it is significant that Roosevelt inserted this reference to economic freedom. Democracy, then, was not solely about political freedom but also had to include economic liberties like making a livelihood, supporting one's family, and, ideally, having access to some degree of financial stability. Freedom from fear meant, in Roosevelt's view, achieving a global reduction of armaments such that nations did not have to worry about acts of physical aggression from their neighbors. Pacifists and conscientious objectors were probably somewhat puzzled by his logic of arguing in favor of increased military production for the ultimate goal of attaining a worldwide arms reduction. In retrospect, the military buildup of the Cold War that immediately followed World War II ultimately overshadowed Roosevelt's initial vision of freedom from fear. Yet, this idea acknowledged the sovereignty of individual nations that was expanded upon in the Atlantic Charter in the summer of 1941 and, ultimately, the charter for the United Nations in 1945.

The Four Freedoms became a rallying call for the war effort. These essential human liberties positioned the Allies as representing a set of values that was fundamentally different from the authoritarianism of Germany, Italy, and Japan. The formulation of the Four Freedoms was referenced by Roosevelt in other speeches. He, for example, compared them to the Constitution and the Magna Carta; he used them to emphasize the urgency of defeating Hitler; and he highlighted them when declaring a "day of mobilization for freedom and human rights" on December 15, 1941.[2] The theme of the Four Freedoms was then depicted in a variety of media for public consumption. For instance, textiles with motifs based on the Four Freedoms designed by Jay Thorpe were available for purchase by patriotic households. The Office of Emergency Management (OEM) constructed a

Figure 2. Representation of the Four Freedoms, Library of Congress, Prints and Photographs Division, FSA-OWI Collection, LC-USE6-D-002992.

sizeable photographic montage by artist Jean Carlu that rendered the Four Freedoms and measured fifteen by thirty feet. It was displayed near Fourteenth Street and Pennsylvania Avenue in Washington, D.C., so that anyone strolling by could take a moment to contemplate the images (see figure 2). When, in 1943, artist Norman Rockwell illustrated the Four Freedoms with scenes from daily American life in the *Saturday Evening Post*, they became indelibly etched in the popular culture of the mobilization for war.

President Roosevelt and Prime Minister Churchill met at sea in August 1941 where they discussed, among other issues, the details of the Lend-Lease declaration that would enable the Allies to purchase munitions from the United States and pay for them later. The two leaders also agreed on a set of principles with regard to the defense of their nations in the face of fascist aggression. The ensuing Atlantic Charter enumerated the common principles for which the Allies stood. In addition to aiding the complete destruction of Nazism, these included: supporting no territorial changes that did not accord with the freely expressed wishes of the people concerned, respect for the right of all peoples to choose the form of government under which they will live, and seeing sovereign rights and self-government restored to those who had been forcibly deprived of them.[3] The spirit of the Four Freedoms was definitely apparent in the Atlantic Charter's emphasis on cooperating for economic security and assuring that all men "may live out their lives in freedom from fear and want." The philosophy of the war (that is, freedom versus tyranny) had now been articulated sufficiently such that Americans knew exactly what the Allies represented ideologically when the United States officially declared war after the attack on the base at Pearl Harbor in early December 1941. National unity was, thus, efficiently achieved for a mobilization effort based on defending the Four Freedoms.

Still, the idea of the Four Freedoms, eloquent though it might have been, was not only vague but fundamentally problematic. From the perspective of African Americans, basic liberties that were supposed to be protected by the Constitution were not being defended. The right to vote was being systematically blocked in the South, and the right to have access to education was obstructed by segregation law. Freedom from want and freedom from fear, especially, had been neglected. Unemployment and job discrimination were consistently acute for African Americans during the Great Depression. New Deal programs, like Social Security, excluded many black workers. Racial violence, such as lynching, was a reality in African American communities. Likewise, the provisions of the Atlantic Charter, while laudable, were imbued with an inherent paradox coming from two nations that had occupied foreign territories and built empires without respecting the sovereign rights of the people therein. Historian Howard Zinn has posed the provocative question: did the Allies "represent something significantly different, so that their victory would be a blow to imperialism, racism, totalitarianism, militarism, in the world?"[4] This query can be pondered from multiple perspectives: Britain was a strong imperialist force and tried to maintain its empire for as long as possible; the Soviet Union, an ally by the summer of 1941, was largely totalitarian under Stalin's rule; the United States' record on race relations was abysmal and would be for many years to come.

Nevertheless, while the United States was terribly compromised with regard to race, it was the African American community that employed the Four Freedoms and the Atlantic Charter as a basis from which to organize during the war. Civil rights activists, in groups like the Southern Negro Youth Congress, pressured the government to live up to the ideas embedded in the Four Freedoms for all American citizens, and anticolonial activists, like those in the Council on African Affairs, lobbied for the Allies to implement the principles of the Atlantic Charter for people in Africa. These were the people who worked to ensure that an Allied victory *would* be a blow to racism and imperialism.

In a very interesting way, the framework outlined in both the Four Freedoms speech and the Atlantic Charter provided a foundation from which black activists could argue persuasively for full civil rights and colonial self-determination. Doxey Wilkerson, a journalist, activist, and member of the Council on African Affairs, observes of the war years, "the events of this period are forging new relationships between the Negro people and the rest of the nation."[5] These new relationships included African Americans serving in the armed forces in large numbers. African American activists also utilized many strategies during the transformative moment of World War II to protest for freedom. The *Pittsburgh Courier* newspaper advocated for a Double Victory, or Double V, which would defeat both fascism overseas and discrimination in the United States.

And through campaigns like A. Philip Randolph's March on Washington Movement, African Americans were agitating for jobs in the defense industries. Randolph's program was largely responsible for pressuring Roosevelt to issue Executive Order 8802 in June 1941, which outlawed racial discrimination in defense hiring and created the Fair Employment Practices Committee (FEPC) to monitor hiring practices. Randolph was not satisfied, however, and called for economic security through union organizing, freedom for Africa, and the dismantling of segregation through nonviolent direct action.[6]

Writer Langston Hughes draws upon Roosevelt's Four Freedoms in a poignant essay from 1944. Hughes laments the ironies of life under segregation as he explains that trains traveling South began the practice of segregated seating at the stop in Washington, D.C. Even if a black passenger had been sitting comfortably in a rail car all the way from New York, he had to move to the Jim Crow car once the train reached the nation's capital. "To a southbound Negro citizen told at Washington to change to a segregated coach the Four Freedoms have a hollow sound, like distant lies not meant to be the truth," Hughes discerns. The rhetoric out of Washington was voided by the injustices that violated the freedoms of African Americans in that very city every day.

Educator Mary McLeod Bethune, who was a supporter of the Southern Negro Youth Congress, also referenced the symbolism of the Four Freedoms to African Americans. She points out in an essay that since "the radios and press of the world" have "drummed" the Four Freedoms into the minds of black Americans, it would lead one to believe "that the world accepts as legitimate" their claims to these rights. "What, then, does the Negro want?" she asks. The "answer is very simple," she notes. "He wants . . . what the Four Freedoms establish."[7]

The Southern Negro Youth Congress and the Council on African Affairs utilized the promises inherent in the Four Freedoms and the Atlantic Charter during the war years. SNYC worked to secure employment and protested against acts of violence in the spirit of the Four Freedoms. The council employed the language of the Atlantic Charter and challenged the Allies to apply those assurances to people in the colonized world. In the eyes of activists in SNYC and the council, the Four Freedoms had to apply equally to the South as well as other parts of the United States just as the Atlantic Charter pertained to Africa as much as it did to the rest of the world.

SNYC 1942–1945: "Freedom's Children, to Arms!"

In the spring of 1942, while the wound of the Pearl Harbor attack was still fresh and gaping in the American consciousness, the United States lurched forward in its mobilization effort now that the country was fully absorbed by the war. Since the conflict had directly penetrated a U.S. base, antifascism became a rallying cry for U.S. citizens who were from a range of political, social, economic, geographic, and ethnic backgrounds. The call against Hitlerism that was sounded by the Southern Negro Youth Congress and other groups sympathetic to the invasion of the Soviet Union in the autumn of 1941 now echoed in near unison across the nation. Since the United States and Soviet Union were officially allied in the worldwide conflagration, those on the left who might have been viewed askance for their vacillating position on the war in 1939–1941 were now in sync with the antifascist position of the majority. When SNYC leader James Jackson implored black youth to take up arms in November 1941 because "our struggle for our people's advancement has become a struggle to win a larger place at the front in the war against Hitler," this may not have been a widely adopted viewpoint.[8] However, by the spring of 1942, the call to arms was widely embraced. (Jackson entered the army in 1943 and served in Asia for a year and a half.)[9]

The hugely successful SNYC conference in April 1942, which focused on the war, illustrated the broad base of support that the group enjoyed. Greetings to the youth congress poured in from cabinet members like Secretary of War Stimson, leaders in the armed forces such as General George C. Marshall, and even President Roosevelt himself. The letter from the commander-in-chief counsels the youth on the grave importance of the war effort. He encourages the young activists: "Your strength, your courage and your loyalty to your country help assure this victory out of which must come a peace built on universal freedom such as many men have not yet known and which all the youth of today shall enjoy as the men and women of tomorrow."[10] Interestingly, Roosevelt's letter does not gloss over the unequal treatment of black Americans in favor of unifying for the war. Instead, he implicitly acknowledges discrimination against the African American community ("freedom such as many men have not yet known") and seems to conclude that the war against fascism will alleviate this contravention of the Four Freedoms he publicly touted.

Upwards of three thousand delegates, students, and townspeople crowded into Tuskegee Institute's Logan Hall for the 1942 conference opening. The lineup of speakers included longtime SNYC supporter Max Yergan of the Council on African Affairs and labor leader Ferdinand Smith, secretary of the National Maritime Union. Yergan spoke of the implications of the war for those living in European colonies who were yearning for freedom. "From the Far East to the deep South," he maintained, "the aspirations of oppressed peoples find their surest promise of fulfillment with the victorious arms of our country and her great allies."[11] Significantly, Yergan positioned the southern United States as part of a global vision of oppressed people who could benefit from the defeat of fascism.

And specifically, Ferdinand Smith warned that the nation "cannot demand of a people that they die for a country which denies them the right to live as free people."[12] As Smith's observation implies, there was some discord over the question of black Americans fully supporting the armed forces, which were still segregated. Additionally, the defense industries had not been forthcoming with jobs for black workers. John Beecher, a representative of the government's Fair Employment Practices Committee (FEPC), assured the crowd that he was fully aware of the discrimination that existed in southern industries. Hartford Knight, of the United Mine Workers, announced that he had been told that the War Production Board had promised jobs for fifty thousand African Americans in the coming months.[13]

In their annual reports to the delegates, SNYC leaders Louis Burnham and Esther Cooper Jackson balanced a call for black youth to assist the mobilization effort with a reminder that the battlefront should be extended to fight for defense industry jobs and desegregation of the armed forces. Burnham asserted that "the youth problem . . . has become a war problem." He insisted that the war was not being fought for the allies alone but that freedom and self-determination for "three-quarters of the world's people" would not be possible if Hitler was not defeated. "We have a real contribution to make to the winning of this war," Burnham urged. Yet he also demanded "the speedy elimination of all barriers" preventing black Americans from participating to their fullest potential.[14] Esther Cooper Jackson outlined an array of programs to be undertaken by SNYC to contribute to the war effort including a victory book drive. She further called for lobbying on the issues of ROTC training for black students, integration in the armed forces, and job training as well as job opportunities for black workers—both men and women—in defense industries.[15]

Though debate at the conference was at times "stormy," the delegates passed a resolution on ending discrimination in the armed forces, and it was agreed that a committee should travel to Washington to lobby on this issue. Delegates also addressed civil rights issues including denouncing segregationist congressmen and calling for continued effort in the anti-poll tax campaign.[16] Thus, the youth congress acknowledged that black youth could play an important role in the war effort. However, they skill-fully connected their call to join the mobilization for war with a sustained cry against Jim Crow. Their fight against segregation was couched in the broader framework of a global fight against fascism that, the youth congress maintained, could not be defeated while racial discrimination persisted. If the United States wanted black youth to join the fight against Hitler, then the nation could not avoid assessing the manifestations of fascism within its own borders.

This position dovetailed with the Double Victory campaign initiated in the *Pittsburgh Courier* newspaper in 1942, which was adopted nationally in the African American community. This initiative underscored the impor-tance of victory abroad over the fascist powers of Germany and Japan but also stressed that victory over domestic forms of discrimination was equally vital. Interestingly, the *Pittsburgh Courier* reported that the resolutions com-mittee at the SNYC conference had failed to officially endorse the Double V campaign. However, Louis Burnham had noted that "If we carry out the things we are planning to do here, there will be a psychological double victory resulting."[17] The fight for victories over fascism both at home and abroad helped undergird a period of cooperation as black Americans, from conservative to progressive and leftist ideologies, took up the mantel against both Hitlerism and, in the words of the SNYC newspaper, "K-K-K-ism."

Probably the most memorable event of the Tuskegee meeting was the performance by Paul Robeson. The applause of the crowd of thirty-two hundred shook the rafters as the delegates, students, soldiers, and working folks "reveled in the deep warmth and fine tonal quality of the unparalleled Robeson voice."[18] The baritone vocalist regaled the audience with selec-tions including "Water Boy," "No John No," and, the song for which he was perhaps best known, "Ole Man River" from the musical *Show Boat*. The desegregated concert at Tuskegee Institute in Alabama set an important precedent in the town and clearly demonstrated the progressive values of the youth congress. In his remarks, Robeson adroitly paralleled economic and political oppression in other countries with the discrimination prac-ticed against black Americans. He noted, "I sang in England before distin-guished people, before 'crowned heads' and was welcomed by them. Then I went into the coal mines of Wales. There I found other people who suffered and I found that they were conscious of our suffering. I learned that the suffering of human beings transcended race."[19] This was a historic occasion in the acclaimed artist's career. Though he had toured widely and was a beloved vocalist and actor around the world in the early 1940s, Robeson had rarely performed in the Deep South. This was an important turning point for him both culturally and politically because he began to more closely identify with southern African Americans and conceive of their political situation as part of the larger African diaspora.

Robeson had witnessed the forces of fascism spreading through Europe firsthand when he had traveled across the continent while touring in the 1930s. He also sang for volunteers who supported the Republican cause on the front of the Spanish Civil War. Robeson's global antifascist perspective corresponded beautifully with the ideology of SNYC. His presence at the 1942 conference solidified his relationship with the youth, which was again reinforced by his appearance at the 1946 conference in Columbia, South Carolina. Moreover, several SNYC activists moved northward after the group disbanded in the late 1940s. Louis Burnham, for example, joined forces with Robeson as editor of *Freedom* newspaper in the early 1950s. In this way, Robeson represented an important link in the black freedom struggle for progressive activists who had organized in the South but then headed to the North when the specter of racist and antiradical repression forced SNYC to dissolve. Still, the 1942 Robeson concert at Tuskegee was also enjoyable on a purely artistic level for "none who heard him" that evening in Alabama would "ever forget" this performance in the South.[20] A follow-up letter from Max Yergan stressed that he and Robeson both felt the conference had been "in every respect significant."[21]

The South and the circumstances of black people there began to figure more prominently in Robeson's political analysis after the SNYC conference in the spring of 1942. Speaking in Louisiana in the autumn of that year, Robeson admitted that he "had never put a correct evaluation on the dignity and courage of my people of the deep South until I began to come south myself.... Deep down, I think, I had imagined Negroes of the South [to be] beaten, subservient, cowed." But spending time with the black community in the South at SNYC events and other engagements demonstrated their strength and courage and made Robeson feel "utterly proud of my people." He decided that he "must come south again and again."[22] And this he did.

Robeson returned to support the Southern Negro Youth Congress and he campaigned in the South for the Progressive Party in 1948. Interacting with African Americans in the South, where poverty was widespread, helped reinforce his commitment to solidarity with the working classes. In a 1949 interview, Robeson pointed out that the wealthy sometimes wondered why he struggled "in behalf of the oppressed" when he could easily isolate himself from the problems of laboring people. He stressed that black people in the South, and in the West Indies as well as Africa, had worked to build the economies of the regions where they lived. Because of that, Robeson declared that he was "fighting for the Negroes on Strivers Row" and for "every Negro, wherever he may be."[23] Robeson, therefore, brought his celebrity in support of SNYC and the youth congress, in turn, helped the acclaimed artist and political advocate establish a closer relationship with his African American brothers and sisters in the South.

The Southern Negro Youth Congress remained active during the war as they implemented the resolutions discussed at the Tuskegee conference. In May of 1942, SNYC sent a delegation to Washington to lobby for full integration of black soldiers in all areas of the armed services. Louis Burnham, Esther Cooper Jackson, and Ernest Wright, a CIO organizer and SNYC vice president, were among the group of six that visited several offices including the War Department, the Department of Justice, the Women's Auxillary Army Corps, and the Office of Civilian Defense. At each meeting, the delegation had interviews with key leaders and discussed "specific proposals as to how Southern Negro youth may be more fully integrated in the nation's fight against Hitlerism."[24] This Washington trip was emblematic of SNYC's continuous agitation during the war for desegregation of the armed forces, jobs for black workers in defense industries, and elimination of the poll tax to alleviate disfranchisement of black voters.

SNYC also kept tabs on how African Americans fared in defense industry jobs once they were hired. This was very important data not just for the safety of workers but to use to put pressure on lawmakers, present to the FEPC, or have on hand in case of future litigation. It was not only essential that black workers have access to jobs, but additionally, SNYC activists maintained, their right to contribute to the war on an equal basis must be protected. For example, Esther Cooper Jackson wrote to Secretary Stimson after reports that three African American "WACs," women in the

Women's Army Corps, had been beaten by policemen in a bus station in Kentucky. She highlighted the significant contribution to the war being made by women in her letter. "At a time when our country is calling for more women volunteers for armed services," she pointed out, "it is impera-tive . . . that Negro Personnel and especially women be given full protection by those in authority."[25] In addition, a paper prepared by James Jackson detailed attacks on black workers in the shipyards of the Alabama Dry-Dock and Shipbuilding Company. He concluded that the government had not completely met the needs of wartime workers as industry rapidly ex-panded. Additionally, Jackson observed, unions had not adequately dealt with white supremacist agitators who now encountered an increasingly diverse population of coworkers.[26]

The attention of SNYC activists to the experiences of black workers was well founded. They no doubt understood that the idea of national unity around the war was more unanimous in theory than in practice. Racial violence erupted in dozens of cities around the country during the war. Un-fortunately, racial bias also continued in many defense plants throughout the mobilization effort. Racially motivated violence during the war per-haps also foreshadowed the surge in lynching numbers that immediately followed the war. The youth congress's documentation of the experiences of black workers during the war demonstrates how the issue of racial dis-crimination complicated the U.S. government's stand against fascism and underscored the need for a double victory.

In keeping with its focus on equal employment access, the SNYC con-ference in Birmingham in the spring of 1943 emphasized the need for en-forcement of Executive Order 8802 and called for the Fair Employment Practices Committee to become a permanent committee.[27] President Roo-sevelt had created the FEPC as an oversight committee in 1941 when he issued Executive Order 8802, which outlawed discrimination in the de-fense industries. These measures had been taken by the president largely to stave off labor leader A. Philip Randolph's call for a mass march on Wash-ington to protest against discrimination in defense employment. Despite Roosevelt's proclamation, many African Americans found few opportuni-ties to work in defense plants except in the most menial positions.

While the committee could collect data and present recommendations, regrettably the FEPC had no real authority to regulate industries that refused to train or hire black workers. As a consequence of an SNYC campaign for defense training opportunities, the Fair Employment Practices Committee held a hearing in Birmingham at which numerous members of the black community advocated for defense jobs for black workers.[28] It was only through persistent campaigning, such as that undertaken by SNYC, that this issue was kept at the forefront of the political discourse. The FEPC faced opposition in Congress from southern Democrats who guarded the poll tax and sought to protect jobs for white workers. In one of several petitions forwarded to Roosevelt, SNYC urged the President to stand firm against segregationist politicians who undermined national unity by stirring race hatred against African Americans during a time of war.[29]

In 1943, SNYC leader James Jackson declared in a speech at a freedom rally in New York, "We must insist that all patriotic forces actively crusade for favorable Senate action on the anti-poll tax bill, in order to restore the cardinal right of citizenship to the southern people."[30] Even though the Geyer Anti-Poll Tax Bill failed to become law, SNYC maintained its efforts to advocate for equal access to the ballot during the war. The southern congressmen who obstructed the FEPC were able to stay in office because of voting impediments such as the poll tax. Continued coverage of the campaign against the poll tax in northern newspapers like the progressive *People's Voice* out of New York demonstrated that the issue continued to have support as it had during SNYC's Anti-Poll Tax Week campaign in 1941. An editorial in the *People's Voice* observed that a "willful minority" of leaders in the South sustained their grip on political power through upholding the poll tax. The editorialist encouraged southern opposition to disfranchisement: "We in the north need to know that there are increasing thousands in the South who do not share the views of those rulers but who are openly and courageously fighting for repeal of the poll tax."[31]

The right to vote was a primary issue addressed at the SNYC conference in Atlanta in 1944. This theme was touched upon in Mary McLeod Bethune's keynote address when she reminded the delegates of the power of the ballot. Bethune was chair of the National Council of Negro Women and served in the National Youth Administration, a federal agency, as director of minority affairs. In her speech, SNYC leader Esther Cooper Jackson contextualized the struggle over the ballot all the way back to the historic collapse of Reconstruction in 1877 after which segregationists began to legislate voting proscriptions such as the poll tax. She insisted, "We are determined that this generation of youth shall be the first full-fledged voting generation of Negro Americans since the odious compromise of 1876."[32] President Roosevelt again sent greetings to the SNYC meeting in 1944 and acknowledged the service of African American youths during the war. In response, SNYC leaders Esther Cooper Jackson and Rose Mae Catchings wrote to FDR and reminded him that black youth had accepted their responsibility to serve but wanted to do so with dignity and equality as "full-fledged voting citizens."[33]

Efforts to secure the franchise continued as the war began to wind down. A local council in Montgomery, Alabama, began a drive in 1944 to register black voters. SNYC efforts also received support from northern allies in the Manhattan Council of the National Negro Congress in New York. For instance, a right to vote dance at the Savoy Ballroom was organized as an SNYC fundraiser.[34] An SNYC pamphlet from this period stressed the African American desire to participate in government but pointed out that "poll taxes, white primaries and registration trickery" deprived millions of their voting rights.[35] The SNYC campaign against disfranchisement was stressed at a rally in May 1945 as the war drew to its brutal conclusion. A speech by South Carolina activist Osceola McKaine looked toward a hopeful future that included expanded implementation of civil rights. He asserted that a global struggle for political rights was underway: "Is not the world wide movement of the oppressed and underprivileged people to obtain a larger measure of freedom to have the four freedoms applied to them also . . . ?"[36]

Invoking Roosevelt's Four Freedoms, which he had devised to rouse support for the war effort, was a politically savvy move on McKaine's part. He deftly utilized the early rhetoric of the war to remind the government that marginalized people who sacrificed for the war were now going to be pushing for full civil rights. The persistent voting rights campaigns through the war illustrated cooperation between activists in the North with SNYC initiatives. Though the battlefields of Europe and the Pacific grabbed larger headlines for the moment, this consistent effort indicated that the fight for civil rights was not losing momentum. In the spirit of the Double V campaign, if a victory over fascism abroad was on the horizon, then victory over racial discrimination could not be ignored.

In an event that foreshadowed the antiradical purges pursued after the war, an African American woman was fired from her position in the War Department in the summer of 1944. Reasons for her discharge included suspicion of being a member of the Communist Party or associating with Communism. SNYC leader Esther Cooper Jackson strongly contested this blatant discrimination in a statement to Secretary of War Stimson. Cooper Jackson determinedly pointed out that SNYC believed that Mrs. Thomas, the sole breadwinner for her mother and two children, "was dismissed from her job solely because of her continuous activities as a member of the United Federal Workers of America and her membership in many organizations of the Negro people." Moreover, Cooper Jackson shrewdly warned that such action could set a dangerous precedent: "If such an unwarranted discharge can be meted out to Mrs. Thomas, any Negro employee may be discharged at the whim of a prejudiced person in charge."[37] SNYC had similarly backed Max Yergan when he was asked to leave the City College of New York in 1941 because of his political views. Asserting that "deeds not words are the test of those who sincerely believe in democracy for the Negro," an editorial in *Cavalcade* suggested a letter-writing campaign be implemented on behalf of the ousted professor.[38]

These actions, though they only warranted small newspaper stories, represented some of the most courageous positions taken by SNYC. As early as 1944, SNYC acutely perceived that charges of political radicalism could be used to isolate and hamper black activists. The group stood strong against red-baiting and refused to back away from defending an activist on the grounds of her political views. Ironically, in the end, it was the lack of support for SNYC in the late 1940s that contributed to their disbanding when Cold War pressure drove away many former supporters.

Finally, the role of women was fundamental to the achievements of the Southern Negro Youth Congress during the war. Women were vital to the group from its founding and especially during the tumultuous war years. The prominent role of women in SNYC made it unique among civil rights organizations, which like the NAACP for example, were traditionally directed by men with a hierarchical leadership approach. Numerous dedicated, articulate black women created spaces for female leadership in the coalitions formed during the Popular Front era such as Claudia Jones in the Communist Party and Louise Thompson Patterson who worked with the International Worker's Order.[39] The grassroots structure of SNYC as a federation of local councils with a national headquarters that employed participatory decision-making was especially suited to fostering female leadership.

In addition, prominent African American women leaders like Mary McLeod Bethune and Charlotte Hawkins Brown had been supporters of SNYC from the first years of its existence. Brown had spoken at the 1938 conference and had even left her mother's bedside "at the point of death" because she wanted to exhort the young people "to press forward, prepare, be sacrificial, vote, work hard, but don't be foolish."[40] The youth congress held a testimonial dinner for Bethune to honor her years of service to the black community in 1945.[41] South Carolina activist Modjeska Simkins helped direct and recruit students to attend SNYC's Leadership Training School in that state in 1946. Many young women were selected as delegates from local councils to the annual national conferences. Several women held leadership positions, such as Rose Mae Catchings, who served as president, and Dorothy Challenor Burnham (wife of Louis Burnham), who sat on the executive board and served as educational director. Women were not confined to making coffee or undertaking domestic chores around the youth congress office. They represented SNYC at international conferences, delivered speeches at youth congress meetings, participated in lobbying trips to Washington, D.C., wrote letters to legislators, and made public statements for the organization. Southern female voices also echoed through the pages of *Cavalcade* in poetry, letters from rural councils, and news articles.

Cavalcade's coverage of Nora Wilson's collision with southern racial barriers illustrated well the segregated relationship between black and white rural women. Wilson had confronted the white plantation owner's wife on behalf of her younger sister, who had been accused of stealing, and it was made clear that questioning authority could be dangerous. Though the plantation owner's wife prevented her husband from shooting Nora, she was thrown into jail. Nora Wilson's case also depicted the networks established between southern black women who were willing to confront white supremacy. The women in the Wilson family forthrightly defended each other. Just as Wilson had stood up for her younger sister, it was Wilson's mother who sought help for Nora's case through the Caravan Puppeteers and ultimately wrote the letter to SNYC headquarters announcing her daughter's release. That letter ended up in the hands of a black female activist, Augusta Jackson Strong, who compassionately rendered Mrs. Wilson's message. Strong eloquently conveyed Nora's story and carefully described her situation within the historical context of Reconstruction and the economic circumstances of debt peonage.

SNYC's grassroots organizational structure coupled with a progressive political perspective that embraced female leadership, especially during the wartime crisis, meant that women played a vital role in the youth congress at the national and local levels. For example, Thelma Dale served as a vice chairman at large and finance director of SNYC. She was later recruited by Max Yergan to help steer the National Negro Congress through the war.[42] Women also worked at the local level of the Southern Negro Youth Congress, like Annie Mae Echols who acted as secretary for the Hamilton Slope Young Southerners Club. This group welcomed steelworkers, miners, domestic workers, and students into its ranks. The cultural programs and political goals of this local council were encouraged by a visit from Esther Cooper Jackson, representing SNYC national leadership.[43] During the war, Echols could be found on the sidewalks of downtown Birmingham selling "Smash Hitler" buttons to raise money for the youth congress.[44]

Augusta Jackson Strong's talent as a writer was reflected in the high quality of *Cavalcade*'s content under her editorship. Even though the newspaper struggled financially, as did the Southern Negro Youth Congress as a whole, throughout its life, *Cavalcade* offered its readers serious, intelligently crafted articles in addition to its evocative poetry and collaborative visual art. In the newspaper's opening issue, she unambiguously states its objective: "to send our message further and clearer throughout the South." What was the message SNYC wished to convey through *Cavalcade?* Simply put, it was that they would work toward freedom, equality, and opportunity for African American youth. "Our message to Southern Negro youth in these pages, and in our councils, and in everything we say and do is one of belief in our own possibilities," the masthead asserted.[45]

The publishing of *Cavalcade*, moreover, was not taken lightly. Strong stressed that the paper was both a "responsibility" and a "necessity" for southern youth. *Cavalcade*, then, during relatively short existence illuminated more than labor struggles, political campaigns, and cultural heritage;

the paper provided a medium of communication for the vulnerable, often overlooked members of southern society. Within its pages, the region's poor, disfranchised, young, and laboring citizens were treated with dignity and were viewed as central to the creation of a more egalitarian community. By the mid-1940s, *Cavalcade* had folded, and Augusta Jackson Strong was regularly contributing to the *People's Voice*, the newspaper in Harlem that was started by Adam Clayton Powell Jr.[46] However, as editor of *Cavalcade*, she had helped mold a uniquely progressive political voice in the South that announced the presence of an articulate, and, at times, militant generation of black Americans.

Ethel Lee Goodman worked for SNYC as chairman of the rural committee in which she oversaw the activities of the local councils in the countryside. She fielded letters on an array of topics and concerns in the rural communities. For example, one concerned SNYC member forwarded the names and addresses of local landlords who were cheating the sharecroppers. Another letter detailed a landowner's request that sharecroppers remove their children from school to labor in the fields at near-starvation wages. One activist worried that a local farmer was caught in a vicious cycle: he could not live on the wages paid by a landlord, so the farmer went to the WPA for assistance, where the administrator advised him to get a job from a local landlord. Other letters observed that their communities had no library or were lacking school buses or had no recreation facilities for their children.[47]

This correspondence shed light on the day-to-day obstacles faced by African Americans living in segregated farming areas. SNYC leaders, like Goodman, offered organizing advice and *Cavalcade* reported on progress made in rural communities. For instance, quilting was utilized as a mechanism for rural people to use their skills and raise money for their local councils. The national SNYC office also sponsored book drives to start libraries. Once the war loomed over the countryside, Goodman explained that farmers had an important role to play in the conflict and should use the opportunity to advocate for better conditions.[48]

Rural folk also vocalized their support for the antifascist cause. Organized farmers in Louisiana wrote to the Department of Agriculture inquiring as to how they could contribute to the need for increased production. At a meeting of SNYC rural delegates, one woman was so moved by the need to mobilize that she exclaimed, "We don't have hardly enough to feed ourselves, clothe ourselves and house ourselves, but we can make some sacrifices however small. As for myself, I'm going to make a quilt and see that it gets across the waters to keep these boys warm!"[49] The fight for the ballot and access to jobs was, of course, crucial, but it was just as essential for the youth congress to help confront the everyday concerns of its membership. Even though the cycles of debt faced by tenant farmers and sharecroppers must have felt like an overwhelming problem to tackle, dedicated SNYC activists such as Ethel Lee Goodman courageously refused to turn away from the devastation wrought by generations of poverty and chose instead to cultivate opportunities, however small, where a fledgling library, or a children's garden, or a quilting bee could offer some measure of improvement in a community.

"With most of the young men at war, the reins [of SNYC] had been taken over by a young woman: Esther Cooper Jackson," Augusta Jackson Strong remembered later.[50] Edward Strong noted the importance of Cooper Jackson's leadership during the war in a letter to Max Yergan. He pointed out that her position in the national office reflected "our policy of having young women become fully integrated into the Congress leadership" so that the work of the group would continue without interruption.[51] Cooper Jackson, originally from Virginia, was a tireless activist who left a strong imprint on the youth congress.[52] Her progressive analysis of economic circumstances in the African American community was refined in her studies at Oberlin College and Fisk University where she wrote a master's thesis on trade unionism and domestic workers. While at Fisk, she met her husband, James Jackson, who urged her to present her thesis to the CIO. Though the CIO did not implement her proposal, she contributed to civil rights and labor issues through her devoted work for the youth congress.[53]

It would have been difficult for anyone affiliated with SNYC during the early 1940s to have missed Cooper Jackson because they might have run into her at the national office, or heard her speak to local trade unions or youth councils, or seen her address a national SNYC conference, or read one of her reports in *Cavalcade*. In various capacities, she was involved at all levels of the Southern Negro Youth Congress's endeavors, from aiding newly formed local councils to clarifying the role of the national office to representing the organization at national and international events. For example, she remarked that she had been "cool as a cucumber" when meeting with First Lady Eleanor Roosevelt to talk about black rural youth.[54] Cooper Jackson also connected with young people from countries around the Western Hemisphere as a delegate to the International Youth Planning Conference in Mexico City in October 1941. The purpose of the meeting was to promote solidarity among young people in the antifascist struggle against Germany.[55]

Indicative of Esther Cooper Jackson's feminist principles was the continued use of her maiden name after her marriage to James Jackson in 1941 and her subsequent adoption of both surnames (Cooper Jackson) rather than solely associating with her married name. Though this became a common practice following the women's movement of the 1960s and 1970s, Cooper Jackson was very much ahead of her time in the way that she nurtured an independent public identity by using both names. Drawing upon this and other examples in her activism, scholar Erik S. McDuffie has postulated that Cooper Jackson's "activism highlights . . . the continuities in black feminist struggles from the 1930s through the 1980s."[56] Cooper Jackson's strong leadership presence in SNYC from the early 1940s until 1946, along with the sustained involvement of other women at the national and local levels, illustrates the existence of feminist ideology on the left at a time when women's issues did not constitute a mass movement, as they did around the early twentieth-century suffrage campaign and the feminist movement of the New Left in the 1960s.

Moreover, female participation in SNYC at all levels provides a vital counterexample to the issue of women's leadership that arose in the most important student-led civil rights group of the next generation, the Student Nonviolent Coordinating Committee (SNCC). Gender relations in SNCC were probably most famously encapsulated in Mary King and Casey Hayden's position paper from the mid-1960s titled "Sex and Caste: A Kind of Memo." This essay pointed out that there was a pattern of women being marginalized and assigned to lowlier jobs such as taking minutes at a meeting or sweeping out an office. Even though SNCC was a grassroots organization that practiced participatory democracy and had been created with important guidance from veteran women activists like Ella Baker, female leaders were not prominent in the leadership core of the national group.[57]

Without a doubt, women were vital to the work of SNCC at the national and local levels. However, the public voice and national agenda of SNCC was primarily expressed through men like Bob Moses, James Forman, John Lewis, Stokely Carmichael, and H. Rap Brown, who made press statements, spoke at major rallies such as the March on Washington, gave interviews, and conducted press conferences. In contrast, SNYC's public face, as seen in spaces like conference proceedings, delegations to Washington, letters to the federal government, and articles in *Cavalcade*, was fashioned through the joint efforts of women and men activists. Because of this, SNYC was able to weather World War II by means of its solid female leadership. In fact, Cooper Jackson, working together with Louis Burnham, made sure that SNYC did not merely survive the war as a bare-bones organization but came through the crisis robust enough to sponsor arguably its most significant national event in the autumn of 1946.

"On the Side of All Peoples Struggling for Their Freedom": The Council on African Affairs, 1942–1945

In the spring of 1942, people in the United States were still coming to terms with the attack on Hawaii, which had dramatically ushered the country into full-fledged mobilization for the war against fascism. While the United States armed forces started island-hopping their way across the Pacific, the European Allies tracked the dessert fox through North Africa. News of battles and troop movements filled the radio broadcasts and dominated the newspapers that were brought into American homes every day. During this time, the Council on African Affairs helped keep the continent of Africa and her people at the forefront of discussions on the war. A pamphlet titled "Africa in the War" cogently placed the continent within the context of the current antifascist crisis.

While Americans were reading newspaper headlines about battles in Africa, this pamphlet written by Max Yergan clarified Africa's role in the war as well as the stakes for which Africans were fighting. Yergan reminded readers that the future of colonized people depended on the outcome of the war. Invoking the promise of the Atlantic Charter, he emphasized the urgency of recognizing "the importance of the colonial peoples, their internal problems, and the relation of these to victory in the war."[58] A double victory strategy was applicable to Africans as well as African Americans. Africans were fighting against fascism in the war and wanted to be on the road to becoming free and independent from European rule once the war was won. In Africa, a double victory was needed over fascism and then colonialism.

The stakes of the war, then, for colonized people could not have been higher. Whether or not the Allies had intended such an interpretation, the antifascist rhetoric that was being broadly employed by the United States and Britain was becoming a rallying cry for anticolonialists. In fact, Yergan placed a statement that President Roosevelt made in February 1942 prominently at the opening of the pamphlet on Africa in the war. It read: "The Atlantic Charter applies not only to the parts of the world that border the Atlantic but to the whole world." The Atlantic Charter proclaimed that sovereign rights would be returned to people to whom they had been denied and that all people had the right to choose the form of government under which they would live. Thus, the antifascist struggle had motivated the United States and Britain to declare that all people had a right to self-government. If the Allied leaders could understand the justice in restoring self-determination to nations invaded by the Nazis, shouldn't the same measure be applied to European colonies in Africa? Even though Roosevelt and Churchill were focusing on nations that had been occupied by the Axis powers and might not have ever meant to apply the Atlantic Charter to colonized people, the Council on African Affairs seized the opportunity to utilize the Allied pledge of freedom as a launchpad in arguing for African independence.

That April, the council sponsored a rally at the Manhattan Center that attracted an interracial crowd of around three thousand. Among the speakers at the meeting were Max Yergan and Paul Robeson of the Council on African Affairs as well as Joseph Curran, head of the National Maritime Union, playwright Lillian Hellman, and author Pearl Buck. The purpose of the rally was to advocate for the arming of Africans and all colonized people so that they could defend themselves against fascist incursions. Robeson underscored the strategic importance of Africa in the scope of the war: "One hundred and sixty million Africans in the very near future may stand between . . . Hitler and New York."[59] Yergan called for a second front in Europe and challenged the Roosevelt administration to live up to the promise of the Four Freedoms by allowing black soldiers and workers to participate fully in the war effort.[60] The substantial crowd as well as the array of speakers on the dais illustrated that the council was a respected advocacy group whose message about Africa was beginning to be heard. Indeed, it was during the war and its immediate aftermath that the Council on African Affairs was at the pinnacle of its influence.

During the war, the council's membership grew and included newspaper publisher Charlotta Bass, labor leader Ferdinand Smith, and professors E. Franklin Frazier and Doxey Wilkerson. The Council on African Affairs also took up residence at its headquarters on West 26th Street during this period and by 1946 its offices grew to include a handsome, spacious library of volumes on Africa.[61] Certainly, the most crucial addition to the council came in 1943 when William Alphaeus Hunton joined the staff as educational director. He also assumed editorial duties of the recently launched newsletter *New Africa*. For the next five years, Hunton, Yergan, and Robeson were the core leaders of the group and steered its programming as well as its ideological direction. Like the other leaders of the group, Hunton's family had deep southern roots that had impacted his intellectual and political development.

Hunton was born in Atlanta, Georgia, into a family whose service and dedication to the freedom struggle of black Americans was distinguished. As Robeson's father had escaped from enslavement in North Carolina, Hunton's grandfather, Stanton, used the underground railroad to flee to Canada. Hunton's father, William Alphaeus Sr., grew up in the abolitionist community of Chatham, Canada, where John Brown had planned part of his famous raid on Harper's Ferry, Viginia. Hunton's father was the first African American secretary for the YMCA and sought to improve race relations during his lengthy career with the Christian organization. In 1906, Hunton Sr. and his young family, including their three-year-old son, were living in Atlanta, but the racist brutality of the riot that year drove the family north to Brooklyn, New York. After earning a doctorate at New York University, Hunton Jr. accepted a post to teach literature at Howard University in 1926.[62]

During his years in Washington, D.C., Hunton observed the segregation, discrimination, inadequate housing, and police brutality that were rife in the nation's capital. These issues moved him to become increasingly politically active in the local branch of the National Negro Congress. Since he saw labor organizing to be "a force for social progress," Hunton also helped to initiate the Howard Teacher's Union.[63] By the time the worldwide antifascist conflagration had commenced, Hunton was applying a Marxist analysis to his study of African history and culture.[64] He then decided that the best way to serve the community of Africans in the diaspora would be by working with the Council on African Affairs. By relocating to New York to support the council full time, Hunton might have been leaving the South geographically, but his analysis of Africa was buttressed by the fight against injustice with which he had been engaged in Washington, D.C. From the North, he was now situated to apply the seriousness of the scholar and the ardor of the activist to the cause of freedom for people in the African diaspora. One of his most important contributions was editing *New Africa*.

"This is your news of Africa." This individualized statement appeared by the name and address of subscribers who received the Council on African Affairs's newsletter, *New Africa*. Historian Hollis Lynch asserts that the council's newsletter, which had a circulation of over three thousand at its peak in 1946, was "the single most important source of information and enlightened opinion on Africa" in the United States at the time it was published.[65] Its influence was certainly greater than its circulation numbers as it was available in libraries and copies would have been passed around among community groups and labor unions. Correspondence printed in its pages indicated that it was known in the United Kingdom and Africa. The Southern Negro Youth Congress used *New Africa* in its leadership training courses and the federal government, no doubt, kept tabs on the council by reading its literature as well.

However, that simple phrase on the outside cover of the newsletter indicating to subscribers that this was *their* news of Africa helped to make its contents personal. The leaders of the organization were conveying that the material—this news of Africa—was written for *you*. In other words, Africa should matter to you. They wanted you, the reader, to be not only informed but invested in the events reported in these pages. The message seemed to gently nudge the reader: now that *New Africa* had enlightened you on these issues, how were you going to get involved? Of course, the newsletter offered multiple ways in which to get involved, from attending lectures and rallies to simply visiting the council's library on Africa. Perhaps the easiest way to offer support was to send in one dollar to renew a subscription.

Issues of *New Africa* were produced about once a month and tended to be around four pages long with photos. The layout, with two or three columns of typesetting per page, allowed for a significant amount of information to be disseminated in a professional and concise format. As its chief organ of propagandizing, the newsletter was probably the most vital tool in the council's arsenal for agitating for Africa. The newsletter covered a range of issues including colonial governance, education, labor, and race discrimination. The dominant themes during the war were demanding that the Atlantic Charter resolutions be applied to all colonized people and requesting that the Allies ensure postwar democracy for all people after the war.

The role African people were playing in fighting the war against fascism was central to the council's argument that the only just and logical conclusion was for colonized people to attain self-government once the peace treaties were signed. In the August 1943 issue, the cover story quoted British Prime Minister Churchill announcing that the war in Africa was over because Benito Mussolini and Adolf Hitler's aims on the continent had been effectively stymied by the Allies. However, the article in *New Africa* queried whether the war in Africa was really over if European domination was to continue. Another issue stated to the Allied leaders: "And let it be remembered that Africa as well as India and the Orient must receive its charter of freedom. *The Africans too want to know what they are fighting for.*"[66] The editor's emphasis on that last sentence stressed that promises for self-government, as directly affirmed in the Atlantic Charter of 1941, must be applied to all people equally. If the Allies were going to talk about freedom, sovereign rights had to be respected and colonial governments had to be dismantled. If this was not going to occur, then the brave Africans and Indians supporting the Allied cause had done so in vain.

In late 1943, Roosevelt, Stalin, and Churchill signed a new charter at the Tehran conference, and its contents were excerpted on the cover of the December issue of *New Africa*. Though not as explicit as the Atlantic Charter, this resolution did assure the world that the Allies sought the cooperation of all nations in securing peace and eliminating tyranny and oppression. That issue of *New Africa* also quoted Robeson from a speech given at a New York Herald Tribune forum on current issues. He reminded the audience and panelists that the participation in the war by Africans and

African Americans should constitute "the measure of the kind of victory and the kind of peace that is in store for them." Early in 1944, council chairman Robeson was hopeful in sending greetings to the new president of Liberia. He confidently pointed to a "new era" that would be characterized by "democratic equality among all nations and peoples in your continent [and] in ours."[67] The leaders of the Council on African Affairs had written numerous articles and delivered speeches in the United States and Canada on the need for extending democracy to colonized people after the war. They broadened the dialogue on this vital issue in the spring of 1944.

In April of that year, the council sponsored a conference for "a new Africa" at its offices on West 26th Street. Throughout the war, the group had been calling for the arming of Africans to defend themselves against fascist invasions as well as for the outlawing of any limitations that prevented the African people from participating in the war effort to the extent of their fullest potential. Toward that end, council officers had "consulted with officials of the Department of State" and "kept in close contact with officials of European governments" with regard to shaping policies toward Africa. Though winning the war was still the paramount objective, the council officers understood that a discourse on the future of Africa must begin in order to "enlist the widest possible endorsement" for implementing a democratic social order and modern economic system in postwar Africa.[68] This interracial and international meeting of over one hundred activists, union organizers, educators, and concerned citizens included representatives of governments of Liberia, the Belgian Congo, France, Belgium, and the Soviet Union. The U.S. State Department felt it was "inexpedient" to send a representative.[69] Other notable participants included West Indians and Africans such as labor leader Ferdinand Smith, Amy Ashwood Garvey, wife of the late Marcus Garvey, and Francis (Kwame) Nkrumah, who would later help lead Ghana to independence.

This gathering was an important precursor to the Pan-African Congress held after the war in England. It was also a vital connector between the congresses of the early twentieth century, which were initiated in part by W.E.B. Du Bois, and the post–World War II conference. The meeting at the Council on African Affairs headquarters was called by African Americans but it was representative of the diaspora. Significantly, the conference included contributions from people like Amy Ashwood Garvey and Kwame Nkrumah, who represented fundamental links to past Pan-African movements (for example, Garveyism) as well as the campaigns for African independence that would occur in the near future. Though his relationship with George Padmore would later be crucial in the development of his Pan-African ideology, Nkrumah's participation in the council's event provided an early opportunity for him to discuss the major issues that Africans would face after the war with people from the diaspora.

In his opening remarks, Paul Robeson took note of two emerging trends in recent literature on Africa. The first school of thought he labeled the "new imperialist" model because it portrayed Africa as a territory of vast resources without taking the people into consideration at all. He described the second school of thought as the "yes, but apologists." This group included people who acknowledged the shortcomings of colonial rule but concluded that overall, much had been accomplished by the Europeans in Africa.[70] It was his hope that new ideas focusing on the future of Africa, including its people and resources, would be generated at the conference in the spirit of international cooperation, which had been modeled at the Allied meetings during the war. Such collaboration, as demonstrated at the Tehran conference, could lay the foundation for democratic self-rule in Africa, in Robeson's view. He further stressed that in order to remain true to the antifascist principles ignited by the war, the Allied public statements made in the Atlantic Charter and at the Tehran, Moscow, and Cairo meetings, which supported the right of self-government, must be applied to the colonized world. These themes resonated throughout the conference discussion and in the resolutions voted upon by the attendees.

In his keynote address, Max Yergan outlined the council's position on the three primary topics of the meeting: increasing Africa's contribution to winning the war, finding solutions to territorial disputes, and determining policies for the general betterment of the African people. These points were then taken up in discussion with the conference participants. With regard to territory disputes, Yergan raised concerns about areas that were under fascist jurisdiction as well as the grouping of land by regional governance. He emphasized that the people should have a voice in any postwar formation of nation-states. Yergan also maintained that any assessment of the future of colonized peoples should not be made in isolation. International cooperation as well as peace, security, and economic prosperity on a global scale should be the framework from which decolonization was considered.

Here Yergan made an interesting analogy: the economically challenged southland was to the United States what Africa was to the world. Both areas were underdeveloped economically, in part because of white supremacist hierarchies. In each place, racial discrimination had gone hand-in-hand with economic policy. In the American South, employment opportunities were tied to race and the overall economic health of the region had historically been guided by race-based enslavement and segregation. Economic policy was determined by the white power structure in both colonized Africa and the American South. Slavery in the Americas and European colonial development had drained much of Africa's resources to enrich other empires.

Yergan's solution was clear: because "the division of the world population into dominant and dependent sections, just as the division of a nation's population into privileged and oppressed sections, breeds friction and conflict," this pattern must be halted and new relationships based on equal terms must be established to ensure security and economic growth.[71] Thus, the way to avoid future conflict and stimulate economic growth was to eliminate the hierarchical systems of colonial dominance in Africa and racial segregation in the United States. The creation of new relationships based on self-determination and equal rights would chart a path to security and productivity for people that had been oppressed.

He argued that the same spirit of cooperation that blossomed in the face of the threat of fascism could now be applied toward the "larger victory of economic and social well-being of all peoples of the world."[72] This collaboration, in the view of the Council on African Affairs, should be fostered by an international body that would oversee the future development of the colonies. However, Yergan was adamant that this body must ultimately be focused on obtaining self-government for colonized people. In the discussion session, Nkrumah was dubious about the competence of any such international body to safeguard the interests of colonized people. Yergan responded that a potential international group would have to be supported from the "roots" of the people in order to be effective.

The question of the role of racial nationalism among African Americans and people of African descent was also raised during the open discussion. Yergan stressed that nationalism alone was not sufficient but that people from the diaspora needed to cultivate allies among labor groups and liberal organizations because a broad-based international, interracial coalition would be most effective in addressing the move to democratic self-governance. At this point, Amy Ashwood Garvey sagely referenced her husband's movement but conceded that she saw "no ill in white allies" as long as the primary "responsibility for striking the blow in the interests for our posterity and ourselves" was taken by "the Negro himself."[73]

Thus, the prepared speeches and lively ensuing discussion presaged a number of postwar developments including the establishment of the United Nations and the emergence of territorial disputes such as that over the former German colony of South West Africa. While the council's conference was largely supported by African Americans with some Africans, Europeans, and West Indians in attendance, the subsequent Pan-African Congress in England in 1945 was strongly backed by Africans and others from the colonized world without much participation from African Americans. The council's meeting signaled a significant moment of change: the momentum for the thrust toward colonial independence was to be taken up by people from the colonies after the war. There was, however, an important role to be played by groups such as the Council on African Affairs in facilitating dialogue and keeping people in the United States appraised of independence campaigns in Africa and the diaspora.

The closing session of the Council on African Affairs' 1944 conference focused on journalistic coverage of Africa in the United States and how it could be improved. One participant perceived a possible solution to be "the increasing prestige and influence" of the council and how that might "result in a more respectful attitude on the part of the daily press in presenting news of the African people."[74] Thus, the presence of an organization that examined African issues in a studious manner impacted public perception of the continent. Even if the resolutions of the conference did not come to pass, and most of them did not, the mere act of treating the future of postwar Africa seriously and disseminating the forum proceedings helped to raise consciousness and liberate Africans from the denigrating caricatures portrayed in the mainstream press. The goal was that Americans would begin to see Africa as more than simply a vast area of exploitable natural resources, which had been labeled "the jackpot of WWII," because of the council's work.[75] In a review of the conference proceedings, distinguished historian Carter G. Woodson characterized the spirit of the council at this time as "invincible."[76]

The Council on African Affairs sponsored another major event in April 1944 that drew thousands of people to the 17th Regiment Armory on Park Avenue. The occasion was Paul Robeson's birthday, and the size of the crowd illustrated his tremendous fame at this point in his career as a vocalist, activist, and, most recently, interpreter of Shakespeare's Othello on the Broadway stage. The *People's Voice* reported that five thousand people had to be turned away from the throng of eight thousand people of "all nations, creeds, and races" that gathered to fete Robeson.[77] An array of entertainers appeared on the program, including Duke Ellington, Hazel Scott, Count Basie, Teddy Wilson, Pearl Primus, and Josh White.[78] Mary McLeod Bethune, a supporter of the council, declared Robeson to be "the tallest tree of our forest."[79] Robeson was stirred by the overwhelming turnout and regaled the crowd with several musical selections, but he also spoke of the important work of the Council on African Affairs, which the audience's donations would go to support. He expressed his hope that his popularity would "serve to further the cause of this very worthy organization."[80] Thus, Robeson's celebrity was an asset to the council with regard to raising the profile of the group as well as obtaining necessary funding. As long as Robeson's name resonated with the populace, so too could the council benefit from his position of artistic prominence.

The Council on African Affairs concluded its work that year by sending a letter to President Roosevelt and Secretary of State Edward R. Stettinius that was signed by over 150 concerned citizens. The range of signatures demonstrated the broad appeal of the council's work among educators, newspaper publishers, writers, politicians, organizers, and philanthropists. The contents of the letter reflected themes discussed at the spring conference and stressed that since "the colonial and subject peoples of Africa have contributed greatly toward the achievement of a United Nations' victory over our common fascist enemies" these people are "justified" in the expectation that they will benefit from the sacrifices they made for the war. The letter did not call directly for independence but highlighted the role the United States might play in an international effort to help raise living standards, promote industrialization, and eliminate discrimination on the continent.[81] Thus, as the war edged toward its conclusion, the council pushed on several fronts to keep Africa at the forefront of postwar dialogue. Even though the decisive battles on the continent had occurred in the early years of the antifascist conflict, the council aimed to ensure that Africa's contribution would not be forgotten.

The Council on African Affairs was also actively involved in lobbying for Africa during the creation of the United Nations governing body. The term "united nations" entered the wartime lexicon in early 1942 after the Declaration of United Nations officially formed a coalition of countries that were aligned against fascism. Global economic policies were outlined at the Bretton Woods conference in New Hampshire in the summer of 1944. Preliminary discussions toward the creation of a worldwide organization were held in the autumn of 1944 at Dumbarton Oaks, a historic estate in Washington, D.C. Representatives from fifty nations then met in San Francisco, California, in 1945 to charter the international body known today as the United Nations. Like other African American organizations, the council followed these developments closely.[82]

In the September 1944 edition of *New Africa*, the council hoped that the talks at Dumbarton Oaks were addressing some form of international cooperation that would help steer colonized people to a brighter future. The article also sharply condemned any usurpation of self-interest and stressed that "selfishness and suspicion" must give way to the common interest of all people.[83] The reply from Secretary of State Stettinius to the council's letter from the previous December also seemed to signal cause for hope. He assured the council that the governments represented at Dumbarton Oaks wished to "protect and promote the welfare of all peace-loving peoples" and that his department was focusing on specific issues related to colonized nations. Stettinius closed by observing that the council's "constructive interest" in the efforts underway to form a peace-time coalition for all people was appreciated.[84]

The United States' ascendancy onto the world stage was evident as Stettinius and Roosevelt met with leaders in Africa and the Middle East in early 1945. *New Africa* published a photo of Roosevelt talking with Haile Selassie on the cover of its March 1945 newsletter. The leaders of the Council on African Affairs hoped that an image of the U.S. president conferring with an African leader represented a "determination and sincerity behind the pledge of international cooperation" in the postwar dialogue on Africa. In the United States, hearings on whether America would participate in the monetary agreements proposed at the Bretton Woods conference were unfolding in Congress in early 1945. In February 1945, Alphaeus Hunton traveled to Washington as one of over a hundred representatives from U.S. organizations who were invited to hear Treasury and State Department officials explicate these monetary agreements. Hunton asked about the impact of the proposed International Monetary Fund (IMF) on colonial people, and an assistant Secretary of the Treasury explained that the IMF would aid people in colonial territories by "expanding world trade" and opening up "profitable markets for the raw materials" from these areas.[85] Hunton assiduously reported on these important economic issues in *New Africa*.

In preparation for the San Francisco conference, the council crafted a statement on colonial issues that was disseminated to delegates at the meeting as well as to the State Department and to anyone else who was interested in the dialogue on postwar Africa.[86] The pamphlet focused on the familiar theme of international cooperation with regard to colonies and dependent territories. The council argued that "world security cannot be achieved" unless there existed an international recognition of the responsibility to enable colonized people to advance toward self-determination. Taking the issue of security a step further, the council declared that "a universal determination" existed "to advance from a laissez-faire world of nationalistic rivalries to a world of collective responsibility and collective security."[87] Though perhaps overly optimistic, this statement illustrated well the deeply felt belief held by many progressives that the antifascist war could alter the global political landscape for the better and that forces for positive change could mold a more egalitarian world in the wake of the terrible conflagration. The defeat of German, Italian, and Japanese fascism could mean that fascism in all of its forms, including imperialism and racial discrimination, was in peril and soon to be eradicated. For the Council on African Affairs, such a vision included the creation of an international colonial commission that would oversee the administration of trade and would facilitate modernization and industrialization as well as the improvement of living standards, health services, and education in colonial territories.

Most important, in the view of the council, such a commission would determine a timetable for individual colonies to attain self-government. After outlining its specific recommendations on the authority of the proposed colonial commission, the council closed its argument with several pages of carefully cited speeches and articles from politicians, intellectuals, and labor leaders from around the world that supported their case. All in all, the pamphlet, which was distributed for free, elaborated on the idea of an international colonial committee that had been suggested at the council's 1944 conference and maintained the position, which the council had held through the war, that the colonial issue was crucial to future world security.

Another Council on African Affairs publication from 1945 synthesizes historical trends as well as the aspirations of the African people. "What Do the People of Africa Want?" was written by Eslanda Robeson with an introduction by Max Yergan, who positioned the author as an expert based on her anthropological study and extensive travel. Unlike the San Francisco pamphlet that laid out a honed argument for an informed audience, Robeson's pamphlet was meant to be accessible to the broadest possible readership. If the San Francisco pamphlet was for the cognoscenti, then Robeson's piece was for the masses. Her writing is straightforward and meant to overturn common misconceptions about Africans by recognizing their ancient civilizations and contributions to world culture. Robeson then deftly situates Africa in the contemporary political climate. Noting that most Africans do not control their own land and resources, she stresses that African soldiers in World War II desire democracy and access to the Four Freedoms. Through this pragmatic, down-to-earth approach, Robeson enables her readers to identify with people in Africa who are millions of miles away. Are they savages living in jungles? No. These are human beings with practical ambitions like quality housing and education, access to food and jobs, and basic political rights. Most important, these people want to have a voice in their government. Any American would be able to relate to such universal aspirations.

However, Robeson closes with the stinging observation that if the colonies are not liberated, "THE WAR NOT ONLY WILL NOT BE WON—IT WILL NOT BE FINISHED."[88] This was a powerful statement especially given its timing. If there was anything that Americans and all of the Allies wanted in 1945, it was for the war to be finished. Yet,

Robeson coaxes the reader to understand that the war was fought to secure the future not only of Europeans and Americans; Africans had also made sacrifices and desired the same freedoms of religion and speech as well as freedom from want and freedom from fear so coveted by all involved in the war effort. Moreover, she maintains that the needs of Africans have to be taken seriously not only because they support the antifascist cause but also because fascism will not truly be defeated if Africans cannot walk in full dignity and enjoy self-government.

Another strong female voice praised Eslanda Robeson's pamphlet. Reviewing the piece in the *People's Voice*, Amy Ashwood Garvey characterizes Robeson's writing as "engaging" and "informative." Though Garvey would have liked the message to have been a more "vibrant song of freedom," she is heartened that an African American woman demonstrated such "precise, pragmatic awareness" and goes on to urge everyone who believes in the need for a "people's peace" to read the piece.[89] This pamphlet is also indicative of Eslanda Robeson's growing profile within the Council on African Affairs in 1945. Her book, *African Journey*, was published that year and she accompanied Yergan as an observer at the San Francisco UN conference.[90]

Several African American organizations sent observers to San Francisco in 1945. Walter White and W.E.B. Du Bois from the NAACP attended as well as Mary McLeod Bethune of the National Council of Negro Women. Ralph Bunche, a former council member, was the only African American in an official capacity working for the Division of Dependent Affairs for the U.S. Department of State. Three nations from the African diaspora were represented at the conference: Liberia, Ethiopia, and Haiti. The Council on African Affairs set up a temporary office on Market Street during the conference. Coverage of the colonial issue became a constant feature in *New Africa* during the meeting from April to June and following the signing of the United Nations charter. As discussions for trusteeship of colonized territories took shape, the hopeful spirit of the council's 1944 conference proceedings slowly gave way to frustration as the United States proved to be more focused on compromising with European colonizers than pushing toward colonial independence.

Observing this trend, editorials in *New Africa* critiqued developments at the San Francisco conference and continued to lobby for colonial oversight that was temporary and helped pave the way to self-government. For example, in May 1945 an editorial worried that a U.S. trusteeship plan did not treat all dependent regions equally. The editorial also called for seats for all five major Allied powers, including China and the Soviet Union, on the Trusteeship Council. That month council chairman Paul Robeson telegrammed newly ascended President Harry S. Truman and Secretary Stettinius that the UN charter should "give clear expression to and support the principle of full freedom within specified time for all colonial peoples."[91]

By September 1946, the Council on African Affairs was concerned that Roosevelt's vision of a peace without colonies was not being fulfilled by the new administration, which was instead "actively aiding and even leading the way in the perpetuation of imperialism." Former Vice President Henry A. Wallace was forced to resign from the position of Secretary of Commerce because of disagreements with the administration's approach to relations with the Soviet Union. This was cited as further evidence that under Truman's watch, the United States was embarking on an aggressive foreign policy that could lead to perpetual war. In the autumn of 1946, the Trusteeship Council remained the only major UN body yet to be organized. The Council on African Affairs, thus, called a meeting in October 1946 to discuss the situation. They urged supporters to send petitions directly to the United Nations and to U.S. Secretary of State James Byrnes demanding representation of colonized African people in the United Nations and guarantees for a timetable for self-government for colonies.[92]

The flurry of council activity regarding the colonial issue in 1945–1946 represented one of the group's most important contributions as agitators for African independence in the United Nations. Reactionary forces became increasingly vocal during this period: staunch segregationists like Secretary of State Byrnes gained prominent political positions in the Truman White House while more progressive voices such as Henry A. Wallace were edged out of Washington. Through it all, the Council on African Affairs consistently and publicly critiqued U.S. policy. As a leader in the postwar world, the council argued, the United States chose to bolster European colonizers rather than foster democracy by helping guide colonies to determining their own futures. The council unflinchingly challenged the U.S. government to live up to the promises of the Four Freedoms and the Atlantic Charter for colonized people even as the democratic rhetoric of

World War II devolved into the red-baiting, antiradical vitriol of the Cold War. As a lobbyist group, the council was the only nongovernmental organization with a regular UN accredited observer attending Trusteeship Council meetings and the General Assembly.[93] With Hunton as a UN observer, the council was able to send reports of UN proceedings to African groups in Britain and on the continent. *New Africa* was one of the only voices keeping Americans informed about positions taken by their government regarding colonized people.

While the United Nations was inching toward progress on the colonial issue, a significant meeting demonstrated that colonized people were nevertheless on the move toward liberation. The question of convening another Pan-African Congress was in the minds of activists who were concerned with the future of colonies in the diaspora. The Council on African Affairs had hosted its international conference in April 1944. In July a group in London, the League of Coloured Peoples, had hosted a meeting that crafted a "Charter for Coloured Peoples," which illustrated the radicalizing effect of the war. The charter demanded economic, educational, and political opportunities for Africans as well as preparations for self-government.[94]

Similarly, W.E.B. Du Bois initiated a meeting on colonial issues under the auspices of the NAACP, which had recently given him an office and the title of director of special research, at the New York Public Library branch on 135th Street in Harlem in April 1945.[95] In planning this symposium, Du Bois had corresponded with Alphaeus Hunton, who had sent him the names of several contacts including Kwame Nkrumah, who was invited and actively participated in the meeting.[96] Du Bois was further intent on reviving the Pan-African Congress movement and wanted the NAACP to support the organizing of a broad meeting of leaders from the diaspora. However, in the spring of 1945 he learned that George Padmore and a group called the Pan-African Federation, which was undergirded by Padmore's International African Service Bureau, was already making arrangements for a congress to be held that year.

Du Bois remained in close touch with Padmore through the autumn as plans coalesced for an October conference in Manchester, England. Padmore scheduled the conference just after the meeting of the World Federation of Trade Unions in Paris so that representatives from the colonies attending that meeting could also attend the Pan-African Congress. Du Bois was concerned about travel arrangements for representatives attending from the Americas as demobilization of troops was tying up most transport services across the Atlantic. However, Padmore was adamant that the meeting be as representative of the masses as possible and felt that coordination with the trade union meeting was crucial. He stressed to Du Bois that a new spirit was burgeoning among Africans and a "unity of purpose" had emerged in which all agreed on the question of self-determination whether their ideologies were more nationalist or Marxist.[97]

Ninety delegates from the Pan-African world attended the Manchester Congress. A news release indicated that the struggles of colonized people had entered a phase characterized by a new mood of "militancy."[98] Padmore was excited that the delegates who attended came with mandates from their organizations to vote on resolutions that made the congress broadly representative. Yet, Du Bois was the only African American to attend this historic meeting. This illustrated a clear shift: the early Pan-African congresses had been strongly supported by African Americans, with Du Bois offering vital leadership, but following World War II the movement was guided by West Indians and Africans.

While the 1945 congress was well attended, clear divisions were nevertheless apparent. Though Anglophone colonies were well represented, at the Manchester meeting the Francophone empire was not. This was because Padmore felt that people under the French "semi-dictatorial regime" had less space in which to maneuver politically than those in the British system, which at least allowed labor and political organizing.[99] Working for freedom in British colonies, then, could be more productive. The League of Coloured Peoples, though based in the United Kingdom, did not participate at Manchester though the group had shown some support for the manifesto that was drawn up in preparation for the congress.[100] Padmore had been critical of the league's "single handed attitude" and seemed to think they might obstruct broad cooperation. Du Bois noted that they were conservative on trade unionization, and trade unionists were fairly prominent at the meeting.[101]

What about the Council on African Affairs? The group did not participate in the meeting. And whether they were invited was not totally clear. Padmore indicated to Du Bois in 1946 that he had indeed invited them.[102] However, in September 1945, just prior to the conference, Padmore wrote that he regretted not having sent invitations to individual organizations in the United States when he realized that there would be little participation from African Americans.[103] If the council was invited, obtaining visas would have been difficult. Moreover, Paul Robeson was scheduled to receive the Spingarn Medal from the NAACP in New York the same week in October that the Pan-African Congress occurred, so he probably would not have been able to attend the meeting in Manchester. In the January 1946 edition of *New Africa*, the Pan-African Congress was not listed among the annual review of important events in African affairs for the previous year. The council might not have known about the congress when this issue went to press. Perhaps they did not want to acknowledge the Pan-African Congress because they were affiliated with the Communist left, and there was tension with Padmore, who was a former Communist. Nonetheless, Du Bois remained a crucial link between the Council on African Affairs and the Pan-African Federation. Hunton knew about the congress by February 1946 when he wrote to Du Bois for a copy of the resolutions passed, and Du Bois commented that he wanted to meet with Hunton to discuss future planning related to what had transpired at the Pan-African Congress.[104] Du Bois also made a statement as a representative of the Pan-African Congress at a rally sponsored by the council in the summer of 1946.[105]

All in all, the Manchester Congress revealed a zeal and commitment for obtaining self-government in the minds and hearts of colonized people. While the United Nations crept toward establishing a committee on colonial trusteeship, the colonized were adamantly resolving to unite and fend off imperial powers by force if necessary. A statement drafted by Kwame Nkrumah for the congress encouraged workers and farmers in the colonies to use tactics like strikes and boycotts to resist European domination. Intellectuals were urged to assist in organizing the masses and Nkrumah himself was soon doing exactly that in the Gold Coast. Historian Imanuel Geiss argues that it was at the council's 1944 conference that Nkrumah, who until then had been a student, made his "debut on the Pan-African stage." It was through the Council on African Affairs that he started a public career that led to the 1945 Pan-African Congress, his intellectual alliance with Padmore, and, ultimately, the toppling of British colonialism in Ghana.[106] Thus, even though the council was not present at Manchester in

1945, it had played an important role initiating dialogue on colonial issues in the postwar environment.

In conclusion, the Southern Negro Youth Congress and the Council on African Affairs mobilized energetically during the war years. In the spirit of Roosevelt's Four Freedoms, SNYC campaigned for equal access to jobs during the war and lobbied for obstructions to be lifted from black voting rights. The group also documented conditions faced by black workers in the defense industries and fostered the leadership of the women in its ranks. By inviting the celebrated artist Paul Robeson to its 1942 conference, SNYC attracted a large integrated crowd to Tuskegee University while also enabling Robeson to connect with the southern African American community. The Council on African Affairs invoked the promises of the Atlantic Charter throughout the war in its case for colonial independence. In addition to publishing its regular newsletter and numerous pamphlets, the organization hosted a crucial conference in 1944 that initiated an international discourse on postwar planning for Africa that helped launch Kwame Nkrumah's public career. The council also actively monitored the meetings where the governing body of the United Nations was established while lobbying on behalf of the right to self-government for colonized people.

The council and SNYC, along with other contemporary activists, were helping to, in the words of Doxey Wilkerson, forge "new relationships between the Negro people and the rest of the nation."[107] These relationships demonstrated the urgency of defeating manifestations of fascism at home as well as abroad and illustrated the hope for a new world based on progressive values that could be born out of the upheaval of the war. Paul Robeson, chairman of the Council on African Affairs, observed in 1943 that "the spirit of Negro youth in the South augurs much for the future." He was heartened that black young people understood their role "in the world wide struggle against fascism." It was also important, in Robeson's view, that African Americans perceive their aspirations and their struggle for freedom within a global context. "Africa will occupy a different position in the post-war world," he asserted, and the United States would have to reevaluate the continued subjugation of black citizens in light of the breakdown of colonialism in India and perhaps even the Caribbean.[108]

What did African Americans desire as outcomes of the war effort? This question was posed in a volume published by the University of North

Carolina Press in 1944. Significantly, the collection was produced at the behest of the press, a southern press. The publisher's introduction affirmed that the country, and especially the South, "ought to know what the Negro wants" as the war came to a close.[109] Fourteen imminent scholars, writers, and activists representing a variety of perspectives across the political spectrum responded to the query. Rayford Logan, a history professor who had spoken at the SNYC conference in 1938, edited the compilation. In his opening, he perceptively framed the contemporary social context. "Race relations," Logan asserted, "are more strained than they have been in many years. Negroes are disturbed by the continued denial of what they consider to be legitimate aspirations. . . ." By contrast, "White Americans express alarm at what they call the excessive insistence by Negroes upon a too rapid change in the *status quo*."[110]

So there would not be any doubt, Logan unequivocally laid out an explanation of "what we want." African Americans wanted first-class citizenship and this idea included equal opportunities, equal pay for equal work, equal protection under the law, equal access to suffrage, equal recognition of human dignity and the abolition of segregation.[111] If the Four Freedoms had been framed to position democracy in opposition to the tyranny of fascism, it was now time to fulfill those freedoms for all American citizens and apply the Atlantic Charter's promise of self-government to all people. As Eslanda Robeson had boldly maintained, if the promises of democratic freedoms were not realized for all people, then not only would the war not be won—it would not be over.

A new front was to be inaugurated wherein oppressed people would fight for their freedom. The Council on African Affairs and the Southern Negro Youth Congress were at the frontlines of this new battle in 1946. Interestingly, in his article in *What the Negro Wants*, Langston Hughes recommended that the government "draft" prominent African Americans such as W.E.B. Du Bois and Paul Robeson to visit the South "carrying messages of culture and democracy." In fact, both Robeson and Du Bois appeared in the South following the war to campaign for the democratic rights of black citizens in a cultural forum. The event that brought these outstanding leaders and proponents of African independence was not, however, sponsored by the government. It was hosted by the Southern Negro Youth Congress.

3

The Cold War Descends

Franklin Roosevelt had introduced the Four Freedoms as a clear representation of the ideology framing America's goals in World War II. Though they appeared to be straightforward and relevant when the United States entered the war, the Four Freedoms became subsumed by the complex postwar political landscape. Following Roosevelt's death in April 1945, the concluding chapter of the war was overseen by Harry Truman. The new president, who had little experience in foreign policy, was at the helm during a significant and transformative moment in global affairs. At the conference between the Allied leaders Joseph Stalin, Winston Churchill, and President Truman in Potsdam, Germany, in the summer of 1945, it was becoming clear that the wartime antifascist coalition between these nations was beginning to unravel. Truman was contemplating the detonation of an atomic bomb on Japan that would not only bring the Pacific war to an end but would also capably demonstrate U.S. military superiority. However, Stalin knew about the bomb and was still adamant about reparations as well as maintaining a buffer zone between his country and Germany. Soon Germany was carved up as the United States and the Soviet Union competed for spheres of influence. In the postwar years, the idea of freedom in Europe was increasingly tied to allegiances between East and West.

Just as the union between the three Allied heads of state was breaking down, the antifascist political consensus that had, by and large, been sustained in the United States during the war years was fraying. Within the United States, the meaning of freedom after the war was a contested space; its definition relied largely upon one's political perspective. As Stuart J. Little has pointed out, American "postwar society churned with dissention"

as people came to interpret the war and its meaning in divergent ways.[1]
Nowhere was the challenge to imbue the idea of postwar freedom with
clear parameters more apparent than in the planning and execution of the
national traveling exhibit aptly named the Freedom Train. Explanations
of the exhibit and reactions to the Freedom Train illustrated contemporary discourses on politics, Communism, and race relations in the wake of
World War II. Through the Freedom Train exhibit, various groups from
the American Heritage Foundation to the Republican Party to African
American activists and conscientious objectors voiced their perspectives
on the course of freedom in the postwar era. Perhaps most illuminating
was the decision to pull Roosevelt's influential Four Freedoms speech out
of the Freedom Train exhibition.[2] After 1945, it seemed that freedom could
not be as tidily summarized as FDR had imagined back in 1941.

The Freedom Train was a traveling exhibit that was organized for the
160th anniversary of the signing of the Constitution of the United States.
It traversed the country by rail departing Philadelphia in September 1947
and terminating its journey in Washington, D.C., in January 1949. In between, the train stopped in hundreds of cities to enable millions of Americans to view its contents. The Freedom Train carried precious cargo: over
one hundred documents that traced the development of the idea of political freedom through such notable manuscripts as the Magna Carta, the
Mayflower Compact, the Bill of Rights, the Gettysburg Address, and the
Emancipation Proclamation. An assistant director of public information in
the Justice Department came up with the idea for a public display focusing
on freedom, but Attorney General Tom Clark felt it was important that the
exhibit be privately funded.

The American Heritage Foundation was incorporated to organize the
project with liaisons from the National Archives. The foundation's board
included an array of corporate leaders, including executives from Chase
Bank and General Electric and the president of the Motion Picture Association of America, which, as critics from the left pointed out, helped
insure the overall message of the Freedom Train "reinforced the purposes
of the Big Business sponsors" by highlighting themes such as mass consumption and free enterprise capitalism.[3] While the documents on display "espoused pluralism," the images in the exhibit showed white and

middle-class citizens and implied that the role of women was primarily that of a homemaker.[4] In short, in its attempt to "sell America to Americans," the American Heritage Foundation made "no attempt to discuss the Civil War, minority rights, economic rights, or social legislation of the twentieth century" in the Freedom Train exhibit.[5] Nevertheless, the exhibit received tremendous popular support. The diverse crowds of school children, working people, professionals, and retirees who waited in line for hours to view the documents defied the Freedom Train's dearth of analysis on race and class issues. Perhaps the two elderly women in Trenton, New Jersey, who stood in line for seven hours and then returned to the line to view the exhibit a second time, as well as the African American woman who fainted upon seeing the Emancipation Proclamation, offered more powerful commentary on the idea of freedom than any single document ever could.[6]

The Freedom Train provoked a range of responses from individuals and political organizations that reflected the contemporary political circumstances and illustrated the extent to which the idea of freedom was subject to conflicting interpretations. For example, Attorney General Clark worried about disloyalty to the government and hoped the exhibit would "tug at the heartstrings of America" while promoting allegiance.[7] President Truman noted that the Freedom Train's implicit message of a "conception of freedom" that was rooted in individualism represented "the world's great hope of lasting peace."[8] In contrast, Republican politicians suspected that the showcase of documents was little more than a publicity stunt in support of Truman's 1948 bid for the presidency. Attorney General Clark was requested to testify before a House committee concerning the funding and purpose of the Freedom Train since, as a Republican representative from Michigan acidly remarked, the administration clearly had not "paid any attention to democracy or freedom."[9]

The Communist Party criticized the corporate nature of the Freedom Train and called on progressive citizens to use the train's visit to organize community activities that supported labor rights and revealed the true nature of the exhibit's "big business backers."[10] Anticommunists, conversely, viewed the Freedom Train as "this country's best weapon against the [communist] doctrine."[11] Nonviolent demonstrators used the Freedom Train as a chance to picket for the release of conscientious objectors who had been imprisoned during the war.[12] NAACP leader Walter White used the announcement of the Freedom Train as an opportunity to point to the continued violence against black Americans. In commenting on a recent lynching in South Carolina in which the accused perpetrators had been released, White lamented that "not only 'an American citizen, but the Constitution' had been lynched."[13] Even as the anniversary of the Constitution was being celebrated, its ethos of democratic rights was being wantonly disregarded in the South. The Freedom Train was, thus, invoked by groups as ideologically diverse as Republicans, Democrats, Communists, anticommunists, conscientious objectors, and African American activists. Each interpreted the Freedom Train's presence and its contents in a way that echoed their political objectives. In the postwar years, defining the idea of freedom was not only partisan but also reflective of deepening fissures in U.S. society. These fractures were devastatingly apparent regarding the issue of segregation and the Freedom Train.

While the exhibition of documents mainly avoided the issue of racial injustice—with the exception of displaying the Emancipation Proclamation—the question of segregation at the Freedom Train stirred controversy. The American Heritage Foundation stated that there should be no segregation at any Freedom Train stop; however, defining segregation became a thorny issue. There were segregated lines to enter the Freedom Train in cities in South Carolina, Virginia, and Georgia while the foundation honed its policy on segregation.[14] In Memphis, city officials wanted separate viewing times based on race, and the stop in that town was cancelled. Similarly, the Freedom Train did not stop in Birmingham, Alabama, or Hattiesburg, Mississippi, because the cities insisted that some kind of segregation be enforced.[15] The fact that city fathers in several southern locales preferred to let the Freedom Train pass by their towns rather than submit to desegregated viewing was indicative of the depth of the vitriol against African American civil rights.

The American Heritage Foundation blocked segregation in some locations after a little nudging from the African American press. However, the deeper issue of the need to protect freedom for black Americans rang hollow on the Freedom Train. No one questioned American society's commitment to economic and political freedom for African Americans at this time more eloquently than Langston Hughes. In his 1947 poem "Freedom Train" Hughes wonders, "am I still a porter on the Freedom Train" and are "there ballot boxes on the Freedom Train?" Hughes also acknowledges the sacrifices recently made by black soldiers. When Jimmy "died at Anzio," Hughes points out, "he died for real." Hughes then puzzles over whether "the freedom they carry on this Freedom Train" is "for real or for show."[16] Paul Robeson recorded the poem, and his reading was produced by the progressive Southern Conference for Human Welfare.[17] Robeson also read the poem at speaking engagements in 1948 during a period in his career when, rather than singing and acting, he was focusing primarily on traveling and engaging with audiences about salient political and social issues. At a meeting of the International Fur and Leather Worker's Union, Robeson commented that the poem "Freedom Train" reflected "so much" about what he felt at the present moment.[18]

African Americans had been determined to employ Roosevelt's Four Freedoms as a metaphor for the freedom they wanted to be fulfilled after the war. Now that the war had concluded, rather than manifesting itself in the concrete form of voting rights, protection from lynching, or equal access to jobs, education, and public facilities, the notion of freedom became entangled with the notion of anticommunism. Competing with the ideas of loyalty and patriotism in the Cold War climate, fighting for freedom became equated with subversion. The Southern Negro Youth Congress and the Council on African Affairs organized and lobbied for a vision of freedom that included jobs, security, political participation, and independence for colonized people. They worked for the fulfillment of the Four Freedoms and the Atlantic Charter in the postwar years. Yet, the global conceptualization of freedom shared by SNYC and the council was not nurtured in the Cold War climate. One visitor to the Freedom Train in Nashville, Tennessee, sagely observed, "The internationalist who looks to the day when people will all be citizens of one world . . . I doubt if he would get much comfort out of the Freedom Train."[19] Defining freedom became a disputed endeavor after the war. The Southern Negro Youth Congress and the Council on African Affairs found that their international vision of freedom for the South and the African diaspora was left behind on the tracks when the Freedom Train departed.

Making "War on White Supremacy": SNYC 1946–1949

Writing on board the USS *General Stewart* returning from the Pacific the-ater of war, James Jackson captured the expectant energy burgeoning in the African American community in the immediate aftermath of World War II. He adroitly referenced Roosevelt's Four Freedoms, which had been crafted as motivations for the U.S. entry into the conflagration. However, African Americans had not enjoyed freedom from fear, freedom from want, or even freedom of speech in the repressive one-party political system of the South. They had fought in the war to liberate Europe and Asia from fascism, and now black citizens wanted to taste these freedoms also. "We like the banner of the Four Freedoms that we have carried to the liber-ated peoples of the world—and we believe in it," Jackson observed, "But we are not stupid. We never have forgotten the limitations imposed upon our people in our native land because of their color." He concluded frankly, "So we want some changes made in America."[20] Here was the second phase of the Double Victory campaign being clearly articulated. Now that fascism abroad had been vanquished, black America wanted to set about defeating all forms of fascism at home without delay.

African American soldiers, like Jackson, must have been crestfallen upon returning to the southern states having defeated Hitler only to find that manifestations of Hitlerism in the United States were thriving. Jim Crow segregation was as entrenched as ever. Disfranchisement continued to go unchallenged by the federal government. Securing employment could be difficult. Probably most disturbing was the upsurge in lynching after the war as terrorists aimed to reinforce white supremacist principles for the sol-diers who might have forgotten the brutal realities of home. The Southern Negro Youth Congress worked to address these unfortunate postwar reali-ties. For instance, SNYC formed a veterans committee that called a confer-ence in the spring of 1946. The goal of the meeting was to start a dialogue to outline a plan that would help tackle the various needs of black veterans in Alabama.[21] The veteran's committee sponsored a march to push for vot-ing rights for those who had served their country.[22] A leaflet in support of the franchise for African Americans appealed to veterans by invoking their brave service and likening the segregationist Senator Theodore Bilbo to the fascist enemies from overseas. It read: "Veterans, you who laid old Hitler low, don't be afraid of old Bilbo. Just like Hitler's friend Tojo, Bilbo has got to go!"[23]

Violence against servicemen was another salient issue in the postwar years. An African American man from Virginia wrote to the SNYC national office in July 1946 disturbed that no action had been taken even though he had reported being the victim of a "near lynching." Esther Cooper Jackson replied that he should contact the Civil Rights Congress immediately for legal assistance and keep SNYC informed on the case.[24] In 1945, scholar Oliver C. Cox had concluded that lynching was endemic to the maintenance of the power structure of white supremacy in the South. He observed that "lynching and the threat of lynching" were contrived "to meet a vital social need" that protected the status quo.[25] The lynching epidemic moved two groups of activists, an American Crusade Against Lynching delegation led by Paul Robeson and a group from the NAACP led by Walter White, to visit President Truman to discuss the crisis.[26] Truman, however, ultimately refused to support an antilynching bill in Congress for fear that it would alienate the southern branch of the Democratic Party. It seemed that the lives of black citizens had to take a back seat to political expediency.

SNYC was also involved with international events as peace talks coalesced and a new world federation was forged. In the spring of 1945, W.E.B. Du Bois sent a telegram to SNYC informing the group that the NAACP was acting as a consultant to the U.S. delegation at the San Francisco conference that laid the framework for the United Nations. Du Bois reported that the NAACP would try to represent all African Americans and urged the youth congress to send along suggested resolutions.[27] The fact that Du Bois, in his capacity working for the largest civil rights organization in the country, contacted SNYC at this important juncture demonstrated the stature of SNYC among activist groups. That year, Esther Cooper Jackson traveled to another world youth conference in England that convened to "discuss the problems and desires of democratic young people from all parts of the world and the responsibility that they bear in helping to secure peace and build a better world." At this conference of 437 delegates from 62 countries, the World Federation of Democratic Youth was founded. In their discussions, the future of people in the colonized world received much attention and the young people resolved that "the first need of youth in the colonial countries is to be free and independent."[28]

The fate of the colonized world was paramount in the minds of activists at this moment. The youth conference that Cooper Jackson attended in London coincided with the Pan-African Congress (PAC) that Du Bois attended in Manchester, England. Du Bois's relationship with SNYC, fostered through Cooper Jackson, also helped connect the Youth Congress with the Pan-African Congress's post–World War II initiatives. Du Bois maintained Cooper Jackson on his list of correspondents in his role as president of the PAC and thus SNYC received a preliminary copy of a petition to the United Nations on behalf of African independence, and the youth congress was invited to cooperate with Du Bois's 1946 project to send consultants for African colonies to the UN assembly.[29] In October of that year, Cooper Jackson, representing SNYC, signed a petition to the United Nations sponsored by the PAC that declared that colonized people should have the right to participate in that world body.[30] Keeping abreast of postwar anticolonial organizing demonstrated SNYC's continued international perspective and solidarity with those fighting oppression, especially in Africa. It was not surprising, then, that SNYC chose to honor the veteran Pan-Africanist and scholar at their 1946 conference in Columbia, South Carolina.

The circumstances of postwar life in black communities ignited an enormous response to the SNYC call for a Southern Youth Legislature in October. In the immediate aftermath of the worldwide conflict, black youth were grappling with issues including diminishing employment and training opportunities as well as physical violence and continued suppression of democratic rights. In order to design a program to deal with such issues, this SNYC conference took the form of a legislature, and each state delegation was asked to assign delegates to various committees. Early registration was urged due to the unprecedented interest once the conference was announced.[31] The SNYC national office in Birmingham was busy with preparations well before the autumn meeting. That summer, Louis Burnham sent out letters to experienced activists asking if they would go to key cities prior to the conference to spread the word and recruit delegates.[32]

A Leadership Training School was also organized by SNYC in South

Carolina during August. The purpose of the school was to "train a corps of fifty or more young Negroes from key southern communities in the methods of effective organizational work."[33] SNYC had held these training courses in the past where they invited local activists to contribute their knowledge to the sessions.[34] Using that model, Louis Burnham collaborated with South Carolinians including Osceola McKaine and Modjeska Simkins for the training school in the town of Irmo, just outside of Columbia. Those participating in the school came from a wide variety of backgrounds. They were college students, teachers, and unionized workers from across South Carolina, Florida, Georgia, and Washington, D.C. Many of them signed up for the training because they aimed to start an SNYC council in their local communities.[35] A young activist from Mississippi, Medgar Evers, registered for the training school, but circumstances prevented him from attending.[36] Evers went on to become field secretary for the NAACP in Mississippi and a tireless activist for black rights before his untimely assassination by a white supremacist in 1963.

At the Leadership Training School, classes covering organizing techniques, public speaking, and writing press releases dovetailed with courses on world affairs and the history of African Americans in politics.[37] Burnham wrote to the SNYC office in Birmingham for back issues of the Council on African Affairs' newsletter *New Africa* in order to discuss recent events in Africa during the sessions on world affairs.[38] Thus, activists who attended the Leadership Training School were well equipped with relevant skills to build a local SNYC council. They were also prepared to start organizing in their communities around the resolutions passed at the youth legislature in October. The youth congress was implementing the second half of the Double Victory by equipping young people across the South with the tactics for fighting discrimination.

More than fifteen hundred delegates poured into Township Auditorium in Columbia when the youth legislature opened. Student representatives arrived from across the South and around the diaspora, including the West Indian island of Haiti and the African nation of Liberia.[39] A local black newspaper, the *Lighthouse and Informer*, which was managed by activist John H. McCray, estimated that five thousand total people came to town, including students, workers, and community organizers.[40] Despite the large crowds, the events were efficiently organized, and lodging was available to delegates in homes in the black community. In his autobiography, Junius Scales recalls arriving in the city with a carful of people from the Southern Conference for Human Welfare. Not knowing exactly where to go, he remembers that the first African American man they saw on the street directed them where to register. He also recalls that while the police were present for the conference events, they remained at a distance.[41]

Along with serious committee sessions on current issues, evening entertainment also drew sizeable crowds. Some of the most famous faces in the African American community were on the programs for Saturday and Sunday nights. Harlem politician Adam Clayton Powell Jr. was on the schedule along with headliners Paul Robeson and W.E.B. Du Bois (though Powell ultimately had to cancel due to illness). The tribute to Du Bois and Robeson's singing attracted people from the surrounding area whether or not they necessarily shared SNYC's political perspective. Scholar Nikhil Pal Singh has discerned that this SNYC gathering was the "biggest interracial gathering in the history of South Carolina" as well as a "high water mark of the civil rights-labor and liberal-radical alliances" of the 1930s and 1940s.[42]

The young people who attended the youth legislature were not only "dedicated to the struggle for freedom" but were also "determined to achieve that freedom" in their lifetimes.[43] Priorities in their program of action focused on becoming "a full-fledged voting generation," securing guarantees for the right to work at all jobs, fighting for antilynching legislation, and insisting upon access to equal housing, health, and educational facilities.[44] The topics discussed in the committee hearings illustrated the broad range of issues that galvanized the young people as well as the educators, labor organizers, and concerned citizens who were present. On Saturday morning, hearings were held on youth and labor, peace, veterans, education, farm problems, voting, and civil liberties.[45] That afternoon, all of the delegates convened to discuss and vote upon resolutions from the sessions.

In the speeches throughout the weekend, the war was consistently invoked as a metaphor. Louis Burnham called for the body of youth and civic leaders in attendance to "make war on white supremacy vandals who seek to turn the clock back on progress."[46] Florence Valentine, secretary of the Miami SNYC council, cogently connected the vital issues of employment and national security: "Since the war many . . . women were laid off, but these women, today, want jobs. What is a job? A job means security—individual—national—world. Security is the best weapon against poverty and disease, the best weapon against defeat at home and abroad."[47] George Blakey, assistant attorney general from Illinois, spoke on civil liberties and effectively invoked the strategy of island-hopping in the Pacific with which the audience would surely have been familiar. He pointed out that when tracing "the long, tedious battle of the Negro to obtain favorable US Supreme Court decisions" one perhaps feels like MacArthur must have felt when facing the "three thousand islands . . . stretching from the Philippines to Tokyo." But just as MacArthur "startled the world" when he recaptured the Philippines after four years, "so too does the Negro hope to get a Supreme Court decision which will declare the Negro free and equal for all time to come."[48]

These speeches redirected the fighting spirit of the war era toward civil rights. In the spirit of the Double V campaign, these speeches declared that the victory against fascism abroad was complete and it was now time to wage the battle against domestic injustice with full force. James Jackson argued that it was time to push for voting rights. "We need and must have the ballot," he declared. "We must have it to vote into office men who will defend our lives and liberties."[49] Clark Foreman, head of the Southern Conference for Human Welfare, took a slightly different approach. He pointed out that if "we blame the German people because they did not resist more effectively the growth of fascism in Germany," then we "cannot sit idly by" and watch fascist tendencies spread in the United States.[50] In that vein, Foreman went on to denounce Secretary of State James Byrnes, a South Carolinian, who was insisting that European nations guarantee rights that were denied to citizens in his home state.

The SNYC legislature went on to pass a resolution against Byrnes that ended up generating some controversy. In addition to Foreman's comments, Du Bois and other speakers had openly criticized Byrnes, who was a segregationist, during the sessions. One of the many resolutions voted upon at the conference called for the immediate removal of Byrnes from office. This provoked the ire of the governor of South Carolina, Ransome J. Williams, who sent out a press release stating that the SNYC was under the influence of "Communistic elements."[51] SNYC's national officers immediately responded to Governor Williams and retorted that his red-baiting was an "obvious attempt to discredit" what had been a "highly successful" conference in his state's capital. The SNYC statement then pointed to Byrnes's reactionary record, observing that "today's Secretary of State was yesterday's Congressman condoning mob violence by his filibuster against the anti-lynching bill."[52]

The youth congress activists saw through the ruse of anticommunist sentiment that the governor had attempted to invoke in order to distract the public from the substance of the civil rights issues addressed at the Columbia conference, including Byrnes's unfitness for office. Branding SNYC as a group that had been infiltrated by reds was Williams's best hope for unraveling the organization. Thus, the Byrnes controversy demonstrated the influence of SNYC at this moment when its largest, most successful meeting garnered national press attention and the indignation of a segregationist governor. However, this exchange also foreshadowed the approaching demise of the Southern Negro Youth Congress as the outspoken, progressive character of the organization made it a target of Cold War vitriol. Governor Williams's strategy of accusing SNYC of being a Communist organization was not an anomaly but was becoming a chief tactic during the rising tide of postwar anticommunist mania. Civil rights groups could be marginalized, or even vilified, in the public discourse if they were brandished with the red label.

Nevertheless, the youth legislature in Columbia solidified SNYC as a unifying force in the African American community. The events sponsored by the group had enabled young activists to collaborate with labor organizers, workers, educators, and middle-class reformers in discussing current issues and passing a set of resolutions. People of all races, ages, and classes had attended the evening sessions and were mesmerized by Paul Robeson's singing. The intergenerational nature of SNYC was especially clear in the moving tribute to the preeminent intellectual and advocate for civil rights W.E.B. Du Bois. The leaders of SNYC understood that it was important to look to the past for vital lessons and to learn from those who had paved the way in the long freedom struggle.

As the program noted, Du Bois inspired their generation and urged them on to "greater strivings for self-improvement." Thus, in paying homage to the "peerless patriarch" the young people honored "not only the man, but our generation as well."[53] The youth congress, then, was aware of its significant position as a bridge connecting the previous cohort of civil rights activists, those who had founded the NAACP and fought lynching after World War I, with the generation whose rite of passage as organizers had been the Great Depression and World War II.

Du Bois used the opportunity of speaking at the SNYC event to emphasize the connections between people in the American South with the African diaspora. Having traveled to England the previous year to participate in the Pan-African Congress, Du Bois had been recently acquainted firsthand with the renewed push for independence in colonial territories. In his speech, "Behold the Land," the "senior statesman of the American Negro's liberation struggle" and "foremost champion" of colonial rights positioned the SNYC's agenda as fitting into the global struggle for self-determination.[54] In arguing that the "future of American Negroes is in the South," Du Bois pointed out that the South was "the firing line" for African Americans as well as people of African descent in the West Indies and on the continent. Defeating the forces of segregation and injustice in the South would also be a blow to colonialism. Leaders such as South Carolina's James Byrnes and South Africa's Jan Smuts must, in Du Bois's eyes, "yield to the forward march of civilization." He viewed the postwar moment as a "chance for young women and young men" to work toward "a civilization which will be free and intelligent."[55] Du Bois concluded following the conference that SNYC was "the most promising organization of young people of which I know."[56]

In the early 1950s, Robeson reflected fondly on his experience at the youth legislature in South Carolina. He affirmed that he had never been as proud of his heritage as when he had had the chance to "sing and inspire these proud descendants of our African forebears, standing as they were with head and shoulders high in the deepest South."[57] As Du Bois did in his 1946 speech, Robeson ably connected the U.S. South with the broader African diaspora. The occasion of the SNYC conference had afforded Robeson an opportunity to connect with young southern African Americans and their demands for "the full fruits of their back breaking toil . . . [and] full freedom" and had made him feel not only pride but also "sure of our future here in these United States."[58]

Despite the huge turnout and enthusiastic community response to SNYC's Columbia conference, indictors of a grim direction in the political landscape were emerging in the late 1940s. It became increasingly apparent that the wartime alliance between the Soviet Union and the United States was not only fraying but also giving way to a potentially dangerous contestation of power between the two nations. While it is debatable whether the Soviet Union, which was still reeling from a tremendous loss of life and destruction of territory from the antifascist war, actually posed an immediate threat to the United States, the Truman administration portrayed the Soviets as well as the ideology of Communism as enemies of the state. A hardline stance was adopted as fascism was dropped in favor of Communism as the most profound threat to capitalist democracy. The policy of containment and the Truman Doctrine positioned the Soviet Union and the United States as being engaged in an ongoing ideological struggle. Illustrations of this trend were rife in the postwar years. Probably no image became more enduring than that of an "iron curtain" cascading between the eastern and western halves of Europe as articulated by former British Prime Minister Winston Churchill in the spring of 1946 on a visit to Truman's home state of Missouri.

The fallout for progressive activists and left-wing organizers, as well as anyone affiliated with or suspected of being linked to the U.S. Communist Party, soon materialized. In the autumn of 1946, Henry A. Wallace, who had served as Roosevelt's vice president, was dismissed from Truman's cabinet for advocating peace with the Soviets. In a move reminiscent of the antiradical Palmer raids of 1919, the leaders of the Communist Party were indicted in 1947 under provisions of the Smith Act and charged with plotting the overthrow of the government. The House Un-American Activities Committee stormed ahead with its antiradical purges, including a cohort of filmmakers who became known as the Hollywood Ten, that same year. Domestically, loyalty oaths were instituted for federal government workers and the Taft-Hartley Act required union leaders to vow their loyalty to the U.S. government. In foreign policy, the Truman Doctrine offered U.S. aid to countries that renounced Communism whether or not they upheld democratic principles. The Marshall Plan bolstered the crumbling economies of European colonizers enabling them to try to maintain control of their empires in Africa.

Amid this political climate, SNYC forged ahead with its 1947 agenda. Momentum from the Columbia conference instigated an effort to dissemi-

Figure 3. Southern Negro Youth Congress delegation to Washington, D.C., meets with Senator Glen Taylor (*center*). Louis Burnham is to the left of Taylor; Esther Cooper Jackson is at the far left. Edward Strong Papers, Manuscript Division, Moorland-Spingarn Research Center, Howard University.

nate Du Bois's speech in the form of a printed pamphlet. Letters streamed into SNYC headquarters from bookstores, libraries, unions, church and fraternal groups, as well as individuals around the United States requesting copies of the speech "Behold the Land."[59] In conjunction with Negro History Week and SNYC's tenth anniversary, the youth congress sponsored a lecture tour by historian Herbert Aptheker in February. Aptheker's groundbreaking book *American Negro Slave Revolts* had just been published a few years earlier. He visited several colleges in North and South Carolina and waived his customary honorarium in favor of promoting interest in the importance of African American history.[60] Perhaps most significantly, an interracial delegation of citizens and activists visited Washington, D.C., under the auspices of SNYC. These potential voters sought an audience with representatives and senators to discuss "a legislative program in the interest of the security and democratic liberties of the American people."

Not surprisingly, many legislators from the South did not make time to meet with the SNYC group. Undaunted, the young people lobbied those politicians who would see them and made a point of visiting Senator Glen Taylor of Idaho, who had spoken out against the notorious segregationist Theodore Bilbo.[61] (In 1945, SNYC had circulated a petition demanding Bilbo's impeachment for inflaming race hatred and mob violence against African Americans, Catholics, and Jews.[62]) This relationship proved to be important for SNYC as Taylor later served as running mate on the Progressive Party's presidential ticket in 1948, and he figured prominently in the SNYC conference held that year. The Southern Negro Youth Congress's networking with Taylor demonstrated the extent of their lobbying to the highest levels of government and their alliances with progressives from across the nation.

SNYC also adopted a slightly more self-protective posture in some of its 1947 activities. For example, in the spring of that year a membership drive was launched that highlighted the importance of organizing for democracy. The local council with the membership roll that grew the most was to be honored at the tenth anniversary banquet.[63] A memo from SNYC special projects director Arthur G. Price urged local councils to hold mass meetings to educate the community on current events and draw new members. Price offered an array of topics that could be discussed at local rallies, such as details on economic trends, pending legislation in Congress that would affect labor policies, and continued discrimination through the poll tax and the white primary. Price's analysis of the Truman Doctrine and its implementation in Greece wondered whether the United States was prepared to support every reactionary movement around the world that positioned itself against forces considered to be a Communist threat. If so, Price encouraged audiences to consider where this incalculable policy might lead and when it would end.[64] Similarly, a flyer for the spring membership drive cautioned "Your Freedom is in Danger" and underscored recent lynchings, cases of police brutality, and the Communist scare being propagated by HUAC as reasons to consider joining SNYC to defend democratic rights.[65]

A new wave of political repression was bearing down on SNYC more directly by December 1947 when it was included on Attorney General Tom Clark's list of subversive organizations. This inventory of about eighty groups included several civil rights organizations, such as the Civil Rights Congress (CRC), the Council on African Affairs, and the National Negro Congress (though it had already been disbanded to merge with the CRC).[66] These particular groups were affiliated with left-wing politics and had some members who were connected to the Communist Party; however, these were all groups that organized on behalf of African and African American rights. In response to the attorney general's action, SNYC's national officers decided at an executive board meeting in January of 1948 to reaffirm publicly the nonpartisan character of the group, which had now been in existence for over a decade. The minutes of the meeting reflected the board's agreement that officers could affiliate with any political party of their choosing as individuals as long as the nonpartisan policy of the organization was not violated. A local SNYC council in Nashville had sent some concerns to the national office regarding the subversive designation, but the executive board assured the members that such lists were primarily meant to feed anticommunist hysteria and that the Communist Party was, in fact, a legal political entity.[67]

A press release from SNYC national headquarters countered the subversive designation by arguing that the youth congress was being targeted because of its outspoken critique of racism. The piece unequivocally stated: "The SNYC is singled out because in its 10-year history it has consistently refused, and refuses now, to participate in the political idiocy of witch-hunting and red-baiting. It is attacked because its growing ranks have always been, and remain, open to all Southerners, of whatever race, religion or party, who will join resolutely in a crusade against lynching, 'white supremacy' terror, and disfranchisement; and against the punitive segregation system and its evil fruits—poverty, ignorance and disease."[68] Indeed, SNYC had been a vocal critic of racism since its inception in 1937 and had never backed down from disparaging any perceived lack of action on the part of the federal government.

For example, in 1939, Edward Strong sent a frank letter to Representative Martin Dies, chair of HUAC, observing that his committee's failure to investigate mob violence in the South indicated that the investigative body "in reality is working to destroy the influence of those organizations in our country which are fighting for the rights of Negroes."[69] In 1946, SNYC had used the global platform of the World Federation of Democratic Youth

(WFDY) to denounce Klu Klux Klan violence. Acting on a motion initiated by Dorothy Burnham, representing SNYC at the Paris conference, the WFDY resolved that terrorism against black Americans was "one of the most active fascist forces in the world" and represented "a threat to the consolidation of peace and the realization of democracy."[70] That same summer, SNYC demanded that Attorney General Tom Clark launch a full-scale inquiry into the Klan in Georgia following the mob killing of four black citizens near Monroe.[71] Thus, the youth congress had consistently and directly challenged federal institutions to protect democratic rights for all citizens. In the charged political climate of the Cold War this was tantamount to subversion.

National events in 1948 were a watershed for progressives. Many activists, like SNYC Executive Secretary Louis Burnham, had supported Henry A. Wallace's bid for the presidency on a third-party ticket with the Progressive Party. Wallace's platform explicitly supported full civil rights for African Americans and peace with the Soviets in lieu of a swelling military-industrial complex.[72] However, the success of Truman initiatives such as the Berlin airlift and the desegregation of the armed forces helped ensure Wallace's crushing defeat in the November election. This meant that Truman's policies were firmly established for another four years. Repression of suspected Communists did not abate, and SNYC was no longer in existence by the time of the next presidential election. The beginning of the end for SNYC was the conference scheduled to be held in Birmingham, the long-time headquarters of the organization, during the first weekend of May 1948.

Significantly, this was also the year that southerners broke from the Democratic Party at their national convention and formed the segregationist Dixiecrat Party that, in a telling display of the national political mindset, actually ended up receiving more votes than Wallace's Progressive Party. The Dixiecrats illustrated that the attitude toward cementing segregation law at any cost was embedded in parts of the South, including Birmingham, Alabama, where the youth congress was preparing to confer. Leading up to the SNYC meeting, terrorism and police brutality against the black community had been relentless. For instance, Klansmen had invaded a Girl Scout camp and threatened the white instructors who worked with African American scouts. Men posing as policemen severely beat an active member of the NAACP in his home. In addition, several black citizens had been killed by police in cold blood.[73] The black-owned *Birmingham World* calculated that police had murdered four African Americans in the thirty days prior to the SNYC conference. This gruesome reality prompted one of the newspaper's editorialists to speculate whether Police Commissioner Eugene "Bull" Connor had "lost control of his police officers."[74]

Aware of SNYC's branding as a subversive organization, Connor was hostile to the group's conference planning. For example, ministers who volunteered church space for events were threatened, a white activist meeting with Louis Burnham in the SNYC office was suddenly arrested, and the police commissioner insisted that segregation ordinances be enforced at the meeting, which contradicted SNYC's history of holding integrated sessions.[75] This treatment differed significantly from the 1939 SNYC conference held in Birmingham, when the group had received an official welcome and was bequeathed a key to the city.[76] In comparison, in 1948, SNYC was grimly warned that the Klan had volunteered to cooperate with Connor in preventing their conference from taking place.[77] With the specter of violence shrouding the conference preparations, a telegram from Louis Burnham urged Attorney General Tom Clark to intervene with Connor on behalf of SNYC's First Amendment right to assemble peacefully.[78] The youth congress's appeal for federal protection of their constitutional rights foreshadowed similar requests from the Student Nonviolent Coordinating Committee (SNCC) a generation later.

Though conference sessions for the May 1948 meeting had been scheduled to meet at the Sixteenth Street Baptist Church, the venue was changed to the Alliance Gospel Tabernacle. For courageously offering his church space, Reverend H. Douglas Oliver was threatened with being ousted from his position on a local radio program. To further complicate matters, white conference attendees were refused hotel accommodations and the Elks Hall, where a dance was to have been held, abruptly canceled under pressure from City Hall.[79] The conference opened on Saturday morning in a most unusual manner with a reading of the city ordinance on segregation. In an unprecedented step to try to maintain peace and safety, the Southern Negro Youth Congress had informed Connor that the separation of the races would be observed during the meeting. Nonetheless, police invaded the afternoon session and arrested Reverend Oliver as well as three white

SNYC supporters, including James Dombrowski of the Southern Conference for Human Welfare. Dombrowski noted in his account that at least one of those arrested was assaulted by the police.[80]

Events unfolding at the Saturday evening session, however, were perhaps even more shocking. Progressive Party vice presidential candidate Glen Taylor of Idaho was the scheduled keynote speaker. The church, a modest single-story structure, was flanked by police as Taylor approached the building. Temporary designations for separate entrances to the premises had been affixed to comply with the segregation ordinance. When Taylor reached to pull open the front door that was marked for African Americans, he was "jostled and shoved by police officers." Subsequently, he was arrested and charged with disorderly conduct.[81] Appalled by this shameful manhandling of a U.S. Senator, Taylor later declared in *Time* magazine, "God help the ordinary man!"[82] When interviewed about the incident, he unabashedly "hoisted his trouser leg" to reveal the four-inch wound he received when the Birmingham police "shoved him into a wire fence."[83] Incongruously, it was Taylor who was charged with disorderly conduct.

Taylor was convicted on three counts, fined fifty dollars, and given a 180-day suspended sentence. Before rendering this decision, Judge Hall announced that racial equality "would bring the white man down to the level of colored people."[84] Meanwhile, the young Reverend Oliver, only twenty-three, who had volunteered his church for the meeting was forced to resign his pulpit.[85] The other activists who had been arrested still faced charges, and SNYC began a drive to raise money for their legal funds because the defendants wished to challenge the constitutionality of the segregation ordinance.[86] Ultimately, they were cleared of all charges. The case hinged, in part, on the section of the city code that ordered a "physical barrier" to be in place in public spaces where both whites and African Americans assembled.[87] In a decision that seemed to underline the absurdity of the very code he ostensibly upheld, Judge Hall decided that the physical barrier could, in fact, be "an imaginary line."[88]

A kind letter from Senator Taylor to Louis Burnham commended the courage displayed by SNYC staff and supporters in the face of southern aggression. Taylor was hopeful that "what happened at that little church in Birmingham will someday help in stamping out the vicious practices we abhor so much."[89] Unfortunately, those sharing Taylor's perspective faced mounting opposition. Beset by negative national press, continued surveillance, financial difficulties, and waning support, the youth congress limped through the summer of 1948. Edward Weaver resigned as SNYC president after being pressured out of his teaching position at a local college.[90] Louis Burnham, a stalwart of the SNYC leadership, prepared to move to New York City. Without money to pay the staff, the Southern Negro Youth Congress faced dissolution by early 1949. Allies of the young activists were dispersing and reactionaries like Connor gained the upper hand. His grip on power in Birmingham did not begin to recede until the 1960s when he was challenged again by another generation of committed civil rights demonstrators.

The Birmingham conference and the case of Senator Taylor exemplified the trampling of basic freedoms—freedom of speech, freedom of assembly—that characterized the anticommunist frenzy of the early Cold War era. Perhaps most brazenly, freedom from fear, which had been accentuated by Roosevelt during the war, was in short supply in places such as Birmingham for civil rights activists as well as the entire black community in the late 1940s. Police violence, unwarranted arrest, and violations of constitutional rights seemed to continue with few consequences. Separating the racist sentiment from antiradical purges proved difficult as the two were almost indivisible. In the eyes of a southern reactionary, civil rights advocates were practically assumed to be Communist infiltrators. The fact that the Wallace-Taylor Progressive Party ticket, the only campaign to advocate both peace with the Soviets and full citizenship rights, had garnered scant national support showed the extent to which anticommunism had taken hold of the American imagination and was animated by racism.

An editorial reprinted from the *Chicago Defender* that lamented Edward Weaver's having been compelled to leave his teaching position summarized the political climate of 1948 well. "Pressure on him to resign," the writer asserted, "was largely the outgrowth of his disposition to think for himself." Furthermore, "If you are against the philosophy of Southern peonage farms . . . then you are a Communist. If you speak out against the lynching of women and men . . . you are a Communist. If you are a sharecropper and want a correct accounting on the proceeds of your crop . . . naturally, you are a Communist." The editorialist observed, "It must be recalled that the Southern Negro Youth Congress had its birth in a desire to train with the hope of freeing themselves from the bondage ... [of] Southern social thought. But they are now branded Communists."[91] This editorialist skillfully pointed out that any engagement against fascist elements in the South was being brushed off as Communist penetration.

While racism played an important role, postwar hostility to civil rights protest was also enabled by the anticommunist frenzy of the era. Since the Communist Party had been the only political party actively organizing in the South in support of civil rights issues since the 1930s, the ideas of Communism and civil rights activism were firmly wedded in much of the public mindset.[92] Thus, the perception of progressive activism as suspicious and anti-American that gripped the region in the late 1940s helped sound the death knell of the youth congress.

* * *

Augusta Jackson Strong, former editor of *Cavalcade*, closed her 1964 article on the Southern Negro Youth Congress on a hopeful note. Writing during an upsurge of nonviolent direct action in the South, Strong postulated that the issues tackled by the young activists had not been pushed aside after the group disbanded. On the contrary, unemployment, voting rights, education, and equal opportunity, around which SNYC had organized, were now being taken up by "the Negro people as a whole."[93] A baton had passed from the group of youthful activists, now veteran organizers, to the communities in which they had organized. In early 1948, SNYC had rolls listing over 4,900 members with local councils in at least eight states and the District of Columbia.[94]

These activists and their supporters left behind a substantial legacy. Young people like James Farmer and Fred Shuttlesworth who were influenced by SNYC events went on to lead lives that focused on civil rights activism.[95] Shuttlesworth became a leader in the Southern Christian Leadership Conference, led by Martin Luther King Jr., and was on hand to stand against police chief Bull Connor's fire hoses in Birmingham in 1963. Progeny of SNYC activists also became engaged in the freedom struggle, such as SNYC supporter Sallye Davis's daughter Angela who came of age as an activist during the Black Power era and became an important scholar studying social and political issues. Perhaps most significantly, as SNYC volunteer and political long-distance runner Jack O'Dell has noted, the youth congress was a forerunner of SNCC, the Student Nonviolent Co-ordinating Committee, which was founded by young people in 1960.[96] Disgusted with the lack of decisive movement against segregation and dis-franchisement, the students of SNCC marched, registered voters, and held sit-ins during the high tide of civil rights resistance in the 1960s.

As vivacious and inspiring as they were, the students of SNCC and the other young activists of the New Left were not completely original. A van-guard of young people had set important precedents as organizers during the crises of the Great Depression and World War II. Playing on SNCC's phonetic nickname, "Snick," Angela Davis has argued that there were actu-ally two "Snicks": SNYC and SNCC.[97] While the second SNCC has oft been examined, the legacy of the first SNYC deserves greater attention. Obviously, SNCC had the crucial advantage of being created during the classical phase of the movement that produced the greatest momentum to-ward civil rights protest in United States history. The group was poised to take advantage of new antisegregation decisions like the *Brown v. Board of Education* ruling and to push for further legislation such as the Civil Rights Act of 1964 and the Voting Rights Act of 1965.

The new medium of television helped influence national public opin-ion to favor the peaceful marches and sit-ins and decry the accompanying backlash of fire hoses and police brutality. Nonviolent direct action was a powerful force, especially when streamed directly into homes and the of-fices of politicians across the country on television screens. In the 1960s, the political landscape was ripe for a degree of change in a way that it had not been for the young activists of SNYC in the 1930s and 1940s. However, it was the consistent efforts of SNYC organizers who had maintained the call for African and African American freedom through those crucial De-pression and war years that had prepared the way for the generation that followed.

The Southern Negro Youth Congress was an early instigator of future change. Their organizing demonstrated that fissures were beginning to crack the stronghold of southern segregation and foreshadowed future change. Just as activists from Du Bois's early generation had influenced SNYC, the freedom fighters of SNYC had made important headway for the student activists of the 1960s. In the narrative of a long civil rights movement, the contributions of every cohort were born of their specific circumstances and left a unique imprint on the overall struggle. The campaigns during the high tide of resistance in the 1950s–1960s were exceptional but should not stand alone in the historical record.

Still, assessing the overall legacy of the Southern Negro Youth Congress is complex. There were few tangible signs of change to reward their hard-fought battles. Segregation signs did not come down while the youth congress was functioning. Neither lynching nor the poll tax was outlawed because of their efforts. Colonial governments in Africa had yet to crumble. Yet, examining the impact of SNYC is fundamentally challenging not only for these reasons but also because its vision of freedom was broad, and much of it still has yet to be fully realized. The youth congress grappled with employment and labor rights as well as with poverty in minority communities; they struggled with the question of equal educational opportunities; they cultivated and embraced female leadership; and they sought solidarity with colleagues across boundaries of race, nation, and age. The primary inheritance bequeathed by the prescient young people of SNYC might be the message that the struggle must be continued. It was this birthright that the students of SNCC embraced wholeheartedly. It is a message that deserves attention even in the age of Barack Obama.

And what became of the SNYC activists, now matured through age and experience, after the breakup of the youth congress? Many became political long-distance runners who remained active in the struggle though repression displaced them to northward regions. Radicalized by the exploitation and discrimination that was rife in the South, these activists continued to respond to the call of Du Bois, who urged in 1946 that they must "make the people of the United States and of the world know what is going on in the South."[98] Northern supporters of SNYC, like Du Bois and Robeson, fostered the work of former youth congress adherents who continued the freedom struggle in New York. Louis Burnham found a home as editor of *Freedom* newspaper, to which several former SNYC members contributed. Esther Cooper Jackson, Augusta Jackson Strong, and others collaborated in the 1960s and 1970s on the journal *Freedomways*, which was based in the North but chronicled the freedom movement in the South while providing "an intellectual bridge to an earlier generation of black activists and organizers."[99]

In his 1946 speech, Du Bois had also connected the U.S. South with the anticolonial struggles that were taking shape around the world. He posited, "Here in this South is the gateway to the colored millions." In other words, the fight for freedom for African Americans was inextricably linked to a broader movement. A freer American South could lead to self-determination for Africa and independence in the West Indies because the freedoms at stake—much like Roosevelt's Four Freedoms—were supposed to be indivisible and the entitlement of all people regardless of race. It was not surprising, then, that some of the most ardent allies of SNYC were dedicated backers of African freedom, as SNYC itself had been. W.E.B. Du Bois, Paul Robeson, and Max Yergan had seen in SNYC an expression of the same anticolonial, antidiscriminatory impulse that had ignited the creation of the Council on African Affairs. For these activists, the southern "gateway" had engaged their unflagging espousal of African self-determination.

Keeping a *Spotlight on Africa* during the Cold War: The Council, 1946–1949

The Council on African Affairs had lobbied for African rights when the United Nations was founded in 1945. Though the council's newsletter *New Africa* provided continuing coverage of UN developments relating to the continent, South Africa took center stage in the Council on African Affairs' 1946 organizing. This year probably represented the peak of the council's influence and was the point at which the group received the greatest public attention. Just as SNYC had launched its most successful conference that year, the Council on African Affairs hosted its largest rallies to aid black South Africans the year after the war ended. Two main issues mobilized the council with regard to South Africa. A dire lack of food and arable land plagued indigenous South Africans, and this chronic situation, which was brought on by the government's land policies, was exacerbated by drought. In addition, the council paid close attention to the UN response when Premier Jan Smuts attempted to annex South West Africa, a former German colony, into the Union of South Africa. Spreading South Africa's discriminatory racial policies was not acceptable in the eyes of the council's leadership.

By early 1946, a critical situation had developed in South Africa. Millions of black South Africans who were segregated and confined onto insufficient plots of land suffered from persistent poverty and disease. A severe drought had heightened the acute danger of starvation. In response, the Council on African Affairs commenced a large-scale food drive that was kicked off with a mass meeting at Harlem's Abyssinian Baptist Church in January. Paul Robeson and vocalist Marian Anderson headlined the program to raise money for famine relief.[100] In lieu of purchasing tickets, concerned citizens were urged to bring canned goods and make donations for the relief effort. The *People's Voice* newspaper regularly published on-the-street responses to questions in its People's Town Hall section. One column in February 1946 published responses from people in Harlem regarding whether Americans should send aid to famine-stricken Africa. The resounding response was in the affirmative. One woman, a secretary, asserted that "every cent and can of food helps."[101]

The scarcity of the war years was hardly a distant memory and a spirit of organizing to help the African cause resonated in the community. Over four thousand people answered the council's call, bringing with them thousands of pounds of food as well as donations of over $1700. Speaking at the mass meeting, Max Yergan paralleled the environmental crisis with the political situation: "The South Africans want us to share with them what we have in food—and they want their freedom."[102] Robeson also addressed a mass meeting in Los Angeles that March that raised money and food aid.[103] Not to be upstaged by charity from the United States, the South African government, while downplaying the severity of the famine, taxed the food sent by the council at an exorbitant 25 percent.[104]

Undaunted, the Council on African Affairs planned an even bigger event at Madison Square Garden that summer. The June 6th rally more explicitly linked the physical starvation facing South Africans with the broader issue of political hunger under the theme "Big Three Unity for Colonial Freedom." On the anniversary of the Invasion of Normandy, the council harnessed the spirit of cooperation that had marshaled the antifascist cause of World War II with the urgent situation in the African colonies. Press coverage of the event was widespread: Robeson appeared on radio programs, letters were mailed to council supporters, and periodicals including the *New York Herald Tribune*, *PM*, the *New York Times*, *New York Post*, and the *Daily Worker* carried notices and articles.[105] Messages of support for the rally came from Broadway stars, the Congress of Industrial Organizations (CIO), Representative Adam Clayton Powell Jr., Councilman Ben Davis, and even from as far away as India, where Jawaharlal Nehru pointed out that the spirit of Nazism and fascism would continue until racial equality and colonialism everywhere were eliminated.[106] The sponsors committee included activists such as Mary McLeod Bethune, W.E.B. Du Bois, Arthur Spingarn, and Charles Houston, as well as luminaries such as Lena Horne and Marian Anderson.[107] In an article in the *New York Herald Tribune*, Robeson pointed out that there was "so little real knowledge" about the lives and struggles of African people disseminated in the U.S. press and that there had been a discrepancy between the pledge for the right of self-determination, as outlined in the UN charter, and implementation of this policy.[108] In addition to responding to the cry for daily bread, the council's leadership believed that Americans had a responsibility to help ensure that the cry for self-government was also heard in the United Nations.

Over fifteen thousand people crowded into the Garden, making the Council on African Affairs' rally the largest meeting ever held in the United States on the subject of colonial freedom. The audience listened to numerous speakers and was treated to entertainment from Katherine Dunham's dance troupe and music from Pete Seeger and Josh White.[109] In his speech, Paul Robeson stressed the postwar moment in noting that "to win total peace there must be total freedom." He characterized the rich undeveloped resources of Africa as a great prize to imperialists that must be defended by anti-imperialists. The emerging policy to "get tough with Russia," Robeson argued, was tantamount to stopping the advancement of colonized people toward independence.[110]

This final theme was underscored in the resolutions passed at the rally as well. The resolutions adopted called for self-determination for all people and asserted that colonized nations should be welcomed into the United Nations so that they might have a direct voice in the proceedings of the world body. Additional resolutions focused on U.S. foreign affairs and called for the country to use its power toward peaceful ends and to adhere to a policy of international cooperation.[111] In July, the African National Congress (ANC) cabled the council to express their "sincerest gratitude" for the famine relief assistance as well as the political stand taken by the Council on African Affairs on behalf of Africans.[112]

The Council also devoted significant time to the question of South Africa's annexation of South West Africa (now Namibia) in 1946. In addition to coverage in the council newsletter *New Africa*, Alphaeus Hunton wrote a pamphlet titled "Stop South Africa's Crimes: No Annexation of S.W. Africa." Hunton painted a detailed picture of the political situation in South Africa where white supremacist policies kept black South Africans mired in poverty, working menial and dangerous jobs without benefit of unionization, segregated, and without access to education, adequate arable land, or voting rights. Continued discrimination against Indians in South Africa as well as inflammatory legislation like the pass laws unified Africans in South Africa, Bechuanaland (now Botswana), and South West Africa against the expansion of a South African empire. Annexing South West Africa, Hunton argued, would only supply South Africa with more cheap labor for the mines while the vast mineral wealth of the region enriched only the small ruling elite. Hunton pointed out that without the backing of U.S. capital, the economy of South Africa would crumble. Thus, because South Africa was obliged to listen to the United States, it was vital that Americans vocalize opposition to Jan Smuts's annexation plan.[113]

The Council on African Affairs worked to help persuade the United Nations to oppose Smuts's proposal for relinquishing South West Africa to his country's jurisdiction rather than to a UN council. Toward this end, the Council on African Affairs initiated a campaign of picketing in front of the South African consulate in the autumn of 1946. Two hundred protesters carried signs denouncing Smuts's plan and calling for an end to racial discrimination in South Africa.[114] This action was supported by numerous activist and trade union groups including the NAACP, the National Maritime Union, and the New York committee of the Southern Negro Youth Congress.[115] By December it seemed clear that Smuts's proposal was not going to hold up in the UN General Assembly after having been soundly defeated in committee.

The council wrote to the U.S. Secretary of State and the U.S. delegation to the United Nations to urge a strong stand against annexation. In a telling response, the State Department informed Robeson that while the United States opposed South Africa's expansionist aims, it was prudent that the

Figure 4. Meeting about lobbying the United Nations in the library of the Council on African Affairs, 1946. Paul Robeson is at the far right; Max Yergan is second from left. *Daily Worker/Daily World* Photographs Collection, Tamiment Library, New York University.

United States use more conciliatory language rather than "adopting a holier-than-thou attitude" toward South Africa.[116] While maintaining its own system of racial segregation, it seemed that the United States did not feel justified in condemning South Africa too harshly. Eliminating all forms of white supremacy, whether in the United States or South Africa, was apparently not going to be on the immediate foreign policy agenda.

In 1947, the council celebrated its tenth anniversary. The previous year had been particularly busy, and the group had enjoyed wide public support. Early in 1947, an article in *New Africa* welcomed over twenty new members to the organization, which put membership over fifty.[117] This was a promising trend that had probably been generated by the high-profile rallies and pickets sponsored by the Council on African Affairs the previous year. For the most part, the council hummed along as usual through early 1947: Hunton continued to observe and publicize developments from the UN

Trusteeship Council meticulously; Yergan spoke on the U.S. stake in colonial freedom at a symposium on non-self-governing territories at Howard University; another pamphlet on South Africa, "Seeing Is Believing," offered detailed explanations of conditions for blacks; and plans for an anniversary program were outlined. However, in April, evidence of mounting reactionism in the United States hit close to home when council chairman Paul Robeson was banned from appearing in Peoria, Illinois, and Albany, New York. Even though a concert would ultimately be held in Albany in May, these events foretold of the political turbulence that lay ahead for the council.

A press release for the Council on African Affairs' anniversary celebration announced that John Latouche, who had written the popular anthem "Ballad for Americans," had penned a dramatization focused on the struggles of African people for independence that would be performed at the birthday event.[118] Warm birthday greetings arrived from all over the globe, including messages from A. B. Xuma, president of the African National Congress in South Africa, Jawaharlal Nehru, Head of India's interim government, Eleanor Roosevelt, and Albert Einstein.[119] Though broad support was still evident at this time, the events in Peoria cast a shadow over the council's anniversary celebration. The City Council of Peoria pressured the manager of the auditorium where Robeson was scheduled to appear and expressed its disapproval of giving a platform to anyone suspected of being affiliated with subversive activities. This clear breach of the freedom of expression was protested by the Council on African Affairs as well as the Civil Rights Congress and the NAACP.

Robeson's keynote address to the audience of 8,500 at the council anniversary event forthrightly linked Peoria with the need for a new antifascist front in the United States. Robeson emphasized that the "heart of the issue" was not whether he was a Communist but whether U.S. citizens would be able to enjoy their constitutional rights regardless of their political beliefs. He further called for strengthening the United Nations as an international body that could promote unity and progress and prevent the dividing of the world into two opposing United States and Soviet camps. Finally, Robeson criticized American foreign policy by stating, "if the only alternative to being a supporter of the Truman doctrine of world domination is to be labeled a 'red,' then I for one welcome that label."[120] Additionally, the crowd adopted resolutions related to the Peoria incident as well as colonial liberation. The rally attendees called on the U.S. government to uphold the democratic rights of its citizens, to give full support to the United Nations, and not subvert its processes when the United States and Europe encountered opposition. The resolution on colonies was particularly incisive. It maintained that current diplomacy was inhibiting the struggles of colonial people for independence and called on the United States to "use its power . . . to promote the welfare of all oppressed and subject peoples."[121]

The Council on African Affairs, then, was determined to remain vocal on colonial and civil rights issues despite the signs that reactionary forces were gaining considerable influence. The council's posture was especially evident when the group repudiated Winston Churchill's infamous "iron curtain" speech. Churchill, fresh off a landslide defeat by the British Labour Party, seemed to have the tacit approval of President Truman when advocating an alliance against the Soviet Union that would help buttress the ailing British Empire. The speech was criticized by numerous black leaders who found Churchill's warmongering rhetoric in defense of imperialism to be quite alarming.[122] The council, in a letter fired off to Truman, considered the speech to be a "deliberate incitement" of war with the Soviets as well as a call for the continued suppression of self-government for colonial people. The United States should be mindful that the Soviets had been a crucial ally in World War II and were consistently supportive of colonial independence in United Nations discussions and votes, the council argued.[123]

The letter to Truman was signed by both Paul Robeson and Max Yergan in the name of the Council on African Affairs, but soon unanimity of purpose in the ten-year-old organization would be dramatically undercut. Just as factions were forming on the global stage, two blocs soon emerged in the council's leadership and caused a split in the group so rancorous that it would drive away long-time members and bring operations nearly to a halt for close to a year. The thronging crowds at council events and *New Africa* subscriber lists dissipated when an iron curtain–like partition materialized between the council's cofounders.

While the Southern Negro Youth Congress was being attacked by external forces in 1948, the Council on African Affairs was being assailed from within its own leadership. Both assaults illustrated the onset of the anticommunist and antiradical purges of the Cold War era in different ways. SNYC leaders and supporters were harassed by police when planning their Birmingham conference because of the organization's antisegregation policy and left-leaning reputation. The subversive designation by Attorney General Clark had caused concern within some of the SNYC local councils but brought more pressure to bear from outside the group. In comparison, being listed as a subversive organization unleashed a fissure within the Council on African Affairs. Conflict over how to react to the subversive label led to a rancorous falling out between Yergan, on one side with some followers, and Robeson and Hunton, who on the other side also had supporters.

Cold War pressure, it seemed, motivated Robeson and Hunton to dig in their heels and defend their constitutional right to affiliate with whatever political philosophy they chose as well as their right to speak out in favor of African self-determination even if that meant criticizing U.S. foreign policy. Yergan, however, adopted a more accomodationist approach. By the early 1950s, after leaving the council, he abandoned his left-wing political connections completely and began testifying about the Communist threat in Africa before congressional committees and making government-supported trips to the continent. This was an era when coalitions born during the Popular Front, like SNYC and the Council on African Affairs, were unraveling. Betrayal by former allies was sometimes a consequence of the divisive political circumstances of the Cold War era.

The fallout within the council had roots in the broader postwar dissolution of the progressive left. In the summer of 1945 Earl Browder, an associate of Max Yergan, was ousted from Communist Party leadership, and the more collaborative Communist Political Association, which Browder had created during the war, was dissolved and replaced by the CPUSA under the more doctrinaire leadership of William Z. Foster. Ironically, the Communist Party became more hard-line at a time when it was increasingly viewed as subversive. The party aligned itself more closely with the Soviet Comintern at exactly the moment when it was most dangerous to do so. In the next few years, alliances within Popular Front era coalitions such as the National Negro Congress were shaken up. The NNC, from which Yergan resigned in 1947, was ultimately merged with the Communist-organized Civil Rights Congress.

Meanwhile, the U.S. government was beginning to crack down on individual radicals as well as left-wing organizations. For example, West Indian Claudia Jones, a vocal member of the Communist Party, was arrested by immigration authorities in 1947. That same year, the *People's Voice* newspaper, under Yergan's direction, fired party member Doxey Wilkerson, who had been editing the paper, and made a public statement of nonpartisanship. In response, Paul Robeson resigned as a columnist. Thus, Yergan's "backpedaling" on his "uncompromisingly militant political stance" was apparent by 1947 according to biographer David Henry Anthony. Though his reversal was perhaps more dramatic than most, Yergan was "not alone in retreating" from the left during this repressive period.[124]

In December 1947, the Council on African Affairs, along with SNYC and other groups, was branded by Attorney General Tom Clark as a subversive organization. Formulating a response to this charge was at the heart of the cleft that developed in the council. At a meeting in early February 1948, the group was to decide on policy and programming. Yergan made a public statement of nonpartisanship that disavowed Communist or fascist ties. Historian Barbara Ransby explains, "Yergan had come to the conclusion that in order for the work of the council to go forward, it had to purge itself of communists and communist sympathizers, mimicking the actions that other liberal reform groups were taking."[125] However, Paul Robeson strongly objected to making such a statement on the grounds that this kind of position merely played into the hands of red-baiters who wanted organizations to go on the defensive. Additionally, at the February meeting Hunton presented a report that charged that as executive director Yergan had failed to promote "collective planning and functioning" and that the "lack of organizational growth" could be attributed to Yergan's ineffective leadership.[126] An article in the *Birmingham World* perceptively suggested that the acrimony between Robeson, Hunton, and Yergan also stemmed, in part, from Wilkerson's dismissal from the *People's Voice*.[127] Wilkerson, a member of the council, was also at the February meeting. W.E.B. Du Bois, also a council member, agreed to chair a committee that would look into Hunton's memo and make overall policy recommendations.

However, the Council on African Affairs remained in disarray for much of the year. At a meeting in March, Yergan was censured. He then resentfully locked Hunton out of his office in the council's headquarters and caustically left a note on the door that Hunton had been fired.[128] By April, Yergan vowed to wrest control of the council away from what he described as a Communist-led minority. Meanwhile numerous members resigned in frustration, as the stated goal of the group to provide information on Africa was being suspended as the leadership bickered.[129] In May 1948, a detailed letter from three members was delivered to Robeson that charged Yergan with malfeasance, citing mishandling of funds and running the group in a "one-man-rule" fashion.[130] That same month, the dispute received embarrassing coverage in the *New York Times* when police were called to the council's offices upon Yergan's allegation that his office had been broken into by Hunton and Wilkerson. Lawsuits were filed with both the Yergan and Robeson factions claiming to be the legitimate leadership of the organization.

Finally, in September, Yergan resigned and severed all connections with the Council on African Affairs following a court agreement that reinstated Robeson's chairmanship.[131] Yergan clarified in a statement following his resignation that he would receive $5,000 from the "Robeson forces" for his court fees and blamed the opposing faction for making the council "an instrument of the communist party."[132] Yet, Yergan had always been well aware of the group's left-wing political affiliations. In the midst of the fracas, for instance, Eslanda Robeson had pointed out that she had first met former Communist Party leader Earl Browder in Yergan's home.[133] And he had for many years collaborated with several groups as well as individuals on the political left. Hunton ultimately concluded that "for his own reasons" Yergan had "decided to withdraw from militant struggles on behalf of the African peoples."[134] The national climate was no longer friendly to progressive coalitions, and Yergan seemed to believe it was expedient to reposition himself politically. In doing so, he chose to leave behind people with whom he had formed friendships and collaborated for many years.

In October 1948, a letter went out to Council members announcing Yergan's departure and listing Robeson (chairman), Du Bois (vice-chairman), and Hunton (secretary) as officers. No issues of *New Africa* had been published since January, and the officers vowed to jump-start the work of the group now that litigation had been finalized.[135] The vitriolic and lengthy nature of the council's split suggests that the emotional investment in the organization was profound on both sides. Yergan's break with progressive activism was complete after his exit from the Council on African Affairs. He went on to become an expert on the Communist threat in Africa for U.S. government committees and an apologist for apartheid in South Africa.[136] Paul Robeson Jr. has made the case in the second volume of his biography on his father that Yergan had acted as an FBI informant.[137] By contrast, the council continued to cite the Soviet Union as being supportive of colonial freedom, which it demonstrated by the votes taken in the United Nations that were published in *New Africa* and, later, *Spotlight on Africa*. Though the group maintained a largely favorable view of the Soviet Union, especially with regard to the colonial question, Hollis Lynch concludes in his study that "there is no evidence that the Council owed its origins or support to the American Communist Party."[138] Indicative of divergent Cold War ideological paths were the lengths of careers enjoyed by the council's right-wing and left-wing factions: Yergan's public career spanned well into the 1960s while the Council on African Affairs sputtered and finally succumbed to McCarthy-style repression in 1955. Yergan's pragmatic embrace of conservative politics helped safeguard his career as a commentator on Africa.

Following the debilitating acrimony of Max Yergan's departure, the Council on African Affairs regrouped in 1949. *New Africa* was up and running again covering the United Nations agenda, events on the continent, and critiquing U.S. foreign policy. In fact, because it was banned by the government, Alphaeus Hunton personally shipped copies of the newsletter to Kenya to a grateful reader who also circulated them among friends.[139] It was also around this time that Paul Robeson's records were banned by the South Africa Recording Corporation. This stemmed from the continued opposition to racial injustice in that country levied by Robeson and the council.[140] On the international stage, alliances between East and West raised the threat of another world war.

During this period, the Council on African Affairs was an outspoken proponent of peace and opposed the formation of NATO, the North Atlantic Treaty Organization. Testifying before the Senate Foreign Relations Committee in May, Hunton argued against NATO on the grounds that it would foster a competitive "two-world system" rather than the international cooperation of a "one-world system" for which the United Nations had been created. Furthermore, he pointed out that the countries in the NATO coalition were those that held "hundreds of millions of colonial peoples in subjection throughout the world." Instead of living in peaceful cohabitation, these nations were currently involved in conflicts to maintain their domination over territories like Vietnam. In addition to financial resources provided via the Marshall Plan, Hunton presciently observed that U.S. troops could be called upon to support European colonial empires in the coming years. Not only would NATO heighten the threat of war with the Soviet Union, Hunton concluded, it would also hamper the quest for independence by colonial people in Africa and Asia.[141]

Nevertheless, voices calling for peace were increasingly marginalized as nationalistic jingoism became closely wedded to the anticommunist fervor building in the mainstream American public discourse. For example, council chairman Paul Robeson was excoriated in the U.S. press after making a few extemporaneous remarks at a worldwide peace conference in Paris in the spring of 1949.[142] The spirit of his comments was that African Americans were not going to support the United States in another conflict, including a war with the Soviets, until they enjoyed full citizenship rights. Immediately following this declaration, Robeson was denounced not only in the mainstream press but also in some of the black press, including *Crisis* magazine, the organ of the NAACP.[143] An editorial in *Crisis* announced that "Robeson speaks for Robeson" alone and that he had little support in the African American community.[144]

Following the publication of this piece, council members were urged to challenge the NAACP's use of their respectable journal for such a "snide and cheap attack."[145] After all, Robeson had been awarded that organization's highest honor, the Spingarn medal, just a few years ago. Yet, the political landscape had evolved since 1945, and the NAACP was now distancing itself from outspoken progressives, such as Robeson and Du Bois, who publicly questioned U.S. foreign policy. Walter White, executive secretary of the NAACP, took a more nuanced position in an article published in the *New York Tribune*. While he asserted that only a "miniscule" number of African Americans shared Robeson's views, he cautioned that Americans should avoid criticizing Robeson until the racial injustices that undergirded his critiques were resolved.[146]

However, in June 1949 the point of the *Crisis* editorialist was undermined by the interracial crowd of five thousand that greeted Robeson at a welcome home rally sponsored by the Council on African Affairs at Rockland Palace in Harlem. The stated purposes of the rally were to demonstrate public support for Robeson in response to the "campaign of vituperation" launched against him and to give him a platform where he could fully explain his Paris statement.[147] Having just returned from a concert tour that included visits across Europe and the Soviet Union, Robeson maintained that the working people in these nations wanted peace. They were far too busy turning out tractors, rather than tanks, and rebuilding their cities to consider entering another war. As for African Americans, Robeson insisted that unity was needed in the struggle for full constitutional rights and that no one wanted "to die in vain any more on foreign battlefields for Wall Street and the greedy supporters of domestic fascism." Then, looking southward, he emphasized, "If we must die let it be wherever we are lynched and deprived of our rights as human beings!"[148]

The mass meeting also helped to clarify the newly revived council's program. In his speech, Hunton underscored that the Council on African Affairs aimed to "rouse" the American public by helping them understand "the major role which the dominant reactionary forces in America are playing in trying to crush the liberation struggles of the African people."[149] The council, then, acted as an important support apparatus for Robeson during an oppressive period. Robeson enjoyed a reciprocal relationship with the council: he had been an advocate for the group since its inception, and now, perhaps more than at any other time during his career, he needed the organizational backing that the council could provide.

W.E.B. Du Bois, who had also attended the peace conference in Paris, pointed out in his speech at Rockland Palace that being in France was "like a bath in clear, cold water" because of the way freedom of speech was being protected. Over there, a man could defend the Marshall Plan and praise the United States while another man could join the Communists and praise Russia without fear of being smeared in the press, "jailed or driven to suicide."[150] In painting this picture of asylum, Du Bois critiqued the repressive political climate in the United States. In contrast to the haven Du Bois experienced in France, Robeson's statements of support for the people of the Soviet Union as well as the indicted leaders of the U.S. Communist Party led not only to acerbic denunciations of him in the press but also to physical attacks on his fans. Nowhere were the forces of reaction more violently apparent than in Peekskill, New York, in the summer of 1949.

On August 27, peaceful concertgoers were assaulted by right-wing vigilantes prior to an outdoor Robeson concert. In the confusion, Robeson was able to escape unharmed, but some attendees were injured from hurled rocks as car windows were broken, fence posts wielded as clubs, cars overturned, and threats such as "No one will leave here alive" shouted by a mob of several hundred.[151] Robeson promised to return in response to the violence, and another concert was planned for early September. This concert took place with tens of thousands of supporters responding to the call to defend not just Robeson but the very principles of freedom of speech and assembly. Famously, a ring of trade unionists encircled the outdoor stage to protect Robeson. After the concert, a mob again gathered and assaulted concertgoers as they exited the grounds.

In his graphic firsthand account, Howard Fast points out that police did little to inhibit the melee and that the bloodiest assaults were targeted at African American men.[152] Indeed, Klu Klux Klan involvement in the mob attack was exemplified by the cross that burned visibly on a nearby hillside.[153] After the second Peekskill attack, a press conference was held in the library of the Council on African Affairs' headquarters. Robeson, Howard Fast, and a procession of over a dozen witnesses and victims, some still bandaged, testified before reporters in the hope that the press would present the story fairly.[154] Despite accounts of concertgoers being beaten not only by hoodlums but also consciously by state police, some newspaper accounts alleged that the concertgoers were to blame for provoking the violence.[155]

The outrageous display of reactionary ire against the peaceful audience at Peekskill shocked activists across the country. The word "Peekskill" became a symbol of right-wing extremism and illustrated the ferocity of domestic fascism. The leadership of the council realized that this was an important moment in which to act. By immediately scheduling a six-city concert tour, audiences in Los Angeles, Chicago, Cleveland, Detroit, Philadelphia, and Washington, D.C., had an opportunity to publicly endorse Robeson. Importantly, all of these cities had significant African American populations, so these communities could demonstrate their support for the council's chairman. Most likely these audience members did not all agree with everything that Robeson advocated, but they upheld his right to express any political belief he so desired. In the repressive post-Peekskill atmosphere, this public confirmation of democratic principles was vital and stood in stark contrast with the appalling hostility revealed in upstate New York.

Under the auspices of the council's tour, Robeson not only delighted audiences with melodies in his unforgettable baritone but also highlighted how the fight for economic security, civil rights, and full equality for African Americans was inextricably linked to the struggles for peace and liberation of colonial people. He also paralleled the Peekskill violence with lynching in the South. For example, in Chicago, after singing "Joshua Fit the Battle of Jericho" to the crowd of four thousand, with two thousand more standing outside, Robeson assured those assembled that he would not keep quiet until "every black man in America can walk with dignity in his own country." He appreciated those who denounced the Peekskill fracas but reminded the audience of continued peril in the South where a black man "never knows when he is going to be the victim of a mob."[156]

Meanwhile, council stalwarts were traveling the globe to peace conferences and reporting on the "battle of Peekskill." Du Bois assured peace proponents in Moscow that he represented a U.S. contingent that was opposed to war. In Mexico City, Eslanda Robeson participated in the American Continental Peace Conference where she told the conferees that domestic peace must be secured before world peace could become a reality. Her husband, she declared, was in the United States fighting "to secure the peace at home."[157]

Newly appointed director of organization for the Council on African Affairs Louise Thompson Patterson was put in charge of arranging logistical details for the post-Peekskill tour. She was a Communist Party member, had served on the executive board of the International Worker's Order (a progressive beneficial organization), and was married to attorney William Patterson, who led the recently formed Civil Rights Congress, which defended many African Americans who were wrongfully accused of crimes and denied due process. Though born in Chicago and closely associated with activist circles in New York City, Louise Thompson Patterson's radicalism had definite southern roots. After earning a bachelor's degree in California, she taught at schools in Pine Bluff, Arkansas, and Hampton, Virginia, in the 1920s, where she discovered that the idea of "separate but equal" as enshrined in the 1896 *Plessy v. Ferguson* decision was nothing more than a "sham calculated to do little more than perpetuate black poverty."[158]

She went on to embrace Marxism and travel to the Soviet Union in 1932 where she worked on a film project that aimed to publicize the circumstances of African Americans in the South. Dispatched as an organizer for the International Worker's Order in the early 1930s, Patterson collided with police in Birmingham, Alabama, who arrested her and warned her that "we ain't going to stand for no interference from you [expletive deleted] yankee reds."[159] Her firsthand experience with the kind of "'justice' meted out to Negroes in the South" only strengthened her belief in "the economic roots of the Negro's oppression" and that "it is impossible to take one step in the direction of winning for the Negro people their elementary rights that is not revolutionary."[160] In her examination of Louise Thompson Patterson's career, Claire Nee Nelson concludes that the years she spent in the South "would inform all her subsequent ventures."[161]

Patterson, then, formulated a radical political philosophy in a similar fashion to Alphaeus Hunton, who spent most of his childhood in the North and became aroused to fight oppression after observing the poverty and racial segregation that subjugated African Americans in the South. Though she served as an officer for only a short period, Louise Thompson Patterson's organizing experience assisted the Council on African Affairs at a pivotal moment when the chairman was beset by negative press and right-wing hostility had been made starkly apparent in upstate New York. Planning security and acquiring venues for a Robeson tour was no simple feat in the fall of 1949, when government surveillance was persistent, police could be unpredictable, and no one knew where the next violent attacks might occur.[162] Louise Thompson Patterson, however, was up to the task and the peaceful post-Peekskill tour demonstrated cross-country support for the council chairman in defiance of right-wing vitriol.

A thoughtful article in the *New York Times* pondered the question of why people thronged to view the contents of the Freedom Train "in an era of uncertainty." An elderly African American man who visited the exhibit asserted of his community, "We have particular interest when you talk about freedom."[163] Black Americans had a strong interest in the Freedom

Train, in part, because they felt keenly the pang of having been denied freedom. African Americans could appreciate the notion of freedom, but they also offered a strong critique of American freedom. Viewing the Constitution in the Freedom Train on its 160th anniversary, black citizens could only conclude that the promise of American freedom had not yet been fulfilled. The author of the *New York Times* article concluded from visiting the Freedom Train that "freedom is a struggle." The writer referred directly to the large number of documents in the exhibit that dealt with war, chiefly World War II. The struggle against fascism had framed the definition of freedom for several years. However, in the postwar years a domestic struggle to define freedom in terms of civil rights and the right to colonial self-determination had ensued. The Southern Negro Youth Congress had been on the front lines of that struggle but had ultimately succumbed to antiradical repression and southern racism. The Council on African Affairs had also struggled for its global vision of freedom in the postwar years. The group suffered a rancorous split and had to downsize while focusing on defending its chairman, Paul Robeson, as anticommunism increasingly animated the political dialogue. Yet, their struggle for African and African American freedom continued.

4

Cold War Consequences

The Council on African Affairs in Decline, 1950–1955

During World War II, Roosevelt's historic speech had not outlined any prerequisites to enjoy the Four Freedoms he described. The Freedom Train exhibit illustrated the increasing contestation of the definition of freedom in the postwar years. By 1950, with the Cold War becoming more entrenched, the idea of freedom was becoming linked with the notion of national loyalty. In the late 1940s, President Truman instituted a loyalty program for federal employees, and the Taft-Hartley Act, passed by Congress in 1947, required union leaders to swear they owed no allegiance to the Communist Party. In 1950, Senator Joseph McCarthy dramatically called into question the loyalty of State Department employees when he publicly claimed to possess a list of spies working in that strategic government agency. That same year, the McCarran Internal Security Bill mandated that groups considered subversive must register with the government and that their members could have passports withdrawn.

As essayist Henry Steele Commager insightfully pointed out at that time, a "new loyalty" was being "etched more sharply in public policy."[1] Rather than protecting one's access to basic freedoms, this new loyalty was constricting. It directed a citizen to prove himself as loyal in order to enjoy the benefits of free society. Conformity, above all, was the basis of the new loyalty and it, in Commager's words, denied "freedom of thought and conscience."[2] Citizens were expected to embrace American society as it was without interrogating its shortcomings.

Groups or individuals who did challenge aspects of American society, like the Southern Negro Youth Congress, sometimes became Cold War casualties. The influential national security paper from 1950 known as NSC-68, which positioned the United States and the Soviet Union as diametrical foes and helped bring about increased military spending, defined a free society as having several clear attributes. The paper indicated that a free society welcomed diversity and derived strength from "its hospitality even to antipathetic ideas."[3] Ironically, the U.S. government was restricting oppositional views even while arguing that the "free trade in ideas" was fundamental to a free society.[4] A consequence of the early Cold War was, thus, an atmosphere that circumscribed freedom of speech and freedom of political association. Critiquing U.S. policy, as the Council on African Affairs did, was not embraced in this political climate. As a result, the council was pushed into a defensive position in the early 1950s in which the organization was forced to contend for its right to function.

Yet, another consequence of the Cold War was resourcefulness in responding to the political environment. The formation of *Freedom* newspaper illustrated a tenacious spirit among activists on the progressive left. Even though the paper lasted but a few years, it showed how organizers and writers persisted in creating outlets from which to advocate for both southern civil rights and colonial freedom for Africa. *Freedom* was part of a near-continuous vision that linked the values and goals of the Southern Negro Youth Congress and Council on African Affairs with an emerging generation of activists who established *Freedomways* journal just a few years after *Freedom* and the council folded in 1955.

A lot of Cold War rhetoric was tinged with an increasingly militaristic tone in 1950. Early that year, in a speech that was later proven to be largely fabricated, Senator McCarthy alleged that the Communist Party had penetrated the Department of State. McCarthy's hawkish anticommunist tone was unambiguous and foreshadowed future armed conflict. Declaring that the "rumblings of an invigorated god of war" were audible, McCarthy evaluated the current political winds by stressing that "this is not a period of peace" but rather time for "the show-down" between "communistic atheism and Christianity."[5] That summer, the formation of Cold War alliances instigated U.S. intervention in a "hot" war on the divided Korean peninsula. The council, and other groups, which had been calling for peace, had to now face the tangible evidence that their pleas had gone unheard.

Undaunted, the Council on African Affairs quickly denounced the

Korean conflict and circulated an antiwar petition that was signed by 150 African Americans.[6] The September issue of *New Africa* also published statements against the war from leaders and activists around Africa. The petition was penned by council vice-chairman W.E.B. Du Bois who was actively involved in the world peace movement. In the summer of 1950, he traveled to Prague for a meeting of the Partisans of Peace, and he worked with the Peace Information Center to disseminate news on the global peace movement in the United States.[7] In the council petition, titled "A Protest and Plea," Du Bois forthrightly stated that the organization stood for peace and demanded that U.S. military intervention in the Korean civil war should be immediately halted in favor of arbitration, which should be undertaken "with the clear understanding that if Koreans prefer socialism or communism they must be free to choose." He then cogently linked the Korean crisis to racial injustice in the United States by pointing out that this country was hardly qualified to intervene on behalf of the rights of "darker peoples" given its record of segregation, disfranchisement, and lynching at home as well as its continued financial support of South African apartheid. Finally, commenting on the domestic political climate, Du Bois noted the federal government had but one response to policy critiques based on sound evidence: they must be evidence of a Communist conspiracy. Nevertheless, he firmly maintained that "it is not treason to work for Peace."[8]

Still, the repressive political atmosphere failed to abate. In the summer of 1950, the Council on African Affairs planned to hold a rally in support of restoring Paul Robeson's right to travel abroad after his passport was revoked by federal authorities. The contract for the event, scheduled to be held at Madison Square Garden, was suddenly canceled on the grounds that a pending bill in Congress would make it illegal for groups on the attorney general's list of subversive organizations to rent the space. At a press conference, council chairman Robeson pointed out that such legislation was being used to "tear up the Bill of Rights and, specifically, the right of free assembly and free speech."[9]

In response, the council called for a protest in front of Madison Square Garden, and over one hundred black and white citizens picketed the site. Noting the public demonstration, the management of the venue granted Alphaeus Hunton an interview but still refused to allow the council to utilize the Garden. Returning to the march, Hunton declared that if constitutional rights can be repressed on the basis of legislation that has not even been passed, "it is not hard to imagine the destruction of our liberties which must follow if these proposals actually become the law of the land."[10] Just as freedom of assembly was curtailed for the Southern Negro Youth Congress in its last year, the Council on African Affairs now suffered from similarly restraining measures. Only four years previously, the council had held one of its biggest mass rallies in Madison Square Garden in support of South African famine relief. However, by 1950, obstruction of progressive coalitions was being more actively pursued. As the U.S. government purportedly defended democratic values in Korea, it systematically curtailed such rights at home, especially for those people and organizations that were critical of U.S. policies. Both Robeson and Du Bois, for example, were deprived of the right to international travel for much of the decade. In Robeson's case, the State Department argued that his advocacy of African self-determination could undermine U.S. policy in the region.[11]

In addition to grappling with civil liberties issues, the council struggled with diminishing financial support as a consequence of the Cold War climate. The organization's deficit prevented the summer issues of *New Africa* from being published.[12] They did offer several publications for sale in 1950, including "Nigeria—Why We Fight for Freedom," a bibliography of resources about the continent, and an overview of current liberation struggles by Alphaeus Hunton titled "Africa Fights for Freedom" with an introduction by Eslanda Robeson. A meticulous combing of sources on Africa was also compiled under the heading "Current Data Concerning Economic, Social, and Political Conditions in Certain African Colonial Territories," which could be distributed to UN officials. In "Africa Fights for Freedom," Hunton outlined the growing resistance in places like Algeria, Uganda, Nigeria, and the Gold Coast, noting that "the Africa of 1950 is not the Africa of 1920 or 1940."[13] In his closing, he adroitly linked the fight against colonialism in Africa with the freedom struggle of African Americans. Hunton argued that just as "the colonial peoples' resistance is at the very core of the present world struggle," "the Negro peoples' struggle for full equality and democracy is at the core of the fight against American fascism." Support for the anticolonial movement was, then, fundamental in guaranteeing "the successful building of a new world order of peace, friendship, and equality among all peoples."[14] Thus, even as the group wrestled with financial woes and government repression, the council continued to disseminate information concerning the continent at a vital moment when colonial independence movements were gaining momentum. Significantly, the council's positions on peace in Korea and colonial freedom were connected to the necessity of obtaining full citizenship for African Americans. The following year, however, was full of even more upheaval for the organization.

In 1951, publication of *New Africa* was again interrupted. This time it was due to the incarceration of council secretary Alphaeus Hunton. A letter to council members and supporters in the summer of 1951 solicited support in securing Hunton's freedom.[15] Hunton's predicament stemmed from his work with the Civil Rights Congress. The CRC, like the other groups on the government's subversive list, was confronting increased government scrutiny. That summer, Hunton, along with three other trustees of a bail fund maintained by the Civil Rights Congress, refused to divulge information about its contributors. For protecting the bail fund's financial supporters, Hunton received a sentence of six months in prison for contempt of court. Having been refused bail, he spent the second half of the year in a segregated penitentiary in Virginia, passing the days by working in the facility's small library.[16]

Discouraging news continued when the cover of the September 1951 issue of *New Africa* confirmed for readers that Hunton was in jail and also announced that council vice-chairman W.E.B. Du Bois was under indictment in federal court for his peace advocacy. He had refused to register as an agent of a foreign government as requested by the Justice Department for his work with the Peace Information Center. This group had circulated petitions against the nuclear bomb and disseminated information on the worldwide peace movement. Du Bois and the other defendants from the recently dissolved Peace Information Center were acquitted in November 1951. But the experience had been jarring for the eighty-three-year-old scholar-activist. Du Bois questioned why the U.S. government would attempt to jail five citizens who had no wealth or power left. He concluded that the State Department had been roused because, despite the government's militarism, "a small group of no influence was bringing out an extraordinary evidence of peace sentiment in this country."[17] By early 1952, Hunton was back at his council desk and noted in an editorial that he was grateful for all of the genial messages that greeted him upon his return to New York from what he euphemistically referred to as his "enforced 'vacation.'"[18] Indeed, an interracial crowd of over one hundred had welcomed Hunton at the airport. Herbert Aptheker directly bestowed his friend with a copy of his new book, *A Documentary History of the Negro People in the United States*, which had been denied to Hunton while in prison on the grounds that it was too incendiary.[19]

After Hunton's return, the group organized several protest campaigns in the spring of 1952. Over one hundred picketers joined the organization in a demonstration in front of the French consulate in New York in support of Tunisian freedom.[20] In April, the Council on African Affairs focused on demonstrating solidarity with the defiance campaigns being waged in South Africa. An editorial from Robeson in *Spotlight on Africa*, the new title of their newsletter, urged African Americans to be inspired by the mass action in South Africa. He implored readers to imagine the black community in the United States unified in a "great and compelling action to put a stop to Jim Crow" just as millions of victims of an even more savage regime were forming a common front of "resolute resistance."[21]

That month, the council called for a moment of silence in all African American churches and communities on the Sunday when the defiance campaigns were launched. The group also sponsored an outdoor rally in Harlem followed by several days of picketing the South African consulate in New York.[22] Signs carried by protesters called for an end to U.S. financial support of the South African government. The mass civil disobedience had been planned by numerous activist and trade union organizations in South Africa as a response to Prime Minister Malan's oppressive administration. The *New York Times* reported that several thousand South African freedom fighters had marched to the voice of Paul Robeson being played over a loudspeaker.[23] The council chairman's unmistakable voice had resonated not only at the street rally in Harlem as he called for South African freedom but also across an ocean in the streets of Johannesburg as South Africans mobilized against the strictures of apartheid legislation.

The defiance campaigns, as well as the social and political circumstances for nonwhite people, were detailed in a 1953 pamphlet distributed by the council titled "Resistance Against Fascist Enslavement in South Africa." In it, the text of a memorandum to the United Nations from the African National Congress and the South African Indian Congress was reprinted, along with a postscript by Hunton where he itemized U.S. financial investments in South Africa and queried, if the United States could not do business with Hitler, "what about Malan?"[24] In calling for support from Americans, Hunton noted that "the problem of Jim Crow" could not be separated "from the problem of Apartheid in South Africa," especially when apartheid laws were paying big dividends to U.S. investors.[25] Finally, Hunton encouraged readers to write to their congressmen or sign the council's petition demanding that the United States stop supporting the repressive administration in South Africa. The African National Congress, one of the groups that led the defiance campaigns, later thanked the Council on African Affairs for its continued acknowledgement and support of their movement. Their efforts had been labeled by the South African government as subversive, just as the council had been classified thusly by the U.S. government.[26]

In the early 1950s, resistance to British imperialism in Kenya prompted what the council labeled a "dirty war" in which scores of Kenyans were murdered and thousands more arrested and imprisoned, including a leader of the struggle, Jomo Kenyatta.[27] In addition to continued coverage of events in *Spotlight on Africa*, the Council on African Affairs hosted a daylong conference on African freedom that highlighted the situation in Kenya in April 1954. Resolutions passed by the conferees included a strong declaration in support of African rights, including self-government. Another statement condemned British crimes in Kenya and called for the immediate release of Jomo Kenyatta and the restoration of civil rights for all Kenyans. This resolution even demanded that the United Nations take action to protect the people from acts of genocide by the British. A message of solidarity was also passed in support of the African National Congress and South African Indian Congress and their consistent efforts to fight racial discrimination in South Africa.[28]

In his keynote address at the meeting, W.E.B. Du Bois lamented that historically African Americans had not been more interested in or supportive of Africa. Outlining the generational distancing of Americans from Africa, he observed that "our help and inspiring understanding of the desperate problems of the dark continent have never been what they should have been." Conversely, European and American imperialists had been engrossed with Africa but only to exploit its vast resources and then fight with each other for a larger share. Du Bois closed by admonishing the participants that it was their duty to "understand thoroughly just what is going on in Africa" and then make some contribution toward black emancipation.[29]

Almost exactly a decade after the council's conference on the future of postwar Africa, the April 1954 meeting struck a more urgent tone. While the April 1944 conference had called for the United States to lead the way in forming an international body that would guide Africa to self-government, ten years later it was clear that the United States was collaborating with European colonizers. Though independence movements were growing in many territories, they did so in spite of Western opposition to self-determination expressed in the United Nations. Continued oppression of nonwhites in South Africa backed by U.S. dollars and the British brutality against Kenyans further illustrated the emptiness of the Atlantic Charter promises with regard to Africa. However, Africans were mobilizing, and this, the Council hoped, would strike a "death-blow to the myth of African inferiority" and provide a "tremendous impetus" to the struggle for African American rights.[30]

As early as 1953, as a consequence of Cold War politics, the Council on African Affairs was vying for its survival. The McCarran Internal Security Act legislated that any organization named subversive must register with the Subversive Activities Control Board (SACB) and Attorney General Herbert Brownell had ordered the council to do so on the grounds that the group was a front for the Communist Party. In response, the council argued that it had not been directed by the party nor was its stated purpose to aid the party. Rather, the group had always functioned to inform the public about Africa and generate support for the welfare of the people there. As evidence, the council cited its activities backing African liberation and supplied correspondence from African activists. Additionally, the group noted that its publications and newsletters were disseminated to libraries, scholars, and United Nations and governmental officials.[31] A council press release also pointedly suggested that the real issue at stake was not its ties to the Communist Party but the right to advocate for the freedom of African people, "including the descendants of Africa who have yet to achieve their full liberty and rights here in the United States."[32]

From 1953 to 1955, the Council on African Affairs was spending more time and resources defending its right to exist rather than carrying out its stated mission. With another hearing before the SACB scheduled for

July 1955, the council's leadership met in mid-June and decided to disband the organization. Summarizing the past and present work of the group, Hunton asserted that "continued government harassment" was making it "difficult if not impossible" to carry on its program and that the upcoming hearing would put "intolerable strain" on the functioning of the organization.[33] Dissolution seemed the pragmatic course under the circumstances. In its final years, Hunton, especially, had worked tirelessly to keep the council operating. At the final meeting of the board, Paul Robeson commended Hunton's service to the cause of African freedom and his personal sacrifices "in the face of great difficulties."[34] The Council on African Affairs had weathered a world war in addition to a rancorous internal split, but government pressure, as well as waning support, signaled the end of the road. Still, the group had pioneered an important path and it was now up to other groups and individuals to stimulate U.S. interest in Africa.

Paradoxically, the Council on African Affairs was disbanded at a promising moment for anticolonial movements on the world stage. The Afro-Asian conference held in Bandung, Indonesia, in the spring of 1955 illustrated a growing momentum toward self-government in the colonized world. In his opening address, President Sukarno of Indonesia recollected that it was exactly 180 years ago that Paul Revere made the historic ride that marked the start of the American War for Independence. This was the first successful anticolonial war, but, Sukarno emphasized, it would not be completely won until colonialism everywhere was eliminated.[35] Ironically, in the one hundred plus years since its revolution, the political climate had evolved and the United States was now allied with the colonizers, including Great Britain.

The Afro-Asian conference galvanized the attention of many in the African American community. In his ruminations on the congress, African American writer Richard Wright noted that the twenty-nine nations gathered at Bandung, who were "the despised, the insulted, the hurt, the dispossessed," seemed to have little in common except "what their past relationship to the Western world had made them feel."[36] These feelings were not ameliorated when President Eisenhower declined to send official greetings to the meeting, though he had been urged to do so by Representative Adam Clayton Powell Jr., who attended of his own accord.[37] Journalist Abner Berry hoped the meeting would inspire a close affiliation between

African Americans and the broader Afro-Asian world. He observed that the principles adopted at Bandung could help African Americans to understand the "essential unity of the demands of the world's colored peoples" and that it would then "be harder for the Negro people to remain separated in their freedom struggles from the majority of the world's peoples."[38]

Enthusiasm for the Bandung meeting was practically palpable in the last two issues of the council's newsletter, *Spotlight on Africa*. The April 1955 issue carried a masthead stating "Bandung: Dawn of a New Era" and asserted that the Council on African Affairs was "proud and privileged" to dedicate an issue to sharing a sample of African and African American opinion on the historic meeting. Though council leaders Robeson and Du Bois wanted very much to attend the conference, continued passport restrictions prevented them from traveling to Indonesia. Still, they each conveyed warm greetings to the conferees. Robeson felt strongly disposed toward the ten principles adopted at Bandung that included respect for fundamental human rights and sovereignty of all nations as well as the equality of all races and abstention from intervention in the affairs of other nations. He reprinted them in his 1958 memoir, *Here I Stand*, declaring that it was upon this platform from Bandung that he took his political stand.[39]

One year following the momentous *Brown v. Board of Education* decision, Representative Powell stated at a press conference in Bandung that racism and second-class citizenship were on the way out in the United States, which sparked a firestorm of commentary in the black press and general approval in the mainstream press.[40] While Powell might have been posturing to counter critiques of American policy that were presented at the conference, the Council on African Affairs maintained that Powell was in a position in which he could be of "service to the colored peoples of America, Africa, and Asia" if he would only focus on that rather than "capitalizing on anti-Communism and hunting headlines."[41] The conference, then, was not devoid of Cold War rhetoric. But, especially as seen in Sukarno's speech, the council believed that the significance of Bandung was its demonstration to a "Cold War weary world" that it was "possible and practicable for Communists, non-Communists, and anti-Communists to live together, meet together, speak together and contribute toward the common good and peace of all mankind." Toward those goals, "Bandung marked a beginning." "Let us begin, too!" the council encouraged its readers.[42]

Those were the last words printed in the final issue of *Spotlight on Africa*. The Cold War climate had made it next to impossible for a group such as the Council on African Affairs, which embraced a Pan-African worldview but was sympathetic to the Communist Party's critique of the twin evils of colonialism and capitalism, to function. In the wake of the council's dissolution, other groups concerned with Africa emerged. For example, the American Committee on Africa (ACOA), formerly known as Americans for South African Resistance, was founded during the defiance campaigns of the early 1950s. Created as a program of the liberal civil rights group the Congress of Racial Equality (CORE), ACOA covered events on the continent in its organ, *Africa Today*. But, unlike *Spotlight on Africa*, the ACOA's newsletter was more critical of African freedom fighters in places like Algeria, Tunisia, and Kenya, revealing what some scholars have characterized as the "limited political horizons" of the group's leadership.[43]

With regard to South Africa, in particular, the council's legacy was perceptible years after its disbanding. Its publications, mass rallies, and the picketing of the consulate had helped to raise national consciousness about the political situation there. The United Nations eventually passed nonbinding sanctions in 1962, and the following year the Kennedy administration stopped selling arms to South Africa.[44] In 1977, an advocacy group that lobbied and provided up-to-date information about Africa to the U.S. public as well as Congress was founded. TransAfrica's educational program was reminiscent of the council's goal to enlighten the public on African issues. Under the leadership of Randall Robinson, in the mid-1980s TransAfrica advanced the campaign to end political repression and U.S. financial investment in South Africa through successful implementation of nonviolent tactics, including sit-ins and long-term picketing of the embassy in Washington, D.C. This action, collectively known as the Free South Africa Movement, ultimately attained a mass following and culminated in congressional passage of the Comprehensive Anti-Apartheid Act of 1986 that applied economic sanctions to South Africa.[45] The call that Alphaeus Hunton had raised in his meticulous pamphlets on the economic underpinnings of fascist enslavement in South Africa had finally been fulfilled. Once the United States passed sanctions, Britain and other European countries followed and the first nails were pounded into the coffin of South African apartheid.

Additionally, recent histories of the Cold War have fleshed out themes that were espoused in the council's body of literature. In his book *The Global Cold War*, Odd Arne Westad argues for the "need to understand the Cold War in light of the colonial experience."[46] The council's publications detailing political and social circumstances in Africa as well as United Nations votes during the early Cold War had helped demonstrate the impact of the East-versus-West mindset on burgeoning colonial independence movements. Historian Robert Dalleck has recently worked to puzzle out why "the most powerful and influential leaders of the twentieth century" failed "to attain the elusive goal of world peace at a time when their citizens were thirsting for tranquility."[47] The council's position in the post–World War II era definitely favored peace, and this message seemed to resonate with audiences at events the group sponsored. Moreover, Dalleck points out that U.S. diplomat George Kennan, whose famous long telegram helped instigate the policy of containment, lamented the fact that his "message of restraint" was less influential than his warnings of the danger of Soviet Communism. Kennan was also distressed by the "hysterical anticommunism of the 1950s" and opposed to the creation of NATO on the grounds that "no military threat existed that required the creation of a multilateral defense organization."[48] Thus, some of the council's positions, such as opposition to NATO, were corroborated within the State Department. Overall, Dalleck's book seems to suggest that another course, away from war and militarism, was lost in the wake of World War II. The Council on African Affairs had seen this at the time when its advocacy for peace went largely unheeded.

The council's call for African self-determination as well as full citizenship for African Americans did not see a groundswell in mass action until after the group's dissolution. These campaigns for civil rights in the United States and independence in Africa were carried out by the generation of activists that succeeded the Council on African Affairs, though some had been influenced by their work, as in the case of Kwame Nkrumah. In her book *Race against Empire*, historian Penny Von Eschen concludes that the silencing of left-wing groups such as the council meant that once the classical phase of the civil rights movement in the United States gained steam, "questions concerning political, economic, and social rights in an international context were neglected in favor of an exclusive focus on domestic political and civil rights."[49] This was an unfortunate reality of the Cold War world. However, what was perhaps more significant than the gap that was left when the Council on African Affairs shut its doors was the way in which the group had functioned as a bridge between the early Pan-African movement, as exemplified in the first Pan-African congresses and Garvey-ism, and the post–World War II movement. Historian Kevin Gaines has pointed out that the "wartime social and political ferment . . . helped align the struggle against segregation in the United States with the African po-litical renaissance of nationalism and anticolonialism."[50] The Council on African Affairs had been very active during the war years and was part of the ferment that helped inaugurate renewed campaigns for African Ameri-can civil rights and independence in Africa in the late 1950s and 1960s.

When the Gold Coast became the independent nation of Ghana under Kwame Nkrumah's leadership in 1957, a phase of Pan-Africanism in the postindependence era was initiated. As the freedom movement in Africa pressed forward, numerous African American activists and artists jour-neyed to the continent and fostered new kinds of political and cultural exchanges.[51] It was in this spirit that Nkrumah invited veteran Pan-Afri-canist W.E.B. Du Bois to Ghana to work on an Encyclopedia Africana. In 1962, Alphaeus Hunton joined Du Bois to collaborate on the project. These former leaders of the Council on African Affairs had linked the cause of African freedom with that of African Americans and subjugated people around the globe. It was truly symbolic and perhaps fitting that both Al-phaeus Hunton and W.E.B. Du Bois ultimately died in Africa. Two great Pan-Africanists were swallowed by the earth of the mother continent.

"Where One is Enslaved, All Are in Chains": *Freedom* Newspaper

In the spring of 1951, not long after the newspaper was founded, an earnest letter arrived at the offices of *Freedom* in New York. Already a reader as far away as Oklahoma felt moved to offer "my thanks to your little paper" and contribute "a few lines about things that are going on here in the deep south against the Negro."[52] The letter writer then explicated grim instances of rape going unpunished and Klu Klux Klan members violently chasing a World War II veteran and businessman out of town. Though it made for an unsettling read, letters such as this, which testified about the true conditions facing African Americans, were central to the consciousness-raising mission that was at the heart of *Freedom* newspaper. This letter was also instructive in that the writer referred to Oklahoma as "the deep south." Indeed, the mind of the South often seeped across geographic boundaries.

Another southerner from Kentucky penned a letter to *Freedom* detailing the impact of the newspaper in the local community. "Until recently," the writer observed, "most of us here in Lexington were little interested in what was taking place in the far corners of the world—except sporting events." However, the letter continued, "Now we are waking up."[53] The writer then explained that a local group was attempting to get a black candidate elected to city council in order to better represent the needs of their constituency. Though their efforts had not yet been fruitful, they were heartened to have gotten some white votes in the last election and were convinced that "eventually we will succeed." The progressive newspaper's coverage of anticolonial struggles and other freedom movements around the world had fostered, in this case, a campaign to institute local democratic reforms.

One final letter from a college student in the South paid tribute to Paul Robeson and W.E.B. Du Bois as leaders who were "putting forth bold effort" to combat current political and social crises.[54] The student urged these freedom fighters to lead on and assured the seasoned activists that his generation, "though weaker in terms of insight and experience," would "measure up in [their] determination" to contribute to the present freedom struggle. This inspired writer, James Kelsaw, went on to write several articles as a southern correspondent for *Freedom*. His letter illustrated well the intergenerational nature of the newspaper. The staff of *Freedom* wanted its readership to be in touch with those who had fought for freedom in the past. Regular articles on history highlighted the insurrectionists who had fought against slavery, like Cinque, Harriet Tubman, and Frederick Douglass, or advocated for African humanity through poetry, such as Phylis Wheatley. In the narrative of *Freedom*, a trajectory of continuous leadership was presented from the freedom fighters of the eighteenth and nineteenth centuries to Du Bois, Robeson, and others in the early and middle twentieth century who were, in turn, conscious that James Kelsaw and his cohort would help foment the next phase of the civil rights revolution in the late 1950s and 1960s. The newspaper, thus, made space available in its pages for young artists and writers to engage in their crafts, and it covered the events that were shaping their generation, such as the Korean War, burgeoning anticolonial movements, and school desegregation.

Freedom newspaper conjoined the primary impulses of both the Southern Negro Youth Congress and the Council on African Affairs by wedding left-wing analysis of the battles for domestic civil rights with global campaigns for colonial self-determination. This coverage was contextualized by rich reportage on history and culture of the Pan-African world. Though based in Harlem, the newspaper assembled a uniquely intergenerational group of contributors from various regions who shared a progressive political perspective and were galvanized by worldwide racial oppression, especially in the southern United States. Most, if not all, of *Freedom*'s contributors were from the South, had relatives down there, or had experience organizing in that region and knew of the profound need for radical change, as the writer from Oklahoma indicated in his letter.

Unlike the council or SNYC, *Freedom* was conceived as a consequence of the Cold War. It was the reactionary nature of skewed reporting in this time period that led to its creation. Ultimately, the struggle for funding as well as antiradical pressure caused it to fold. For the few years of its existence, from 1950–1955, however, *Freedom* carved out a space for a progressive voice that denounced war, advocated for full freedom, and called for labor rights. The newspaper's unapologetically left-wing, internationalist perspective informed readers of global events and sometimes inspired them to act at home, like the letter writer from Kentucky. Most important, by its very name, the newspaper challenged the definition of freedom during a period of intense domestic repression and warmongering overseas. According to these activists, full freedom meant having the ability to speak in favor of African liberation without recrimination; and it meant being able to join or affiliate with the political party of one's choosing; it meant exercising all democratic rights enshrined in the U.S. Constitution; it meant being able to travel abroad regardless of one's political perspective; it meant having the opportunity to organize on behalf of working people. Evoking a previous era of oppression with its masthead, "Where One is Enslaved, All Are in Chains," *Freedom* reminded its readers that the task that the great abolitionists had initiated was not yet complete.

*   *   *

As anticommunism gained prominence in the public discourse, black activists, such as Paul Robeson, who outspokenly critiqued the Truman Doctrine, the Marshall Plan, or other Cold War legislation were maligned in the mainstream press and sometimes dissociated by the black press, as had occurred after the 1949 peace conference in Paris. Recent scholarship has found that by the late 1940s, there was more coverage of world Communism than European colonialism in most national black newspapers.[55] Media voices from the left were becoming increasingly rare. For example, the *People's Voice* newspaper in New York disbanded in 1948. The *Daily Worker* out of New York was a mainstay of the Communist left and a few smaller regional papers, like Charlotta Bass's *California Eagle*, provided a reliable progressive perspective. Of the major national black newspapers, the *Pittsburgh Courier*, Baltimore *Afro-American*, and the *Chicago Defender*, the *Afro-American* was probably the most sympathetic to left-wing viewpoints. At the other end of the spectrum, *Pittsburgh Courier* columnist George Schuyler was relentlessly disparaging of radicalism.

Events in 1950 were also troubling for radicals. For instance, Robeson was banned by NBC from participating in a political broadcast with Eleanor Roosevelt in which he was slated to represent the Progressive Party's position on civil rights. This was also the first year of Robeson's enforced domestic confinement due to his passport revocation. Perhaps most disheartening was the outbreak of war on the Korean peninsula, which flew in the face of the international movement for peace. In the midst of the growing antiradical climate, Robeson and other progressive activists collaborated on a new monthly publication called *Freedom*. Though well intentioned and staffed by talented writers, the project faced considerable obstacles. Not only were the early 1950s difficult for radical publications but this was also the beginning of a period of general decline for black newspapers. As mainstream publications began to integrate more coverage on African American communities, it was challenging for black-owned newspapers to compete. The heyday of black newspapers was coming to an end.

In addition, the new mode of television soon challenged the dominance of print media.[56]

Financial solvency was also a perpetual difficulty for *Freedom* newspaper. In fact, the first issue noted that the project got up and running on a "shoestring" budget.[57] The paper was largely supported by subscriptions with help from the United Freedom Fund. The United Freedom Fund was a coordinating committee formed to raise money for progressive groups including the Council on African Affairs, *Freedom* newspaper, and the National Negro Labor Council. It sponsored the benefit concert tours Robeson undertook in the early 1950s.[58] However, these initiatives failed to generate adequate revenue, in part, because newspaper subscriptions and concert ticket prices were intentionally kept at rates that would be accessible to the broadest possible audiences.[59] In the spring of 1955, a financial appeal to its readership urged subscribers to renew, but the paper was forced to fold by summer.[60]

Though modest in size and relatively short-lived, *Freedom* left an impressive body of work. As one of few progressive newspapers, it was able to attract top-notch contributors from the political left. The team was headed by editor Louis Burnham, who had turned northward after SNYC was dissolved and following his stint as a southern organizer for Henry A. Wallace's Progressive Party campaign. Lorraine Hansberry poetically characterized Burnham, an important influence on her, as having a deep voice that was "so rich, so strong, so very certain" and imbued with a "profound literacy." In Hansberry's memory, he sat in his office on 125th Street and occasionally glanced out the window, which "let him look at Harlem while he talked to me." She concluded movingly that "the thing he had for our people was something marvelous . . . it was an open and adoring love that mawkishness never touched."[61]

The general manager was George B. Murphy Jr., who had the newspaper business in his blood coming from the family that owned the *Afro-American*. Thelma Dale, who had worked with the Southern Negro Youth Congress and the National Negro Congress, took over that job toward the end of the paper's run. Members of the editorial board included labor organizer Revels Cayton, writer Shirley Graham, southern activist Modjeska Simkins, and Alphaeus Hunton with Paul Robeson serving as chairman. Beginning in November 1950, the staff produced regular issues, with some interruptions, until the summer of 1955. During that time, articles were contributed by W.E.B. Du Bois, historian Herbert Aptheker, William Patterson of the Civil Rights Congress, Councilman Ben Davis, and writers Howard Fast, John O. Killens, John Henrik Clarke, and Lloyd Brown.

Figure 5. George B. Murphy Jr. and Adele Young pose with *Freedom* newspaper. *Daily Worker/Daily World* Photographs Collection, Tamiment Library, New York University.

Known for his novel *Iron City*, Brown penned a pamphlet in support of Robeson's passport fight, "Lift Every Voice for Paul Robeson," and collaborated on Robeson's featured column, "Here's My Story." Activists from the Pan-African world submitted articles on their local freedom struggles. For example, Walter Sisulu and Z. K. Matthews offered editorials on South Africa, Robert F. Williams called for a student movement in North Carolina, Janet Jagan summarized the people's movement in British Guiana, and Jamaican trade unionist Harry Drayton chronicled labor organizing in the West Indies.

A prominent aspect of *Freedom*'s legacy was the vital role of radical women. Recent research has demonstrated the significance of the work of activists from the political left who helped lay the groundwork for the new wave of feminism that emerged in the 1960s.[62] Like the men who worked with the paper, many of these women were members of or affiliated with the Communist Party. Eslanda Robeson, who supported the Council on African Affairs, wrote articles on international politics, paying particular attention to events in Africa. Shirley Graham, who married the venerable Du Bois in the early 1950s, contributed articles in addition to serving on the editorial board. Women such as Dorothy Burnham, Yvonne Gregory, Vicki Garvin, Thelma Dale, and Beulah Richardson helped establish and maintain the valuable progressive journalism on culture, civil rights, and labor issues with which *Freedom* was identified. Their reporting often paid particular attention to women in an era when this practice was far from commonplace. An article by Dorothy Hunton after her husband Alphaeus's release from prison was particularly illuminating in this regard. After enduring the hardship of his incarceration, Dorothy reflected that the experience had actually been an "opportunity and gain" in that it had made her a "new wife" because she had learned that her true place was with those who endeavored "to make this a decent world in which to live." She urged others to join her: "The time has come when we Negro women, especially, must unite and work together for the freedom and dignity of our people."[63]

In addition to providing an important space for progressive authors and historians to practice their crafts, *Freedom* nurtured the careers of developing writers who became significant African American voices in the literary community. Alice Childress's fictional, but remarkably vibrant and realistic "Conversations from Life" series was one of the most memorable and enduring features in *Freedom*.[64] Childress, born in South Carolina, was three generations removed from enslavement. She grew up in New York and worked for a time as a domestic laborer, which helped inform the depiction of Mildred in her *Freedom* column. Mildred is a working-class protagonist somewhat akin to Langston Hughes's Jesse B. Simple character. Childress imaginatively outlines a uniquely one-sided dialogue between Mildred, a daytime domestic worker, and her friend Marge. Though Marge's voice is never heard directly, the reader can picture her clearly from Mildred's lively reactions. Through these well-crafted vignettes, Childress addressed labor and political issues in a way that was poignant and accessible to readers. Mildred ruminated on class, gender, and familial relationships, as well as racial identity, from the perspective of one of the folk. For example, Childress's envisioning of Mildred's feelings about attending a meeting on African freedom could convey a personal, nuanced viewpoint on the anticolonial movements that was not necessarily possible through straight reporting.

Mildred's good humor, which espoused dignity against the daily assaults wrought by segregation and low-wage labor, imbued *Freedom* with a potent female voice that was powerful, in part, because of her straightforwardness and unpretentious humanity. As a consequence of her left-wing political affiliations, Childress's columns were largely overlooked when they were collected into a single volume in 1956. Historian Mary Helen Washington has thoughtfully observed that the "sharp political critique" of the individual columns was lost in the collection, as was the reciprocal relationship between the columns and the content in *Freedom*. Mildred was an ally for the newspaper who aimed to educate its audience because she could complement "the political energy of the paper" from a working-class female perspective.[65] Childress's inspired portrayal of a working-class heroine without condescension presaged literary characterizations of black women in the 1970s and 1980s.[66]

Probably the most celebrated career that was cultivated, in part, through her experience at *Freedom* was that of writer Lorraine Hansberry. She was only twenty years old when she first sat before the editor's desk and she was glad to be working for "*the* journal of Negro liberation."[67] Hansberry grew up in the African American community on the South Side of Chicago, but she was not unfamiliar with the southern states from which her family migrated. Her parents were both from the South and her family history included the painful memory of an uncle who was lynched during the Arkansas riot of 1919.[68] As a girl, Hansberry traveled to Tennessee to visit her mother's birthplace and meet her maternal grandmother. Having been born during slavery, the grandmother Hansberry encountered was, in her words, "wrinkled as a prune," but she "could still rock and talk" and her memories of that previous era "didn't sound anything like *Gone with the Wind*."[69] Hansberry's parents were both college educated and active in the Chicago community, which was bustling with artists, intellectuals, and activists. During Lorraine's adolescence, her father Carl Hansberry fought against housing segregation, and his presence is embedded in her most profound literary and commercial success, *A Raisin in the Sun*.[70]

She became involved with the Communist Party during a short stint at the University of Wisconsin, but it was in New York working for *Freedom* that Hansberry's writing and her burgeoning political consciousness were guided by seasoned intellectuals and organizers. The strong female presence at the newspaper fostered her dedication to women's issues, and it was Louis Burnham who encouraged her playwriting.[71] Two highlights of her rapid ascent from clerical staff to associate editor were her coverage of the Sojourners for Truth and Justice march in the autumn of 1951 and her participation in a peace conference in Montevideo, Uruguay, the following year.

The Sojourners for Truth and Justice were 132 wives and mothers from fifteen states that had been victims of racism. They journeyed together to Washington to lobby for redress. These women knew the pain of having family members lynched, sons lost in Korea, relatives viciously beaten, and passports capriciously revoked. According to Hansberry, the slogan of the sojourn became "Negro women, dry your tears and speak your mind."[72] Her full-page story described with care the narratives the women brought with them to the nation's capital and their meeting with a representative in the Justice Department. Hansberry's empathy for these women was apparent in her conscientious rendering of the sense of purpose imbued in their assembling.

Hansberry attended the Inter-Continental Peace Congress in Uruguay in the spring of 1952 and conveyed greetings from Paul Robeson who could not travel internationally.[73] With 250 delegates representing nine countries, the conference carried on despite intimidation from the U.S. State Department. Thousands of miles from home, she penned in her article, a crowd of five thousand stood cheering when Hansberry graced the stage to relay Robeson's message to the meeting. In those first years at *Freedom*, her writing was honed as her output grew and the conviction of a young activist undergirded her words on the page.

Just as her interaction with the *Freedom* family was central to Hansberry's political and literary development, her contributions were vital to the journalistic integrity of the newspaper. Hansberry's clear prose connected the reader with the core issues of her pieces, whether on the freedom struggle in Egypt or the dearth of dignified African American roles on television. By 1953, bolstered with greater confidence as a writer, she began devoting more time to her own projects. By the end of the decade, she was propelled into the international spotlight as the young recipient of the New York Drama Critics' Circle Award for the best American play of 1959. By chance, Hansberry and Robeson were featured on the same page of the *Afro-American* in the spring of that year.[74] A generational shift was inadvertently but poetically implied: a lengthy article and large photo trumpeting the success of *A Raisin in the Sun* dominated the page where a comparatively tiny piece announced the opening of Paul Robeson's *Othello* in England. Robeson's portrayal fleshed out the dignity in Shakespeare's Moor, a character conceived in the early seventeenth century. Hansberry, in comparison, had created a modern portrayal of black identity that was both grounded in realism and tenderly human. The playwright, whose early writing career had blossomed at Robeson's newspaper, was now at the pinnacle of her profession, while the seasoned artist-activist was nearing the end of his life on the stage.

The men and women contributors to *Freedom*, then, represented a coalition of progressive-minded writers and activists who, in spite of FBI surveillance and other forms of pressure, offered a left-wing analysis of contemporary issues. In fact, their work was significant not only because they functioned in spite of Cold War reactionism but because they came together in response to right-wing vitriol and defamation by the mainstream media. The contributors voiced with conviction an internationalist perspective based on a strong sense of history while paying close attention to anticolonial rumblings. Their shared southern roots and experience organizing in the South meant that the burgeoning freedom movement in that region was a central focus of the newspaper. While the Southern Negro Youth Congress and the Council on African Affairs confronted Cold War politics as well-established organizations, *Freedom* was born as a consequence of the unsettling circumstances of domestic repression and was short-lived.

An editorial in the inaugural issue connected *Freedom* with the journalistic roots of *Freedom's Journal*, the first African American newspaper in the United States, founded in 1827. The piece pointed out that African Americans in 1950 remained "sorely aggrieved," as their forebears had been in the early nineteenth century. The founders of *Freedom* pledged to make the newspaper "an instrument for our people's unity and for their cooperation with our true friends in labor and progressive social action."[75] In his opening column for the introductory issue, Robeson outlined the vision of the newspaper. Framed by an encounter with a man on the street who inquired whether he was born in Russia, Robeson's account acutely surveyed the Cold War media landscape. He reminded the reader that the question of his national origin reflected the characterization by "the masters of the press and radio" that "a person who fights for peace, for the admission of People's China to the UN, for friendship with the Soviet Union, for labor's rights and for full equality for Negroes now cannot be a 'real' American, [he] must have been 'born in Russia.'" Robeson emphasized his southern heritage and his father's enslavement while arguing vehemently against the new enslavement that prevented many African Americans from having access to "decent homes, decent jobs, and the dignity that belongs to every human being." By advocating for peace, labor, and civil rights, *Freedom* could be "the real voice of the oppressed masses of Negro people."

As the specter of war drew closer to the United States in early 1941, President Roosevelt outlined Four Freedoms that conveyed the importance of entering the antifascist struggle against Germany and Japan. These freedoms—freedom of speech, freedom from want, freedom from fear, freedom of religion—helped juxtapose democracy with fascism and explain the purpose of the war in basic terms with which all Americans could readily identify. During World War II, the SNYC had utilized the idiom of the Four Freedoms to argue in favor of civil rights for African Americans. Similarly, the Council on African Affairs had employed the Four Freedoms as a metaphor in contending for African freedom. After the close of the war, it became clear that full freedom for Africans and African Americans was not going to be included in immediate postwar planning. In fact, as the Cold War descended, the rhetoric of freedom changed significantly. For example, rather than wait for the United Nations to act, Africans began campaigns to achieve freedom from colonial rule through political movements (as in the Gold Coast) and by militant action (as in Kenya). The political landscape for the African American struggle for civil rights was complicated by suppressions of freedom in the name of anticommunism as seen in the hostility toward SNYC's 1948 Birmingham conference.

Thus, when *Freedom* newspaper was born during the Cold War, the meaning of freedom had evolved considerably since World War II when FDR's Four Freedoms had offered such a clear definition. In examining the pages of *Freedom* over approximately five years, the themes that emerge present an instructive interpretation of the meaning of freedom during one of the most repressive periods in United States history. Whereas

Roosevelt's Four Freedoms stood in defiance of fascist ideology overseas, the four freedoms conveyed in *Freedom* newspaper countered expressions of international fascism as well as manifestations of domestic fascism that were specific to the Cold War context. They were: Freedom for the colonial world, freedom to organize, freedom from persecution, and freedom from Jim Crow. Had Roosevelt's Four Freedoms been sincerely implemented during the war and the immediate postwar era, there might have been no need for *Freedom* newspaper.

The call for freedom in the colonial world was an unmistakable component of the international perspective of *Freedom* newspaper. This conception included both independence from European colonizers as well as political and social freedom from the strictures of the South African apartheid system. Though the paper did not last long enough to celebrate the birth of Pan-African freedom in Ghana in 1957, articles in *Freedom* carefully followed anticolonial developments around the world. Coverage included the West Indies, British Guiana, Guatemala, the Gold Coast, Egypt, Kenya, Nigeria, South Africa, and the Bandung conference. Special correspondents submitted numerous articles, which meant that reports from places such as the West Indies and British Guiana were firsthand. Not surprisingly given the contributions of Hunton, Du Bois, and both Robesons, reporting on South Africa was detailed with special attention paid to the defiance campaigns in the early 1950s and the freedom charter of 1955. Messages of solidarity from the African National Congress paralleled the apartheid system with racial segregation in the United States.

Perhaps most notable was the June 1953 issue that was dedicated to Africa. Under the headline "Africa: Key to War or Peace," articles elucidated African culture and the historical scramble to control resources as well as contemporary events. Significantly, the issue also included a section on African leaders titled "Let Africans Speak for Africa!" Along with photos and brief biographies, excerpts from speeches illuminated an African perspective on issues such as Communism, nationalism, the Mau Mau movement, and the role of the United States on the continent. A large map occupying two full pages plainly defined the meaning of colonialism and identified military bases as well as strategic mineral deposits while clarifying the political status of specific regions. So as not to leave any doubt about the role of the United States on the continent, a sidebar next to the map described how American companies like Monsanto, Union Carbide, and Gulf Oil were reaping huge profits from raw materials while the masses of Africans remained impoverished. Alice Childress's "Conversations from Life" column adroitly demonstrated an African American connection to the continent when Mildred depicted her visit to a community meeting on Africa. She was moved to learn how South Africans were defying segregation and was aroused by the discussion about the future of Africa. "All of a sudden," Mildred relayed, "I jumped straight up and hollered, 'There ain't no mystery about that! Africans want to be free!'" It was no mystery either that *Freedom* newspaper aimed to educate and unite Americans on the cause of colonial freedom.

Also, maintaining the freedom to organize was expressed in the newspaper through coverage that backed labor organizing as well as restoring the freedom to support organizing on behalf of peace. *Freedom* disseminated information on the National Negro Labor Council (NNLC), which was a coalition of African American workers from various CIO unions allied with sympathetic whites and nonunionized blacks to improve the economic and social status of all working Americans. The newspaper covered, for example, racial bias against railroad workers as well as efforts on behalf of fishermen in Virginia and sugarcane workers in Louisiana. However, labor organizing in the South was not promising at this time. During the late 1940s through the early 1950s, the CIO had undertaken a major campaign to organize in the South, which historically had the least unionized workforce in the country. Their campaign, however, was ultimately unsuccessful as the region remained largely resistant to organizing. Moreover, New Deal labor coalitions were weakening in the postwar period and the shift to conservatism and anticommunism in both mainstream and political culture inhibited southern organizing.[76]

Additionally, in the early 1950s, when *Freedom* was published, the labor movement was undergoing a shift to the right. The Taft-Hartley Act of 1947 had restricted union organizing and obstructed radical leaders through means such as loyalty oaths.[77] The CIO purged from its alliance many left-wing unions, including the International Longshore and Warehouse Union and the International Union of Mine, Mill, and Smelter Workers, which had grown with energetic participation from Communist Party members and affiliates in the 1930s and 1940s.[78] Its partnership with the AFL, solidified in the mid-1950s, sealed the CIO's break with the left after having expelled scores of female and nonwhite members in the purges. In one of *Freedom's* final issues, Vicki Garvin wondered whether the AFL-CIO merger would signal new hope for black labor. She acknowledged the potential for a larger membership base to foster "decisive struggles to end job discrimination" for black and women workers but cautioned that "continuous struggles must be waged" within the labor movement to ensure "greater protection for all workers."[79] Unfortunately, in hindsight, historians have pointed out that following the merger, the AFL-CIO was no more effective at organizing in the South; furthermore, the expulsion of left-wing unions from the CIO resulted in fewer campaigns to unionize women and workers of color.[80] The response to Garvin's question, then, was decidedly in the negative.

Freedom also advocated organizing for peace especially during the war in Korea. Criticism of the war was rarely printed in other black newspapers.[81] Paul Robeson contended that decisive effort toward civil rights would not occur while the nation was preoccupied by war. In a May 1951 column, he emphasized that African American soldiers were "not helping to tear down one single 'Colored Only' sign by dying in Korea." *Freedom* printed a speech before a NNLC meeting in which Robeson connected labor interests and the peace movement. Encouraging workers to condemn the anticommunist warmongering foreign policy that their tax dollars were supporting, Robeson observed that it was not foreign Communists but southern landlords that were exploiting black sharecroppers.[82] In an interview published in *Freedom*, a wounded Korean War veteran made a similar point. He urged the public to "sit down and think" about "what their sons are fighting for." And maybe then Americans would also "get their heads together and stop all this segregation."[83]

Freedom also reported on international peace meetings such as the one Hansberry attended in Uruguay. Dorothy Burnham reported on the meeting of the World Congress of Women that convened in Denmark in 1953. Burnham noted that on several occasions at the conference, the U.S. delegation was directly confronted and prodded to "bring the majority of the US actively to our side."[84] Coverage of the indictment of Du Bois for his support of the Peace Information Center accentuated the community groups, labor unions, and individuals who rallied to his support.[85] In a *Freedom* article in his defense, Du Bois stressed that he had "the right within the law . . . to fight for peace."[86] Robeson's position for peace also presciently contended that current U.S. policy was only going to lead to more war. He worried that support for European colonizers would entangle American forces in other Asian or African nations. "We must insist," Robeson declared in 1953, "that the French rule in France and leave the Vietnamese to govern themselves."[87] Regrettably, the Vietnamese would face many more years of conflict.

Finally, the need for freedom from persecution was apparent in *Freedom*'s coverage of cases of wrongful imprisonment that were rooted in racial discrimination. The prosecution of citizens for their political views under the Smith Act was also a recurring theme in the newspaper. For example, New Orleans native Roosevelt Ward was arrested for evading the draft in 1951, but he understood that the charges actually stemmed from his involvement with the labor movement. While in a southern jail, he wrote to *Freedom* that his fellow prisoners all agreed that injustice was regularly meted out to African Americans who were politically active. "Any little old frame-up, especially for a Negro, is good enough," Ward concluded when he realized how many inmates were incarcerated on "flimsy charges."[88]

In 1951, the newspaper reported on two southern rape cases: those of Willie McGee and the Martinsville Seven. Louis Burnham traveled to Mississippi to investigate the McGee case in 1945 and had written a thorough report that was "one of the most reliable things ever written about the case."[89] Despite cries against the dubious guilty verdict from the all-white jury, McGee was executed in 1951, as were each of the African American youths from Martinsville, Virginia.[90] *Freedom* urged readers to support parole for Georgia mother Rosa Lee Ingram and her two sons who had defended themselves from the violent attack of a white farmer in the late 1940s.[91] Attorney William Patterson, of the Civil Rights Congress, which supported the defendants in many of these cases, encouraged a movement on behalf of Robert Wells Brown. His sentence was vastly out of proportion with the crime that had been committed and illustrated that such cases of injustice were, in Patterson's words, "an inseparable part of struggles of greater political depth and scope."[92] The extradition order for Edward Brown to return to a Georgia chain gang was ultimately withdrawn, in part because of support from *Freedom*, which published Brown's shocking account of the tortures to which he was subjected while in custody.[93] Thus, by advocating for justice in cases such as these, *Freedom* demonstrated, in keeping with the spirit of its masthead, that legal action for individuals was an indelible component of the broader movement for civil rights.

Several articles in *Freedom* connected the repression of perceived radicals with racial discrimination since both manifestations of injustice aimed to subjugate the democratic rights of citizens. In an article decrying the lack of support for Ethel and Julius Rosenberg in the African American community, William Patterson pointed out that the Rosenbergs advocated for peace and could have been important allies in the struggle for colonial independence and domestic civil rights. After all, Patterson concluded, it was the same court system that framed the Jewish couple that had framed Rosa Lee Ingram, Willie McGee, and other African Americans.[94] In an insightful article examining the Smith Act, W.E.B. Du Bois contended that the prosecutions in the name of this law were punishing mere thought crimes. While the United States purported to stand for democracy, it was clamping down on anyone who tried to understand and explain how "the technical processes of production and wealth" could be made more equitable. Because so many people were "comfortable and powerful" due to the current system of production and its unequal distribution of wealth, the Smith Act aimed to silence adherents of dissenting political ideologies.[95]

An article on Alabama-born activist Pettis Perry, a Smith Act defendant, explained why this African American from a sharecropping family joined the Communist Party. He had witnessed racial violence in his youth but was intrigued when the International Labor Defense (ILD) took on the case of the Scottsboro boys in the 1930s. Perry then attended a picnic sponsored by the ILD where a sheriff threatened the mostly white group, demanding that the blacks with them had to disperse. The whites refused and Perry recalled his reaction: "I'd never seen a mass of white people standing together for Negro rights. [It] made quite an impression on me."[96] Another article focusing on African American targets of the Smith Act, like Claude Lightfoot, Ben Davis, and West Indian Claudia Jones, cogently linked the law with the issue of protecting minority rights. The piece contended that radical alteration of American life was necessary to uphold African American rights. Moreover, whether that change took place "along the lines [that] Communists advocate is not the point at issue. The point is that any law which prohibits Communists from saying what they please . . . can be used to justify similar prohibitions against other minorities and against Negroes."[97]

The prosecution of radicals, then, was a vital theme in *Freedom* because such defendants could be champions of African American rights. In addition, the prosecution of radicals for their political beliefs could lead to further obstruction of the rights of minority groups, including African Americans. Paul Robeson's passport case was a good example: it was not his affiliation with Communist Party members but his advocacy for African liberation that led to his passport revocation.[98] All citizens, *Freedom* insisted, should be wary when one group is persecuted, because a similar rationale could easily be levied against other minority groups.

Finally, freedom from Jim Crow was a theme that percolated across the pages of *Freedom* newspaper. Its coverage of segregation was broad. Articles uncovered slums in New York, segregation in government jobs, the need for hospitals in Brooklyn, and discrimination against dark skinned immigrants. Reporting on schools, both in the North and South, was prominent in *Freedom* as the *Brown v. Board of Education* decision meandered through the court system. As the backlash against the Supreme Court decision grew more violent, *Freedom* correctly predicted that a mass movement was necessary to enforce the ruling. Just as *Brown* consolidated cases of school segregation from around the country, *Freedom's* articles on schools in New York illustrated that inequities in public education were not only a southern phenomenon. For instance, a piece by Lorraine Hansberry detailed the overcrowding and underfunding of Harlem schools.[99] Kenneth B. Clark, who actively supported the *Brown* case, traced the history of public education in New York and called for a new study to shed light on conditions in northern schools.[100]

In November 1953, about seven months before the *Brown* decision, a lengthy cover story explained the history and significance of the cases. In this article, Harriet Bourne observed that new legal precedent could be set: not since the *Plessy v. Ferguson* ruling over a half-century ago had the Supreme Court grappled with the constitutionality of segregation law. She also insightfully pointed out that southern lawmakers were already laying plans to circumvent integration should the decision rule against racial segregation. The following August, three months after the May 1954 ruling, another cover feature called for a popular movement to push for enforcement of *Brown*. Surveying the scant progress toward compliance with the decision in seventeen states, the article concluded that "the law of the land remains primarily where the justices put it—on paper."

A March 1955 article by Thelma Dale chronicled the southern counterattack. While state legislatures passed measures like preventing money from being budgeted for desegregated schools, White Citizen's Councils were being formed to apply pressure to African Americans who advocated implementation of *Brown*. For instance, a doctor in Mississippi who had publicly supported the decision started losing business. His patients had been warned that if they did not find another doctor, they would lose their jobs or their credit. Dale also skillfully linked the issue of continued disfranchisement with the desegregation order. If whites protected their political power base by preventing black voting, she pointed out, they could more effectively obstruct local and state integration of schools.

In its final issues in the spring and summer of 1955, alongside coverage of the Bandung meeting, *Freedom* documented an acute situation: the *Brown* ruling was in danger and terrorism was growing in the South.[101] That spring, when the court heard arguments on a timeline for *Brown*, Thurgood Marshall was dismayed that "only the Negro attorneys argued for immediate enforcement of last year's decision." Thelma Dale summarized the grim circumstances: southern states were "fighting integration with every weapon" while border states "straddled the fence" and the Eisenhower administration seemed to be in league with the Dixiecrats. The final issue of *Freedom* reported that a southern "offensive" had "gained murderous momentum" in the wake of the Supreme Court's ruling. The unprosecuted lynching of Lamar Smith, an African American activist in Mississippi, was indicative of the hostile attitude toward the *Brown* decision. In a pamphlet published by Freedom Associates, Louis Burnham foresaw the unfortunate long-term consequences of the *Brown* rulings. "It is generally recognized," Burnham wrote, "that the Supreme Court decrees of May 31, 1955 . . . encouraged nullification of its original decision by placing implementation in the hands of . . . the Southern racist politicians with no specific time-limit for compliance."[102] Indeed, the follow-up decision rendered that spring, which infamously called for implementation "with all deliberate speed," ensured that little to no significant progress toward school desegregation would be made for years. Reflecting fifty years later, legal scholar Derrick Bell mused that *Brown* had become "the legal equivalent of that city on a hill to which all aspire without any serious thought that it will ever be attained."[103]

Freedom folded prior to Eisenhower's dramatic backing of the Little Rock Nine and the groundswell of nonviolent direct action inaugurated in Montgomery, Alabama, for the bus boycott. However, the newspaper's insistence on freedom for the colonial world, freedom to organize, freedom from persecution, and freedom from Jim Crow shed light on the Cold War political landscape of the early 1950s. As certainly as FDR's Four Freedoms offered justification for entering World War II, these four freedoms advocated a path away from war and toward a more democratic nation with a more enlightened foreign policy. The newspaper staff knew that safeguarding these four freedoms was most crucial in the South where the assault against them was most vicious.

As Du Bois had contended in 1946 at the Southern Negro Youth Congress meeting, the southern United States was a gateway to the Pan-African world. In that spirit, *Freedom* newspaper crafted a narrative based on a progressive analysis of issues and events from across the African diaspora, which paid particular attention to the acute circumstances of southern African Americans. The radical critique of *Freedom* was grounded in the southern heritage and experiences of its founders and contributors. *Freedom* had been created as a consequence of slanted Cold War reporting, and the newspaper disbanded just as the classical phase of the civil rights struggle in the South was commencing. Many of the political long-distance runners who had been involved with SNYC and the Council on African Affairs as well as *Freedom* came together once again to establish a quarterly journal that chronicled the rising tide of nonviolent direct action.

Epilogue

The formation of *Freedomways* journal elucidates well the continuing legacy of the Southern Negro Youth Congress and the Council on African Affairs in a long civil rights movement. *Freedom* newspaper had engaged activists who wrote about southern civil rights in a global perspective in the early years of the Cold War. In the years following *Freedom*'s dissolution in 1955, there was a historic upsurge in nonviolent campaigns for southern civil rights. Anticolonial movements in Africa were also signaling a wind of change. *Freedomways* was based on a similar impulse to that which had guided its predecessor. From 1961 to 1985, this publication focused on civil rights in the United States and documented freedom struggles around the world. Art, culture, and history of the Pan-African world were also featured.[1]

Freedomways was an ideological and organizational heir of *Freedom*, as it came from the political left and was founded by activists who had been involved with *Freedom* as well as various popular front coalitions, like SNYC and the council, that were started during the Great Depression. Edward Strong and Louis Burnham had a hand in conceiving *Freedomways* though, sadly, they did not live to steer the project to fruition. Upon its inaugural issue, Shirley Graham and Alphaeus Hunton served as editors and Esther Cooper Jackson was managing editor. W.E.B. Du Bois acted as an important advisor for the new publication.[2] The first issue invited intellectuals, students, artists, and writers to contribute to a dialogue on domestic civil rights and global anticolonial movements. An opening editorial explained that *Freedomways* was created as a "vehicle of communication" to disseminate viewpoints on the "many sided struggles of the Negro people" in addition to providing "*accurate* information on the liberation movements in Africa itself."[3]

Freedomways encapsulated the spirit of *Freedom* through its internationalist perspective and high quality content. Its coverage of the contemporary movement and invitation to students to contribute articles recalled a previous generation of youth activism manifested in the Southern Negro Youth Congress. The emphasis on accurate coverage of independence campaigns in the African diaspora reflected the aim of the Council on African Affairs' newsletters and other publications. *Freedomways* originated in a time of considerable social upheaval when the thrust for revolution was reaching a pinnacle. In the words of the editors, "We are born in a time of tremendous change. Though white racists in [the] South United States and South Africa respond to the Negroes' demands with frenzied violence their castles are tumbling about their feet as the earth rumbles with change."[4]

The roots of that transformative period, however, were deep in the African American community: they reached back to the activism that was inspired to alleviate southern oppression during the Depression years and all the way back to the spread of colonialism in Africa. The activists of the 1960s and 1970s were part of a much longer freedom struggle; they were not the first advocates of social and political change, nor would they be the last. Nikhil Pal Singh has thoughtfully observed that the commentary and analysis in *Freedomways* "provided early insight into and also helped to shape the contours of a 'long civil rights movement' with roots in the left-labor internationalism of the 1930s and 1940s."[5] The contributors to *Freedomways*, then, many of whom had come out of the black-labor-left coalitions of the late 1930s, understood their work as part of the long-term "great and holy crusade" that Du Bois had conceived in "Behold the Land" in 1946.

Perhaps nowhere was *Freedomways*'s conceptualization for a long civil rights struggle better illustrated than in the Winter 1964 issue. This issue came out at a pivotal moment: the Southern Christian Leadership Conference's (SCLC) historic direct action campaign in Birmingham in the spring of 1963 had persuaded President Kennedy to take his strongest stand yet in calling upon Congress to pass a new civil rights bill. The momentum from nonviolent direct action campaigns around the South culminated in the March on Washington that summer; however, tragedy also ensued with the deaths of four young girls in a church bombing in Birmingham in September, followed by the assassination of JFK in November. In the winter of

1964, the Civil Rights Bill and the Voting Rights Act had yet to materialize. In that issue, the editors of *Freedomways*, including Alphaeus Hunton and Esther Cooper Jackson, pledged extended coverage of "the southern battle fronts." In fact, they ambitiously promised that their history and reporting would be "the most comprehensive coverage of the Freedom Movement in the south ever to appear in a single issue of an American magazine."[6]

The content of the Winter 1964 edition of *Freedomways* did not fail to deliver. It outlined the scope of a long movement in the South, which included both an international component and a strong intergenerational perspective. Activists who had been leaders in SNYC or influenced by its campaigns were clearly represented alongside discussions of recent organizing. For example, Jack O'Dell, who had been an SNYC member and later an advisor to Martin Luther King Jr., contributed a piece on southern political power, and Fred Shuttlesworth, who had been a young man when SNYC was headquartered in Birmingham and later a leader in SCLC, wrote an assessment of the current struggle in that city. Augusta Jackson Strong's insightful history of the youth congress provided a strong underpinning for the articles on the contemporary movement in the South. Contextual essays from political long-distance runners who had considerable organizing experience, such as Septima Clark and Anne Braden, highlighted their long-term experiences with issues like literacy and antiradicalism. These pieces added not only chronological depth but also a crucial sense of historical memory, especially when published adjacent to recent field diaries from volunteers with the Student Nonviolent Coordinating Committee who were aiding the movement in towns like Gadsden, Alabama, Danville, Virginia, and Jackson, Mississippi. In a public symposium on SNYC in the early 1980s, Esther Cooper Jackson remarked that the organizing of the generation that lived through the Great Depression and fought in World War II had helped make the struggles of the 1960s possible.[7] Reading in *Freedomways* the substantive analysis of youth congress adherents like O'Dell and Strong next to the journals of the young SNCC volunteers demonstrates the potency of her observation.

An acknowledgement of the return of Council on African Affairs stalwart Paul Robeson to the United States following an extended period abroad was a "happy coincidence" that fit well into the span of the Winter 1964 issue. In honoring Robeson's homecoming, the editors recognized the fact that he "was the inspiration and idol of a whole generation of Negro youth, who grew to adulthood in the early struggles of the CIO (Congress of Industrial Organizations) and the New Deal."[8] Additionally, Shirley Graham Du Bois's decision to remain in Accra, Ghana, and continue working with educational programming there following the death of her husband highlighted the international reach of *Freedomways*. Even though "the godfather" of the journal, W.E.B. Du Bois, had passed away, she agreed to remain a contributing editor who would work from overseas in Africa.[9] In conveying the importance of Du Bois's final research project, the Encyclopedia Africana, and Robeson's long history of activism, *Freedomways* helped introduce these titans to the generation that was coming of age during the classical phase of the movement. Finally, it was perhaps Du Bois's own words that cemented the long view of the movement portrayed throughout the journal. The editors of *Freedomways* chose this moment to reprint the 1946 speech "Behold the Land," which had expressed the hopefulness of the immediate postwar era and exhorted the young people of SNYC to continue the struggle. Du Bois's conception of a southern gateway to the broader African diaspora was now laid bare for a new generation of freedom fighters to ruminate upon. With Du Bois's counsel, this youthful cohort might now better understand their role in the long movement to forge a "Path to the Greater, Freer, Truer World."

Appendix

Always articulate and memorable, the venerable W.E.B. Du Bois was especially eloquent and forthright on this 1946 evening in Columbia, South Carolina. The evocative preface added in the pamphlet version of the speech that was published by SNYC details the setting of the occasion as well as the presentation made to the elder scholar/activist prior to his speech. The large audience drawn to the event demonstrated the high esteem in which Du Bois was held by both young and old in the southern black community. This was especially important in light of the antiradical repression that impacted Du Bois's career in subsequent years and ultimately led to his repatriation to Ghana. In the speech, the Pan-Africanist located the center of struggle for African Americans to be in the southern farming economy, but he was careful to contextualize his analysis within the broader fight for colonial independence worldwide. Naturally, he conveyed these ideas in a particularly inspired, poetic fashion, as only Du Bois could do.

W.E.B. Du Bois, "Behold the Land"

Preface

The text which follows, for all its brevity, or possibly because of it, bears all the marks of a classic statement of one of America's most persistent problems. In slightly more than two thousand words, the author, with the incomparably brilliant insight which characterizes all his works, illuminates the basic nature of the social, political and economic life of the South.

As notable as his analysis of socio-economic forces in the South is, Dr. Du Bois' hardly equaled appeal and challenge to the South's youth, white and black. With the full force of his great intellectual and combative powers, the renowned scholar, teacher, and people's leader sounds the democratic tocsin for the emerging generation.

And these two salient features of the work—the analysis of the South's condition and the exhortation to its youth—are couched in language whose grandeur and simplicity explain why Dr. Du Bois is regarded as one of the great literary stylists of our times.

The reader will be interested in the circumstances under which the address was delivered. At the closing public session of the Southern Youth Legislature, 861 delegates, Negro and white, crowded into Antisdel Chapel of Benedict College in Columbia, South Carolina. They were joined by a large and sympathetic public who stood in the aisles, jammed the doors and listened through loudspeakers outside the auditorium.

A hush fell over the audience as youth prepared to express "the great obligation of reverence and respect which (they) cherish for . . . the senior statesman of the American Negro's liberation struggle . . . the noble and peerless patriarch of our steady climb out of slavery's darkness into the light of full freedom."

Softly, the Organ swelled with the tones of "Battle Hymn of the Republic." And throughout the spellbound room a Voice was heard to say:

"White Men said that Black Men could never be their equals because they were the Sons of the condemned Ham; and many Black Men believed them.

But in frosty New England a Hamite was born who did not believe the White Men. His mother named him William Edward Burghardt and his family's name was Du Bois. William at an early age decided to prove the White Men liars by attaining a wisdom and a culture equal to that of the most learned among them.

Thus armed, he said to the White Men, 'Am I not the equal of your finest?' But the White Men scoffingly replied: 'You are a phenomenon, a miracle, an accident. Can you not see that your fellows are still hewers of wood and drawers of water? Cannot you see that you are alone?'

And William was sorely hurt and disappointed. However, other Hamites had been inspired by his aim and determination. These he called around him and bound them together as the Talented Tenth and gave them a mission to create a Movement with the force of Niagara to fight for the recognition of the equality of Black Men.

William was no longer alone; but his group was alone. And the White Men when asked for equality for Black Men still pointed to the countless Black Men who could not solve the mysteries of the symbols which made sound and those which determined measures.

William was challenged.

And down from the Ivory Towers of the Talented Tenth came swiftly the sensitive, suffering, crusading William; down from the Ivory Towers to the Good Earth. Here he mingled with the laborers of the fields, of the mines, of the factories; laborers who stank with sweat made sweet by honest toil. He touched them tenderly, passionately, brotherly.

He asked them to let him join them in the struggle for their daily bread and a fuller life; and to join with him in the great struggle for Equality.

They smiled him a warm welcome.

Then he turned to the Talented Tenth who had watched him with misgiving and cried: 'I am now without the Veil! The Talented Tenth Alone will never prove the White Men liars. But with all of us working together the truth will establish itself. Together we can challenge destiny and move the Earth; separately each of us shall perish!'

A voice in the multitude cried, 'Close ranks!'

And God smiled."

As the Voice and the Organ returned the chapel to a tense silence, Dr. Du Bois rose to the accompaniment of enthusiastic applause and received from the hands of Miss Esther Cooper, retiring executive secretary of the Southern Negro Youth Congress, youth's award for his "unparalled achievements . . . monumental labors . . . and principled struggle . . . on behalf of the Negro people of the United States and the unfree peoples of the world."

Setting aside a book of reverence signed by all the delegates of the Southern Youth Legislature, Dr. Du Bois then delivered the address which follows.

Behold the Land

The future of American Negroes is in the South. Here three hundred and twenty-seven years ago, they began to enter what is now the United States of America; here they have made their greatest contribution to American culture; and here they have suffered the damnation of slavery, the frustration of reconstruction and the lynching of emancipation. I trust then that an organization like yours is going to regard the South as the battle-ground of a great crusade. Here is the magnificent climate; here is the fruitful earth under the beauty of the Southern sun; and here if anywhere on earth, is the need of the thinker, the worker and the dreamer. This is the firing line not simply for the emancipation of the American Negro but for the emancipation of the African Negro and the Negroes of the West Indies; for the emancipation of the colored races; and for the emancipation of the white slaves of modern capitalistic monopoly.

Allies in the White South

Remember here, too, that you do not stand alone. It may seem like a failing fight when the newspapers ignore you; when every effort is made by white people in the South to count you out of citizenship and to act as though you did not exist as human beings while all the time they are profiting by your labor; gleaning wealth from your sacrifices and trying to build a nation and a civilization upon your degradation. You must remember that despite all this, you have allies and allies even in the white South. First and greatest of these possible allies are the white working classes about you. The poor whites whom you have been taught to despise and who in turn have learned to fear and hate you. This must not deter you from efforts to make them understand, because in the past in their ignorance and suffering they have been led foolishly to look upon you as the cause of most of their distress. You must remember that this attitude is hereditary from slavery and that it has been deliberately cultivated ever since emancipation.

Slowly but surely the working people of the South, white and black, must come to remember that their emancipation depends upon their mutual cooperation; upon their acquaintanceship with each other; upon their friendship; upon their social intermingling. Unless this happens each is going to be made the football to break the heads and hearts of the other.

White Youth is Frustrated

White youth in the South is peculiarly frustrated. There is not a single great ideal which they can express or aspire to, that does not bring them into flat contradiction with the Negro problem. The more they try to escape it, the more they land into hypocrisy, lying and double-dealing; the more they become, what they least wish to become, the oppressors and despisers of human beings. Some of them, in larger and larger numbers, are bound to turn toward the truth and to recognize you as brothers and sisters, as fellow travelers toward the dawn.

James Byrnes, the Favorite Son of this Commonwealth

There has always been in the South that intellectual elite who saw the Negro problem clearly. They have always lacked and some still lack the courage to stand up for what they know is right. Nevertheless they can be depended on in the long run to follow their own clear thinking and their own decent choice. Finally even the politicians must eventually recognize the trend in the world, in this country, and in the South. James Byrnes, that favorite son of this commonwealth, and Secretary of State of the United States, is today occupying an indefensible and impossible position; and if he survives in the memory of men, he must begin to help establish in his own South Carolina something of that democracy which he has been recently so loudly preaching to Russia. He is the end of a long series of men whose eternal damnation is the fact that they looked *truth* in the face and did not see it; John C. Calhoun, Wade Hampton, Ben Tillman are men whose names must ever be besmirched by the fact that they fought against freedom and democracy in a land which was founded upon Democracy and Freedom.

Eventually this class of men must yield to the writing in the stars. That great hypocrite, Jan Smuts, who today is talking of humanity and standing beside Byrnes for a United Nations, is at the same time, oppressing the black people of Africa to an extent which makes their two countries, South Africa and the Southern South, the most reactionary peoples on earth. Peoples whose exploitation of the poor and helpless reaches the last degree of shame. They must in the long run yield to the forward march of civilization or die.

What Does the Fight Mean?

If now you young people instead of running away from the battle here in Carolina, Georgia, Alabama, Louisiana and Mississippi, instead of seeking freedom and opportunity in Chicago and New York—which do spell opportunity—nevertheless grit your teeth and make up your minds to fight it out right here if it takes every day of your lives and the lives of your children's children; if you do this, you must in meetings like this ask yourselves what does the fight mean? How can it be carried on? What are the best tools, arms, and methods? And where does it lead?

I should be the last to insist that the uplift of mankind never calls for force and death.

> There are times, as both you and I know, when
> Tho' love repine and reason chafe,
> There came a voice without reply,
> 'Tis man's perdition to be safe
> When for the truth he ought to die.

At the same time and even more clearly in a day like this, after the millions of mass murders that have been done in the world since 1914, we ought to be the last to believe that force is ever the final word. We cannot escape the clear fact that what is going to win in the world is reason if this ever becomes a reasonable world. The careful reasoning of the human mind backed by the facts of science is the one salvation of man. The world, if it resumes its march toward civilization, cannot ignore reason. This has been the tragedy of the South in the past; it is still its awful and unforgivable sin that it has set its face against reason and against the fact. It tried to build slavery upon freedom; it tried to build tyranny upon democracy; it tried to build mob violence on law and law on lynching and in all that despicable endeavor, the state of South Carolina has led the South for a century. It began not the Civil War—not the war between the States—but the War to Preserve Slavery; it began mob violence and lynching and today it stands in the front rank of those defying the Supreme Court on disfranchisement.

Nevertheless reason can and will prevail; but of course it can only prevail with publicity—pitiless, blatant publicity. You have got to make the people of the United States and of the world know what is going on in the South. You have got to use every field of publicity to force the truth into their ears, and before their eyes. You have got to make it impossible for any human being to live in the South and not realize the barbarities that prevail here. You may be condemned for flamboyant methods; for calling a congress like this; for waving your grievances under the noses and in the faces of men. That makes no difference; it is your duty to do it. It is your duty to do more of this sort of thing than you have done in the past. As a result of this you are going to be called upon for sacrifice. It is no easy thing for a young black man or a young black woman to live in the South today and to plan to continue to live here; to marry and raise children; to establish a home. They are in the midst of legal caste and customary insults; they are in continuous danger of mob violence; they are mistreated by the officers of the law and they have no hearing before the courts and the churches and public opinion commensurate with the attention which they ought to receive. But that sacrifice is only the Beginning of Battle, you must re-build this South.

There are enormous opportunities here for a new nation, a new Economy, a new culture in a South really new and not a mere renewal of an old South of slavery, monopoly and race hate. There is a chance for a new cooperative agriculture on renewed land owned by the State with capital furnished by the State, mechanized and coordinated with city life. There is a chance for strong, virile Trade Unions without race discrimination, with high wage, closed shop and decent conditions of work, to beat back and hold in check the swarm of landlords, monopolists and profiteers who are today sucking the blood out of this land. There is chance for cooperative industry, built on the cheap power of T.V.A. and its future extensions. There is opportunity to organize and mechanize domestic service with decent hours, and high wage and dignified training.

Behold the Land

There is a vast field for consumers' cooperation, building business on public service and not on private profit as the main-spring of industry. There is chance for a broad, sunny, healthy home life, shorn of the fear of mobs and liquor, and rescued from lying, stealing politicians, who build their deviltry on race prejudice.

Here in this South is the gateway to the colored millions of the West Indies, Central and South America. Here is the straight path to Africa, the Indies, China and the South Seas. Here is the Path to the Greater, Freer Truer World. It would be shame and cowardice to surrender this glorious land and its opportunities for civilization and humanity to the thugs and lynchers, the mobs and profiteers, the monopolists and gamblers who today choke its soul and steal its resources. The oil and sulphur; the coal and iron; the cotton and corn; the lumber and cattle belong to you the workers, black and white, and not to the thieves who hold them and use them to enslave you. They can be rescued and restored to the people if you have the guts to strive for the real right to vote, the right to real education, the right to happiness and health and the total abolition of the father of these scourges of mankind, *poverty*.

The Great Sacrifice

"Behold the beautiful land which the Lord thy God hath given thee." Behold the land, the rich and resourceful land, from which for a hundred years its best elements have been running away, its youth and hope, black and white, scurrying North because they are afraid of each other, and dare not face a future of equal, independent, upstanding human beings, in a real and not a sham democracy.

To rescue this land, in this way, calls for the *Great Sacrifice*; This is the thing that you are called upon to do because it is the right thing to do. Because you are embarked upon a great and holy crusade, the emancipation of mankind black and white; the up building of democracy; the breaking down, particularly here in the South, of forces of evil represented by race prejudice in South Carolina; by Lynching in Georgia; by disfranchisement in Mississippi; by ignorance in Louisiana and by all these and monopoly of wealth in the whole South.

There could be no more splendid vocation beckoning to the youth of the twentieth century, after the flat failures of white civilization, after the flamboyant establishment of an industrial system which creates poverty and the children of poverty which are ignorance and disease and crime; after the crazy boasting of a white culture that finally ended in wars which ruined civilization in the whole world; in the midst of allied peoples who have yelled about democracy and never practiced it either in the British Empire or in the American Commonwealth or in South Carolina.

Here is the chance for young women and young men of devotion to lift again the banner of humanity and to walk toward a civilization which will be free and intelligent; which will be healthy and unafraid; and build in the world a culture led by black folk and joined by peoples of all colors and all races—without poverty, ignorance, and disease!

Once a great German poet cried: "Selig der den Er in Sieges Glanze findet." "Happy man whom Death shall find in Victory's splendor."

But I know a happier one: he who fights in despair and in defeat still fights. Singing with Arna Bontemps the quiet, determined philosophy of undefeatable men:

I thought I saw an angel flying low,
I thought I saw the flicker of a wing
Above the mulberry trees; but not again,
Bethesda sleeps. This ancient pool that healed
A Host of bearded Jews does not awake.
This pool that once the angels troubled does not move.
No angel stirs it now, no Savior comes
With healing in His hands to raise the sick
And bid the lame man leap upon the ground.

The golden days are gone. Why do we wait
So long upon the marble steps, blood
Falling from our open wounds? And why
Do our black faces search the empty sky?
Is there something we have forgotten? Some precious thing
We have lost, wandering in strange lands?

There was a day, I remember now,
I beat my breast and cried, "Wash me God,"
Wash me with a wave of wind upon
The barley; O quiet one, draw near, draw near!
Walk upon the hills with lovely feet
And in the waterfall stand and speak!

The Atlantic Charter, 14 August 1941

This declaration by Franklin Roosevelt and Winston Churchill, leaders of the United States and the United Kingdom, stated the positions of these nations with regard to the war in Europe. Though the US did not officially join the war until December, this declaration was an important statement of purpose from the allied nations. The Council on African Affairs referred consistently to the set of principles outlined in this declaration to argue for colonial freedom. Whether Roosevelt would have been more inclined to abide by the spirit of the Atlantic Charter after the war is debatable since he died as the war was winding down in April 1945. The Truman administration, however, was inclined to bolster the economies of European colonizers rather than apply these declarations to colonial people after the war. Notice the inclusion in item six of the freedoms from fear and want, which were also included in Roosevelt's formulation of the Four Freedoms, along with the freedoms of speech and religion, in his speech before Congress in January of 1941.

The Atlantic Charter
The President of the United States of America and the Prime Minister, Mr. Churchill, representing His Majesty's government in the United Kingdom, being met together, deem it right to make known certain common principles in the national policies of their respective countries on which they base their hopes for a better future for the world.
1. Their countries seek no aggrandizement, territorial or other.
2. They desire to see no territorial changes that do not accord with the freely expressed wishes of the people concerned.
3. They respect the right of all peoples to choose the form of government under which they will live, and they wish to see sovereign rights and self government restored to those who have been forcibly deprived of them.
4. They will endeavor with due respect for their existing obligations, to further the enjoyment by all States, great or small, victor or vanquished, of access on equal terms to the trade and to the raw materials of the world which are needed for their economic prosperity.
5. They desire to bring about the fullest collaboration between all nations in the economic field with the object of securing, for all, improved labor standards, economic advancement and social security.
6. After the final destruction of the Nazi tyranny, they hope to see established a peace which will afford to all nations the means of dwelling in safety within their . . . boundaries, and which will afford

assurance that all the men in all the lands may live out their lives in freedom from fear and want.

7. Such a peace should enable all men to traverse the high seas and oceans without hindrance.

8. They believe that all the nations of the world, for realistic as well as spiritual reasons, must come to the abandonment of the use of force. Since no future peace can be maintained if land, sea or air armaments continue to be employed by nations which threaten, or may threaten, aggression outside of their frontiers, they believe, pending the establishment of a wider and permanent system of general security, that the disarmament of such nations is essential. They will likewise aid and encourage all other practicable measures which will lighten for peace-loving peoples the crushing burden of armament.

Notes

Introduction

1. *Birmingham World,* 25 October 1946.

2. *Lighthouse and Informer,* 20 October 1946.

3. W.E.B. Du Bois, "Behold the Land" (Birmingham, AL: Southern Negro Youth Congress, 1946), 5.

4. Ibid., 3–4.

5. Ibid., 5.

6. Ibid., 3.

7. Martha Biondi, *To Stand and Fight: The Struggle for Civil Rights in Postwar New York* (Cambridge: Harvard University Press, 2003), 147. The idea of a black-labor-left coalition refers to alliances, particularly during the Popular Front era in the late 1930s, that organized around both African American civil and labor rights and incorporated a left-wing perspective but also included a range of progressives, liberals, and New Dealers. Biondi and other scholars also use the term "Black Popular Front" to describe the intersection between civil rights and labor organizing. See, for example: Biondi, *To Stand and Fight,* 6; Jacqueline Dowd Hall, "The Long Civil Rights Movement and the Political Uses of the Past," *Journal of American History* 91 (March 2005): 1245; Michael Denning, *The Cultural Front: The Laboring of American Culture in the Twentieth Century* (New York: Verso, 1996).

8. Du Bois, "Behold the Land," 7–15.

9. Calhoun famously resisted federal intervention in favor of states' rights, which was the same political platform that defended slavery. The Hampton family had earned its significant wealth through plantation slavery. Wade Hampton III fought in the Civil War, strongly opposed Reconstruction reforms, and was prominent in the Democratic "Redeemer" movement. "Pitchfork" Tillman was a vocal proponent of white supremacy in the late nineteenth century.

10. W.E.B. Du Bois, *Dark Princess: A Romance* (Jackson: University Press of Mississippi, 1995), 257.

11. W.E.B. Du Bois, *Black Reconstruction in America, 1860–1880* (New York: Free Press, 1998), 5.

12. Du Bois, *Dark Princess*, 297.

13. W.E.B. Du Bois, *The World and Africa* (New York: International Publishers, 1972), vii.

14. Robin D. G. Kelley, *Hammer and Hoe: Alabama Communists during the Great Depression* (Chapel Hill: University of North Carolina Press, 1990); Glenda Elizabeth Gilmore, *Defying Dixie: The Radical Roots of Civil Rights* (New York: W. W. Norton, 2008); Erik S. Gellman, *Death Blow to Jim Crow: The National Negro Congress and the Rise of Militant Civil Rights* (Chapel Hill: University of North Carolina Press, 2012).

15. Dayo F. Gore, *Radicalism at the Crossroads: African American Women Activists in the Cold War* (New York: New York University Press, 2011); David L. Lewis, Michael H. Nash, and Daniel J. Leab, eds., *Red Activists and Black Freedom: James and Esther Jackson and the Long Civil Rights Revolution* (New York: Routledge, 2010); Nikhil Pal Singh, ed., *Climbin' Jacob's Ladder: The Black Freedom Movement Writings of Jack O'Dell* (Berkeley: University of California Press, 2010).

16. See, for example: Hollis R. Lynch, *Black American Radicals and the Liberation of Africa: The Council on African Affairs, 1937–1955* (Ithaca, NY: Cornell University Africana Studies Research Center, 1978); Penny M. Von Eschen, *Race against Empire: Black Americans and Anticolonialism, 1937–1957* (Ithaca, NY: Cornell University Press, 1997); Brenda Gayle Plummer, *Rising Wind: Black Americans and U.S. Foreign Affairs, 1935–1960* (Chapel Hill: University of North Carolina Press, 1997); James H. Meriwether, *Proudly We Can Be Africans: Black Americans and Africa, 1935–1961* (Chapel Hill: University of North Carolina Press, 2002). Biographies of leaders in the Council on African Affairs include: David Henry Anthony, *Max Yergan: Race Man, Internationalist, Cold Warrior* (New York: New York University Press, 2006); David L. Lewis, *W.E.B. Du Bois: The Fight for Equality and the American Century 1919–1963* (New York: Henry Holt, 2000); Martin B. Duberman, *Paul Robeson: A Biography* (New York: Ballantine Books, 1989); Paul Robeson Jr., *The Undiscovered Paul Robeson: Quest for Freedom, 1939–1976* (New York: John Wiley and Sons, 2010); Barbara Ransby, *Eslanda: The Large and Unconventional Life of Mrs. Paul Robeson* (New Haven: Yale University Press, 2013).

17. Dowd Hall, "The Long Civil Rights Movement," 1234.

18. Jeanne Theoharris and Komozi Woodard, eds., *Groundwork: Local Black Freedom Movements in America* (New York: New York University Press, 2005), 3. For similar discussions of an expanded civil rights paradigm, see also: Dowd Hall, "The Long Civil Rights Movement," 1235; Jeanne Theoharris and Komozi Woodard, eds., *Freedom North: Black Freedom Struggles Outside the South, 1940–1980* (New York: Palgrave Macmillan, 2003), 3; Nikhil Pal Singh, *Black Is a Country:*

Race and the Unfinished Struggle for Democracy (Cambridge: Harvard University Press, 2004), 52–53; Robert O. Self, *American Babylon: Race and the Struggle for Postwar Oakland* (Princeton: Princeton University Press, 2003), 6.

19. Thomas J. Sugrue, *Sweet Land of Liberty: The Forgotten Struggle for Civil Rights in the North* (New York: Random House, 2008), xxi.

20. Theoharris and Woodard, *Freedom North*, 2.

21. Sundiata Keita Cha-Jua and Clarence Lang, "The 'Long Movement' as Vampire: Temporal and Spacial Fallacies in Recent Black Freedom Studies," *Journal of African American History* 92 (Spring 2007): 265. For an assessment of the long thesis and its critics, see also: Walter B. Hill Jr., "Researching Civil Rights History in the 21st Century," *Journal of African American History* 93 (Winter 2008): 94–99.

22. Cha-Jua and Lang, "The 'Long Movement' as Vampire," 274.

23. Dowd Hall, "The Long Civil Rights Movement," 1239.

24. Ibid., 1235.

25. Ibid., 1248.

26. Robbie Lieberman and Clarence Lang, eds., *Anticommunism and the African American Freedom Movement* (New York: Palgrave Macmillan, 2009), 5. See also: Biondi, *To Stand and Fight*, 152; Gilmore, *Defying Dixie*, 8; Carol Anderson, *Eyes Off the Prize: The United Nations and the African American Struggle for Human Rights, 1944–1955* (Cambridge: Cambridge University Press, 2003), 5; Thomas Borstelmann, *The Cold War and the Color Line: American Race Relations in the Global Arena* (Cambridge: Harvard University Press, 2001), 3–4; Mary L. Dudziak, *Cold War Civil Rights: Race and the Image of American Democracy* (Princeton: Princeton University Press, 2000), 12–13.

27. Lieberman and Lang, *Anticommunism and the African American Freedom Movement*, 12.

28. Gore, *Radicalism at the Crossroads*, 8–9.

29. Robin D. G. Kelley, "'But a Local Phase of a World Problem': Black History's Global Vision, 1883–1950," *Journal of American History* 86 (December 1999): 1047.

30. Ibid., 1048–49.

31. Ibid., 1067. See also, for example: Du Bois, *The World and Africa*; Plummer, *Rising Wind*; Von Eschen, *Race against Empire*; Cedric J. Robinson, *Black Marxism: The Making of the Black Radical Tradition* (London: Zed, 1983).

32. Meredith L. Roman, *Opposing Jim Crow: African Americans and the Soviet Indictment of U.S. Racism, 1928–1937* (Lincoln: University of Nebraska Press, 2012), 7.

33. See, for example: Anthony, *Max Yergan*; Kelley, *Hammer and Hoe*; Mark Naison, *Communists in Harlem during the Depression* (New York: Grove, 1983); Nell Irvin Painter, *The Narrative of Hosea Hudson: His Life as a Negro Communist*

(Cambridge: Harvard University Press, 1979); Harry Haywood, *Black Bolshevik: Autobiography of an Afro-American Communist* (Chicago: Liberator Press, 1978); Langston Hughes, *I Wonder as I Wander* (New York: Hill and Wang, 1993); William Patterson, *The Man Who Cried Genocide* (New York: International Publishers, 1971); Paul Robeson, *Here I Stand* (Boston: Beacon, 1988); Kate Baldwin, *Beyond the Color Line and the Iron Curtain: Reading Encounters Between Black and Red, 1922–1963* (Durham, NC: Duke University Press, 2002); Joy Gleason Carew, *Blacks, Reds, and Russians: Sojourners in Search of the Soviet Promise* (New Brunswick: Rutgers University Press, 2010).

34. Singh, *Climbin' Jacob's Ladder*, 23.

35. Meriwether, *Proudly We Can Be Africans*, 43.

36. Philip Foner, ed., *Paul Robeson Speaks* (New York: Citadel Books, 2002), 104.

37. Painter, *The Narrative of Hosea Hudson*, 17.

38. Roman, *Opposing Jim Crow*, 13.

39. James C. Cobb and William Stueck, eds., *Globalization and the American South* (Athens: University of Georgia Press, 2005), xii. Also: "The US South in Global Contexts: A Collection of Position Statements," *American Literature* 78 (December 2006): 691–739.

40. Herbert Aptheker, "American Imperialism and White Chauvinism," *Jewish Life* (July 1950): 22.

41. Natalie J. Ring, *The Problem South: Region, Empire, and the New Liberal State, 1880–1930* (Athens: University of Georgia Press, 2012), 9.

42. Ring, "Linking Regional and Global Spaces in Pursuit of Southern Distinctiveness," in "The US South in Global Contexts: A Collection of Position Statements," *American Literature* 78 (December 2006): 712.

Chapter 1. Origins

1. Augusta Jackson (Strong), "Free At Last," *Cavalcade* 1 (June 1941): 3.

2. Ibid.

3. "Civil Liberties Breach Attacked by S.N.Y.C.," *Cavalcade* 1 (April 1941): 1.

4. "Rural Club Aids Nora Wilson," *Cavalcade* 1 (May 1941): 4; Johnetta Richards, "The Southern Negro Youth Congress: A History," PhD diss., University of Cincinnati, 1987, 82–83.

5. Jackson (Strong), "Free At Last," 3.

6. Singh, *Climbin' Jacob's Ladder*, 199.

7. *Southern Workman* 65 (February 1936): cover.

8. Report reprinted in *Southern Workman* 66 (May 1937): 150.

9. John P. Davis, "A Survey of the Problems of the Negro under the New Deal," *Journal of Negro Education* 5 (January 1936): 12.

10. Gellman, *Death Blow to Jim Crow*; Horace R. Cayton and George S. Mitchell, *Black Workers and the New Unions* (Chapel Hill: University of North Carolina Press, 1939), 415–24; Gunnar Myrdal, *An American Dilemma* (New York: McGraw Hill, 1964), 817–19; Lawrence S. Wittner, "The National Negro Congress: A Reassessment," *American Quarterly* 22 (Winter 1970): 883–901.

11. Herbert Newton, "The National Negro Congress," *Negro Worker* 6 (May/June 1936): 22–27.

12. Wittner, "The National Negro Congress," 886.

13. Quoted in Cayton and Mitchell, *Black Workers and the New Unions*, 416.

14. Robert Cohen, *When the Old Left Was Young: Student Radicals and America's First Mass Student Movement, 1929–1941* (New York: Oxford University Press, 1993), 1.

15. Ibid., 219.

16. Ibid., 221.

17. Maurice Gates, "Negro Students Challenge Social Forces," *Crisis* 42 (August 1935): 251.

18. Juanita E. Jackson, "Young Colored America Awakes," *Crisis* 45 (September 1938): 307.

19. Walter White, "The Youth Council of the NAACP," *Crisis* 44 (July 1937): 215.

20. Edward E. Strong, "The Negro Youth Offensive," *Negro Worker* 7 (May 1937): 8.

21. Audio recording of Southern Negro Youth Congress forum, 6 February 1984, Oral History of the American Left Collection, Tamiment Library/Robert F. Wagner Labor Archives, Elmer Holmes Bobst Library, New York University.

22. Edward E. Strong, "I Visited Spain," *Crisis* 43 (December 1936): 358.

23. For a discussion of local Communist organizing, see, for example: Naison, *Communists in Harlem during the Depression*; Kelley, *Hammer and Hoe*.

24. "Negro Editors on Communism," *Crisis* 39 (April 1932): 117.

25. Painter, *The Narrative of Hosea Hudson*, 21.

26. For example, Ralph Bunche quoted in Myrdal, *An American Dilemma*, 819.

27. Painter, *The Narrative of Hosea Hudson*, 380.

28. Junius Irving Scales and Richard Nickson, *Cause at the Heart: A Former Communist Remembers* (Athens: University of Georgia Press, 1987), 119.

29. Gilmore, *Defying Dixie*, 236.

30. Wilson Record, *The Negro and the Communist Party* (Chapel Hill: University of North Carolina Press, 1951), 162–63.

31. Richards, "Southern Negro Youth Congress," 157.

32. Southern Negro Youth Congress Papers, Moorland Spingarn Research Center, Howard University, Washington, DC, and George Marshall Papers,

Manuscripts, Archives, and Rare Books Division, Schomburg Center for Research in Black Culture, New York Public Library, New York, NY.

33. Box 35, Folder 1, George Marshall Papers.

34. Martha Biondi describes the relationship between the Communist Party and a broad range of "people's organizations" in that it exerted influence but did not necessarily represent a majority of the membership or control the agenda. Biondi, *To Stand and Fight*, 5.

35. Edward E. Strong, "The Negro Youth Offensive."

36. Augusta (Jackson) Strong, "Southern Youth's Proud Heritage," *Freedomways* 4 (Winter 1964): 46, 48.

37. Richards, "Southern Negro Youth Congress," 132. This is clear when looking through the folders on the local councils in the SNYC papers.

38. Files on local councils, Box 5, Southern Negro Youth Congress Papers, Manuscript Division, Moorland-Spingarn Research Center, Howard University, Washington, DC.

39. SNYC constitution, Box 1, Southern Negro Youth Congress Papers.

40. Claudia Jones, "Southern Parley Heralds Negro Youth Emancipation," *Sunday Worker Magazine Section*, 14 February 1937.

41. Audio recording of Southern Negro Youth Congress forum, 6 February 1984, Oral History of the American Left Collection.

42. James Farmer, *Lay Bare the Heart: An Autobiography of the Civil Rights Movement* (New York: Arbor House, 1985), 129–31.

43. (Jackson) Strong, "Southern Youth's Proud Heritage," 38.

44. Farmer, *Lay Bare the Heart*, 132.

45. James W. Ford, "Negro and White Youth Join in Southern Parley," *Daily Worker*, 15 February 1937.

46. Edward E. Strong, "The Negro Youth Offensive."

47. SNYC manual, Box 4, Southern Negro Youth Congress Papers.

48. "Conditions of the Negro Wage Earner" in Myrdal, *An American Dilemma*, 1107–10.

49. Augusta Jackson (Strong), "A New Deal for Tobacco Workers," *Crisis* 45 (October 1938): 322–24, 330. For more on tobacco workers, see chapter 2 in Robert Korstad, *Civil Rights Unionism: Tobacco Workers and the Struggle for Democracy in the Mid-Twentieth Century South* (Chapel Hill: University of North Carolina Press, 2003).

50. Audio recording of Southern Negro Youth Congress forum, 6 February 1984, Oral History of the American Left Collection.

51. "Report of the Credentials Committee," Official Proceedings: Second All Southern Negro Youth Conference, Chattanooga, Tennessee, April 1–3, 1938, 31.

52. Augusta Jackson (Strong), "Southern Youth Marches Forward," *Crisis* 45 (June 1938): 170–71.

53. Official Proceedings: Second All Southern Negro Youth Conference, Chattanooga, Tennessee, April 1–3, 1938, 9 and 13.

54. Ibid., 16.

55. Ibid., 11.

56. James Smethurst, *The Black Arts Movement: Literary Nationalism in the 1960s and 1970s* (Chapel Hill: University of North Carolina Press, 2005), 321.

57. (Jackson) Strong, "Southern Youth's Proud Heritage," 43.

58. "Sharecroppers' Lives Pictured," *Cavalcade* 1 (May 1941): 3.

59. Richards, "Southern Negro Youth Congress," 119–20.

60. Augusta Jackson (Strong), "Youth Meets in Birmingham," *Crisis* 46 (May 1939): 178.

61. (Jackson) Strong, "Southern Youth's Proud Heritage," 42.

62. Lee Coller, "Not Since Reconstruction," *New Masses*, 30 May 1939, 13.

63. Albert Whitfield, "A Boy and His Mule," *Cavalcade* 1 (April 1941): 3.

64. Waring Cuney, "Organize Blues," *Cavalcade* 1 (April 1941): 4.

65. Eugene B. Williams, "New Songs from Dixie," *Cavalcade* 1 (May 1941): 3.

66. Cordelia P. Key, "Two Were Born: One White, One Black," *Cavalcade* 1 (April 1941): 4.

67. Eugene B. Williams, "Drafted Blues," *Cavalcade* 1 (June 1941): 4.

68. Pernell Collins, "Culture and Labor," *Cavalcade* 1 (June 1941): 4.

69. For example: *Cavalcade* 1 (June 1941): 4; *Cavalcade* 1 (October 1941): 2.

70. Audio recording of Southern Negro Youth Congress forum, 6 February 1984, Oral History of the American Left Collection.

71. Angelo Herndon, "Peace, Democracy Set as Twin Goals for Negro Youth," *Daily Worker*, 20 April 1940.

72. "Our Battle for the Ballot," Series 11, Box 14, Folder 14, James E. Jackson and Esther Cooper Jackson Papers, Tamiment Library/Robert F. Wagner Labor Archives, Elmer Holmes Bobst Library, New York University, New York, NY.

73. Audio recording of Southern Negro Youth Congress forum, 6 February 1984, Oral History of the American Left Collection.

74. "Negro Youth Leader Calls for Widespread Anti-Poll Tax Drive," *Daily Worker*, 2 May 1941.

75. "Thousands to Participate," *Cavalcade* 1 (April 1941): 1.

76. "Education and the Poll Tax," *Cavalcade* 1 (May 1941): 1.

77. Letter from Irving Cohen of the Bronx Anti-Poll Tax Committee to James Jackson, Series 11, Box 14, Folder 6, James E. Jackson and Esther Cooper Jackson Papers.

78. Letter from Lee Geyer to SNYC, Box 2, Southern Negro Youth Congress Papers.

79. "Anti-Poll Tax Week a Success," *Cavalcade* 1 (June 1941): 1.

80. SNYC Press release, 17 July 1941, Box 3, Edward Strong Papers, Manuscript

Division, Moorland-Spingarn Research Center, Howard University, Washington, DC.

81. "Report of Delegation to Santa Clara Province," Box 3, Edward Strong Papers.

82. Angelo Herndon, "Dr. Yergan Warns Negro Youth of War," *Daily Worker*, 21 April 1940.

83. "American People at People's Parley," *Cavalcade* 1 (May 1941): 3.

84. "All Out for Democracy," *Cavalcade* 1 (October 1941): 4.

85. For a more complete discussion of the Communist Party and the war, see Maurice Isserman, *Which Side Were You On? The American Communist Party during the Second World War* (Middletown, CT: Wesleyan University Press, 1982).

86. "Let's Do Our Part," *Cavalcade* 1 (November 1941): 6.

87. Richards, "Southern Negro Youth Congress," 137. Also: Southern Negro Youth Congress F.B.I. Files, Tamiment Library/Robert F. Wagner Labor Archives, Elmer Holmes Bobst Library, New York University, New York, NY.

88. "Youth Congress on Dies' Black List," *Pittsburgh Courier*, 27 January 1940.

89. Angelo Herndon, "Peace, Democracy Set as Twin Goals for Negro Youth," *Daily Worker*, 20 April 1940.

90. For more on the NNC split, see Gellman, *Death Blow to Jim Crow*, 149–64.

91. John Baxter Streater, "The National Negro Congress, 1936–1947," PhD diss., University of Cincinnati, 1981; Cicero Alvin Hughes, "Toward a Black United Front: The National Negro Congress," PhD diss., Ohio University, 1982.

92. Wittner, "The National Negro Congress," 900–901.

93. Richards, "Southern Negro Youth Congress," 138–40.

94. "Profile," *Cavalcade* 1 (October 1941): 2.

95. "This Makes Us Happy," *New Africa* 5 (December 1946): 4.

96. *Spotlight on Africa* 12 (13 August 1953): 6.

97. *New Africa* 9 (May/June 1950): 3.

98. Reprinted in Dorothy Hunton, *Alphaeus Hunton: The Unsung Valiant* (privately published, 1986), 60–61.

99. Meriwether, *Proudly We Can Be Africans*, 10. See also chapter 1 on Ethiopia.

100. Von Eschen, *Race against Empire*, 8; Meriwether, *Proudly We Can Be Africans*, 8.

101. Ralph J. Bunche, "French and British Imperialism in West Africa," *Journal of Negro History* 21 (January 1936): 31.

102. Lynch, *Black American Radicals and the Liberation of Africa*, 17.

103. Anthony, *Max Yergan*, 7.

104. Ibid., 154–55.

105. Termination notice, 31 March 1941, Box 13, Folder 7, George Marshall Papers.

106. Robeson, *Here I Stand*, 33.

107. Audio recording of Robeson interview with Elsa Knight Thompson on *Paul Robeson: Words Like Freedom* (San Francisco: The Freedom Archives, Inc., 2008).

108. Foner, *Paul Robeson Speaks*, 260.

109. See, for example: Baldwin, *Beyond the Color Line and the Iron Curtain*; Carew, *Blacks, Reds, and Russians*.

110. Eslanda Robeson, *African Journey* (New York: John Day, 1945), 13.

111. Letter from Eslanda Robeson to Council members, 17 April 1948, W.E.B. Du Bois Papers, microfilm edition, reel 61, frame 762, Special Collections and University Archives, W.E.B. Du Bois Library, University of Massachusetts, Amherst, MA; Ransby, *Eslanda*, 134–35.

112. Letter from Max Yergan to members of ICAA, 31 August 1937, Council on African Affairs Organizational Files, W. A. Hunton Papers, microfilm edition, Schomburg Center for Research in Black Culture, New York Public Library, New York, NY.

113. See, for example: Meriwether, *Proudly We Can Be Africans*; Von Eschen, *Race against Empire*; Biondi, *To Stand and Fight*; Plummer, *Rising Wind*. Recent biographies of Council on African Affairs leaders are also illuminating: Anthony, *Max Yergan*; Lewis, *W.E.B. Du Bois: The Fight for Equality*; Paul Robeson Jr., *The Undiscovered Paul Robeson*; Ransby, *Eslanda*.

114. For example: Harold Cruse, *The Crisis of the Negro Intellectual from Its Origins to the Present* (New York: William Morrow, 1967), 177–78.

115. Lynch, *Black American Radicals and the Liberation of Africa*, 7. Drake wrote a very thoughtful introduction to Lynch's study of the council.

116. Meriwether, *Proudly We Can Be Africans*, 62.

117. See, for example, these very interesting studies: Kevin K. Gaines, *African Americans in Ghana: Black Expatriates and the Civil Rights Era* (Chapel Hill: University of North Carolina Press, 2006); Mary G. Rolinson, *Grassroots Garveyism: The Universal Negro Improvement Association in the Rural South, 1920–1927* (Chapel Hill: University of North Carolina Press, 2007).

118. Imanuel Geiss, *The Pan-African Movement: A History of Pan-Africanism in America, Europe and Africa*, translated by Ann Keep (New York: Africana Publishing, 1968), 3–8.

119. George Padmore, *Pan-Africanism or Communism?* (New York: Doubleday, 1971), xvi and xix.

120. For example: W.E.B. Du Bois, *The Autobiography of W.E.B. Du Bois: A Soliloquy on Viewing My Life from the Last Decade of Its First Century* (New York: International Publishers, 1968), 271–76; Du Bois, *The World and Africa*, 336–38; W.E.B. Du Bois, "The Pan African Congresses: The Story of a Growing Movement," in *W.E.B. Du Bois: A Reader*, edited by Lewis, 670–75.

121. Du Bois, "A Second Journey to Pan Africa," in *W.E.B. Du Bois: A Reader*, edited by Lewis, 667.

122. Cedric Robinson, *Black Marxism*, 297.

123. For more on the self-determination thesis and the Negro Question, see, for example: Cedric Robinson, *Black Marxism*, 301–10; Philip Foner and Herbert Shapiro, eds., *American Communism and Black Americans: A Documentary History, 1930–1934* (Philadelphia: Temple University Press, 1991); Harry Haywood, *Negro Liberation* (New York: International Publishers, 1948); "The National Question: Outline and Study Guide for Five Session Course," prepared by New York State Communist Party, 1949; Timothy Johnson, "'Death for Negro Lynching!' The Communist Party, USA's Position on the African American Question," in *Red Activists and Black Freedom*, edited by Lewis, Nash, and Leab, 73–84.

124. Geiss, *The Pan-African Movement*, 322–25.

125. George Padmore, *Africa and World Peace* (London: Frank Cass, 1937), vii. See also: James Hooker, *Black Revolutionary: George Padmore's Path from Communism to Pan-Africanism* (New York: Praeger, 1967).

126. Padmore was denounced as a counterrevolutionary in the pages of the newspaper he had edited. See: Helen Davis, "The Rise and Fall of George Padmore as a Revolutionary Fighter," *Negro Worker* 4 (August 1934): 15–17.

127. Padmore, *Pan-Africanism or Communism?*, introduction.

128. Padmore, *Africa and World Peace*, x.

129. Padmore, *Pan-Africanism or Communism?*, xvi. Interestingly, Hunton's position in chapter 16 of his 1957 book *Decision in Africa*, though written after the Council on African Affairs disbanded, was not too far from Padmore's. His chief concern seemed to be independence for African nations so that their leaders might decide for themselves with whom they wanted to align, whether it was the East, the West, or as a neutral state. W. Alphaeus Hunton, *Decision in Africa* (New York: International Publishers, 1957).

130. Padmore, *Pan-Africanism or Communism?*, 293; Herbert Aptheker, ed., *The Correspondence of W.E.B. Du Bois, Vol. III: Selections 1944–1963* (Amherst: University of Massachusetts Press, 1978), 148.

131. Letter from Max Yergan to members of ICAA, 31 August 1937, Council on African Affairs Organizational Files, W. A. Hunton Papers.

132. Max Yergan, "Gold and Poverty in South Africa" (New York: International Industrial Relations Institute, 1938), 2.

133. Ibid., 24.

134. Max Yergan, "The Status of the Natives in South Africa," *Journal of Negro History* 24 (January 1939): 44–56.

135. Ibid., 54.

136. Letters between Yergan and Mary van Kleeck, who was director of the International Industrial Relations Institute, indicate that the pamphlet was sent to

members of that organization in the United States, Europe, and Africa and that it was advertised in periodicals on these continents. Copies were also requested from a bookshop in Johannesburg. Mary van Kleeck Papers, Sophia Smith Collection, Smith College, Northampton, MA.

Chapter 2. The World at War

1. Samuel I. Rosenman, *The Public Papers and Addresses of Franklin D. Roosevelt*, Vol. 10 (New York: Harper and Brothers, 1950), 672.

2. Ibid., vol. 10, 66, 192, 498.

3. Ibid., vol. 10, 314–15.

4. Howard Zinn, *A People's History of the United States, 1492–Present* (New York: Harper Collins, 2003), 408.

5. Doxey A. Wilkerson, "Freedom—Through Victory in War and Peace," in *What the Negro Wants*, edited by Rayford Logan (Chapel Hill: University of North Carolina Press, 1944), 214.

6. A. Philip Randolph, "March on Washington Movement Presents Program for the Negro," in *What the Negro Wants*, edited by Logan, 133–62.

7. Mary McLeod Bethune, "Certain Unalienable Rights," in *What the Negro Wants*, edited by Logan, 252–53.

8. James E. Jackson, "Freedom's Children, to Arms!" *Cavalcade* 1 (November 1941): 3.

9. Esther Cooper Jackson, *This Is My Husband: Fighter for His People, Political Refugee* (Brooklyn, NY: National Committee to Defend Negro Leadership, 1953), 27.

10. Letter reprinted in *Cavalcade* 2 (May 1942): cover.

11. "Notes from Speakers," *Cavalcade* 2 (May 1942): 2.

12. Gerald Horne, *Red Seas: Ferdinand Smith and Radical Black Sailors in the United States and Jamaica* (New York: New York University Press, 2005), 81.

13. "Dixie Youth Congress Has Three-Day Confab," *People's Voice*, 25 April 1942.

14. Louis Burnham, "We Fight for America," *Cavalcade* 2 (May 1942): 3.

15. Esther V. Cooper (Jackson), "Organize for Victory," *Cavalcade* 2 (May 1942): 4.

16. *People's Voice*, 25 April 1942.

17. "Youth Congress Fails to Endorse 'Double V' Campaign," *Pittsburgh Courier*, 2 May 1942.

18. "Paul Robeson Sings, Speaks," *Cavalcade* 2 (May 1942): cover.

19. "Notes from Speakers," *Cavalcade* 2 (May 1942): 2.

20. "SNYC War Meet Draws Thousands," *Cavalcade* 2 (May 1942): cover.

21. Letter from Max Yergan to Esther Cooper, 4 May 1942, Box 2, Edward Strong Papers.

22. Foner, *Paul Robeson Speaks*, 143.

23. Ibid., 225.

24. "Washington Memo: A Report of Interviews with Federal Agencies, Conducted by Representatives of the Southern Negro Youth Congress, May 28–30, 1942," Box 31, Folder 9, George Marshall Papers.

25. SNYC press release, 2 August 1945, Box 8, Southern Negro Youth Congress Papers.

26. "Mission to Mobile," Series XI, Box 14, Folder 14, James E. Jackson and Esther Cooper Jackson Papers.

27. Hughes, "Toward a Black United Front," 181; "Invitation to the Greater Birmingham Negro Youth Conference May 14, 15, 16, 1943," Box 31, Folder 9, George Marshall Papers. (As reported in the *Afro-American*, there was no national SNYC conference in 1943 but several regional conferences were held instead. "SNYC Calls Off Its Spring Conference," *Afro-American*, 28 November 1942.)

28. Augusta (Jackson) Strong, "Southern Youth's Proud Heritage," 45; Richards, "Southern Negro Youth Congress," 60–62.

29. "Stop Hate Sheets Youths Ask FDR," *People's Voice*, 8 July 1944; Richards, "Southern Negro Youth Congress," 64.

30. Cooper Jackson, *This Is My Husband*, 27.

31. Reverend Richard Morford, "Thousands in South Support North on Anti-Poll Tax Bill," *People's Voice*, 22 April 1944.

32. "Youth Stress Right to Vote," *People's Voice*, 9 December 1944.

33. Letters reprinted in Official Proceedings of 1944 conference, Box 3, Edward Strong Papers.

34. Richards, "Southern Negro Youth Congress," 103–4; "Congress Group to Aid Youth," *People's Voice*, 17 June 1944.

35. "Would You Smile?" Birmingham, AL: Southern Negro Youth Congress, no date.

36. "For Victory at the Ballot Box," Southern Negro Youth Congress Monthly Bulletin, May 1945.

37. "Youth Congress Protests Firing," *People's Voice*, 1 July 1944.

38. "Reinstate Dr. Yergan," *Cavalcade* 1 (June 1941): 2.

39. See, for example: Kate Weigand, *Red Feminism: American Communism and the Making of Women's Liberation* (Baltimore: Johns Hopkins University Press, 2001); Gore, *Radicalism at the Crossroads*.

40. Official Proceedings of 1944 conference, 17.

41. Proceedings of testimonial dinner for Mary McLeod Bethune, 19 July 1945, Box 2, Southern Negro Youth Congress Papers. (Interestingly, the dinner was held in the facilities of the Council on African Affairs at 23 W. 26th Street in New York. Bethune was a supporter of both the council and SNYC.)

42. Streater, "The National Negro Congress: 1936–1947," 300; Gore, *Radicalism at the Crossroads*, 36–38.

43. Annie Mae Echols, "Industrial Youth Club Launched," *Cavalcade* 1 (June 1941): cover.

44. *Cavalcade* 1 (October 1941): 5.

45. *Cavalcade* 1 (April 1941): 2.

46. Robin Kelley notes that Edward and Augusta (Jackson) Strong moved to New York in 1945 in Kelley, *Hammer and Hoe*, 224.

47. "From the Rural Mailbag," *Cavalcade* 1 (April 1941): 3; *Cavalcade* 1 (June 1941): 3.

48. Ethel Goodman, "Tenants, Croppers, and Defense," *Cavalcade* 1 (October 1941): 7.

49. "Louisiana Farm Youth Meet," *Cavalcade* 1 (November 1941): 4.

50. (Jackson) Strong, "Southern Youth's Proud Heritage," 44.

51. Letter from Edward Strong to Max Yergan, 18 October 1940, Box 1, Edward Strong Papers.

52. For more on the Jacksons, see Lewis, Nash, and Leab, eds., *Red Activists and Black Freedom*.

53. Cooper Jackson, *This Is My Husband*, 25–26; "Meet Esther Cooper," *Cavalcade* 1 (May 1941): 3.

54. "They Tell Us," *Cavalcade* 1 (April 1941): 4.

55. Esther V. Cooper (Jackson), "Hitler's Foes—From Canada to the Cape," *Cavalcade* 1 (November 1941): 5.

56. Erik S. McDuffie, "'No Small Amount of Change Could Do:' Esther Cooper Jackson and the Making of a Black Left Feminist," in Dayo F. Gore, Jeanne Theoharis, and Komozi Woodard, eds., *Want to Start a Revolution? Radical Women in the Black Freedom Struggle* (New York: New York University Press, 2009), 27.

57. For more on women in SNCC, see Faith S. Holsaert et al., eds., *Hands on the Freedom Plow: Personal Accounts by Women in SNCC* (Champaign: University of Illinois Press, 2010).

58. Max Yergan, "Africa in the War" (New York: Council on African Affairs, 1942), 4. Yergan touched on similar themes in his column on Africa in the *People's Voice* in February and March 1943.

59. "Appeal to Arm Africans Made at Rally Here," *New York Herald Tribune*, 9 April 1942.

60. "4000 Call for Arming of Colonial Peoples," *Daily Worker*, 10 April 1942.

61. *New Africa*, January 1944 and September 1946.

62. Dorothy Hunton, *Alphaeus Hunton*, chapter 1.

63. Doxey A. Wilkerson, "William Alphaeus Hunton: A Life that Made a Difference," *Freedomways* 10 (Third Quarter 1970): 254.

64. George B. Murphy Jr., "William Alphaeus Hunton: His Roots in Black America," *Freedomways* 10 (Third Quarter 1970): 249.

65. Lynch, *Black American Radicals and the Liberation of Africa*, 24.

66. *New Africa* 2 (October 1943): 4.

67. *New Africa* 3 (January 1944): 3.

68. Program of the Council on African Affairs published in *For a New Africa: Proceedings of Conference on Africa, April 14, 1944* (New York: Council on African Affairs, 1944), 38.

69. "Conference on Africa," *People's Voice*, 22 April 1944.

70. "Opening Statement of Conference," in *For a New Africa*, 10.

71. "Africa—New Perspectives," in *For a New Africa*, 13–21.

72. Ibid., 17.

73. "Summary of Conference Discussion," in *For a New Africa*, 28.

74. "Africa in the American Press," in *For a New Africa*, 35.

75. "Future of Colonies Affects US," *Daily Worker*, 15 April 1944.

76. Carter G. Woodson, review of "For a New Africa," *Journal of Negro History* 30 (July 1945): 347.

77. "Police Called to Handle Crowds at Paul Robeson Birthday Party," *People's Voice*, 22 April 1944.

78. "Yergan Talks About Robeson's Birthday," *Daily Worker*, 10 April 1944.

79. "Chairman of the Council Honored," *New Africa* 3 (May 1944): 4.

80. Fredi Washington, "Headlines and Footnotes," *People's Voice*, 15 April 1944.

81. "Africa and Postwar Security Plans," 15 December 1944, Council on African Affairs Organizational Files, W. A. Hunton Papers; also published in *New Africa* 3 (December 1944): 4.

82. See, for example, the role of the NAACP in Anderson, *Eyes Off the Prize*.

83. "The Colonial Question and Plans for Lasting Peace," *New Africa* 3 (September 1944): 1.

84. Reprinted in *New Africa* 4 (February 1945): 2.

85. "Bretton Woods Proposal," *New Africa* 4 (March 1945): 1.

86. A draft was circulated prior to publication and feedback from all council members was solicited. Letter from Yergan to council members, 30 March 1944, Box 31, Folder 3, George Marshall Papers.

87. "The San Francisco Conference and the Colonial Issue" (New York: Council on African Affairs, 1945), 5.

88. Eslanda Robeson, "What Do the People of Africa Want?" (New York: Council on African Affairs, 1945), 23.

89. Amy Ashwood Garvey, "Pamphlet Urges New Day for Africa," *People's Voice*, 14 July 1945.

90. Lynch, *Black American Radicals and the Liberation of Africa*, 29.

91. "Council Urges Independence for Colonies," *New Africa* 4 (June 1945): 2.

92. "Resolutions on Issues Affecting Africa," *New Africa* 5 (October 1946): 3.

93. Lynch, *Black American Radicals and the Liberation of Africa,* 34. He notes that Hunton was the regular observer with Eslanda Robeson sometimes substituting.

94. Geiss, *The Pan-African Movement,* 386–87; *New Africa* 3 (September 1944): 4.

95. *New Africa* 4 (April 1945): 3; Lewis, *W.E.B. Du Bois: The Fight for Equality,* 499–500.

96. W.E.B. Du Bois Papers, microfilm edition, reel 57, frames 387–93; Lewis, *W.E.B. Du Bois: The Fight for Equality,* 500.

97. Letter from Padmore to Du Bois, 17 August 1945, W.E.B. Du Bois Papers, microfilm edition, reel 57, frames 1040–41.

98. W.E.B. Du Bois Papers, microfilm edition, reel 57, frame 1056.

99. Letter from Padmore to Du Bois, 17 August 1945, W.E.B. Du Bois Papers, microfilm edition, reel 57, frames 1040–41.

100. Geiss, *The Pan-African Movement,* 390–91.

101. Letters dated 12 April and 9 July 1945, W.E.B. Du Bois Papers, microfilm edition, reel 57, frames 1033–37.

102. Aptheker, *The Correspondence of W.E.B. Du Bois, Volume III,* 148.

103. Letter dated 18 September 1945, W.E.B. Du Bois Papers, microfilm edition, reel 57, frame 1048.

104. Letters dated 19 February and 10 May 1946, W.E.B. Du Bois Papers, microfilm edition, reel 58, frames 1046–47.

105. Letter dated 6 June 1946, W.E.B. Du Bois Papers, microfilm edition, reel 58, frame 751.

106. Geiss, *The Pan-African Movement,* 367–68.

107. Logan, *What the Negro Wants,* 214.

108. Foner, *Paul Robeson Speaks,* 144.

109. Logan, *What the Negro Wants,* ix.

110. Ibid., vii.

111. Ibid., 14.

Chapter 3. The Cold War Descends

1. Stuart J. Little, "The Freedom Train: Citizenship and Postwar Political Culture, 1946–1949," *American Studies* 34 (Spring 1993): 38.

2. Ibid., 49.

3. Ibid., 40–41, 46; *New York Times,* 11 September 1947.

4. Little, "The Freedom Train," 47.

5. Ibid., 40 and 43.

6. A description of Freedom Train crowds can be found in *New York Times,* 25 January 1948.

7. Ibid., 23 May 1947.

8. Ibid., 17 September 1947.

9. Ibid., 3 June 1947.

10. Ibid., 11 September 1947.

11. Ibid., 18 September 1947.

12. Ibid., 26 September 1947.

13. Ibid., 23 May 1947.

14. Little, "The Freedom Train," 58–59.

15. *The Southern Patriot* 6 (April 1948): 46; *New York Times*, 20 November 1947.

16. Arnold Rampersand, ed., *The Collected Poems of Langston Hughes* (New York: Vintage Books, 1994), 323.

17. *Voices of Black America: Historical Recordings of Poetry, Humor and Drama, 1908–1947* (Franklin, TN: Naxos Audio Books, 2002). The poem was first published in *New Republic* in September 1947.

18. Foner, *Paul Robeson Speaks*, 184.

19. *New York Times*, 25 January 1948.

20. Cooper Jackson, *This Is My Husband*, 29.

21. "Flyer for First Alabama State Conference of Negro Veterans," Series 11, Box 14, Folder 20, James E. Jackson and Esther Cooper Jackson Papers.

22. "Birmingham War Vets March Through Streets for Voting Rights," *Chicago Defender*, 2 February 1946.

23. Audio recording of Southern Negro Youth Congress forum, 6 February 1984, Oral History of the American Left Collection.

24. Letter from Edgar Holt to Louis Burnham, 31 July 1946, and reply from Esther Cooper Jackson, 7 August 1946, Series 11, Box 14, Folder 7, James E. Jackson and Esther Cooper Jackson Papers.

25. Oliver C. Cox, "Lynching and the Status Quo," *Journal of Negro Education* 14 (Autumn 1945): 588.

26. For more on the NAACP and lynching in the postwar years, see, for example: Anderson, *Eyes Off the Prize*. For more on the American Crusade Against Lynching, see, for example: Foner, *Paul Robeson Speaks*, 173–78; William Patterson, *We Charge Genocide: The Crime of Government against the Negro People* (New York: International Publishers, 1970).

27. Letter from Du Bois to Esther Cooper Jackson, 14 April 1945, Series 11, Box 14, Folder 6, James E. Jackson and Esther Cooper Jackson Papers.

28. "Historic London Conference Unites Youth of World," Box 5, Edward Strong Papers.

29. Letters from Du Bois to Esther Cooper Jackson, 24 July 1946, 22 August 1946, 3 September 1946, Series 7, Subseries A, Box 9, Folder 14, James E. Jackson and Esther Cooper Jackson Papers.

30. "Petition to the UN," Series 11, Box 14, Folder 2, James E. Jackson and Esther Cooper Jackson Papers.

31. "Youth Congress President Urges Early Conference Registration," *Birmingham World*, 4 October 1946.

32. Letters from Louis Burnham to organizers in several cities, Box 6, Southern Negro Youth Congress Papers.

33. Letter of invitation from Dorothy Burnham, 11 July 1946, Box 2, Edward Strong Papers.

34. "Youth Institute to Open," *People's Voice*, 8 July 1944.

35. Registration forms from third Leadership Training School, Box 2, Southern Negro Youth Congress Papers.

36. Letters between Medgar Evers and SNYC office, July 1946, Box 2, Edward Strong Papers.

37. "Flyer for SNYC Third Leadership Training School," Series 11, Box 14, Folder 20, James E. Jackson and Esther Cooper Jackson Papers.

38. Letter from Louis Burnham to Esther Cooper Jackson, no date, Series 11, Box 14, Folder 5, James E. Jackson and Esther Cooper Jackson Papers.

39. "Youth Meet Draws Upwards of 1500," *Birmingham World*, 22 October 1946.

40. "Five Thousand Visitors Expected for Weekend SNYC Meeting," *Lighthouse and Informer*, 20 October 1946.

41. Scales and Nickson, *Cause at the Heart*, 163.

42. Singh, *Climbin' Jacob's Ladder*, 16.

43. "Southern Youth Legislature Program," page 1, South Caroliniana Library, University of South Carolina, Columbia, South Carolina.

44. Ibid.

45. "Southern Youth Legislature Program," 6.

46. "Youth Summoned to Organize Against Human Exploitation," *Birmingham World*, 25 October 1946.

47. Florence Valentine, "Remarks on Job Training for Negro Women," Box 3, Edward Strong Papers.

48. "Remarks on Civil Rights," John H. McCray Papers, microfilm edition, South Caroliniana Library, University of South Carolina, Columbia, South Carolina.

49. "Excerpts from Speech by James E. Jackson, Jr.," 19 October 1946, John H. McCray Papers.

50. "Text of Address by Clark Foreman," John H. McCray Papers.

51. "Youth Congress Ends in Wrangle with Governor," *Birmingham World*, 29 October 1946.

52. Copy of letter to Governor Williams, 21 October 1946, John H. McCray Papers.

53. "Southern Youth Legislature Program," 7.

54. Ibid.

55. Du Bois, "Behold the Land," 7, 9, 14.

56. Letter from Du Bois to SNYC leaders, 28 October 1946, Series 7, Subseries A, Box 9, Folder 14, James E. Jackson and Esther Cooper Jackson Papers.

57. Foner, *Paul Robeson Speaks*, 289.

58. Ibid.

59. Correspondence in "Behold the Land" folders, Box 8, Southern Negro Youth Congress Papers.

60. Folders on Aptheker tour, Box 2, Southern Negro Youth Congress Papers.

61. SNYC press release, 13 January 1947, Box 8, Southern Negro Youth Congress Papers.

62. Petition against Theodore Bilbo, 1945, Box 2, Southern Negro Youth Congress Papers.

63. Invitation to banquet, Box 2, Southern Negro Youth Congress Papers.

64. "Every Member Get a Member Mass Meetings," 9 April 1947, John H. McCray Papers.

65. Flyer titled "Your Freedom is in Danger," John H. McCray Papers.

66. Allan Morrison, "Organizations Say Charges by Attorney General False," *People's Voice*, 13 December 1947.

67. Minutes from Executive Board Meeting, 3 January 1948, Box 1, Southern Negro Youth Congress Papers; also *Birmingham World*, 16 April 1948.

68. SNYC press release, 8 December 1947, Box 8, Southern Negro Youth Congress Papers; statement also published in: *Young South* 1 (February 1948): 3.

69. Letter from Edward Strong to Martin Dies, 31 October 1939, Box 1, Edward Strong Papers.

70. SNYC press release, 5 August 1946, Box 8, Southern Negro Youth Congress Papers.

71. SNYC press release, 26 July 1946, Box 8, Southern Negro Youth Congress Papers.

72. "Peace, Freedom and Abundance: The Platform of the Progressive Party as adopted at the Founding convention, Philadelphia, July 23–25, 1948" (New York: Progressive Party, 1948).

73. "Fascism in USA," *Southern Patriot* 6 (May 1948): 4.

74. Examples of continued coverage of police brutality in the *Birmingham World*: 30 April 1948; 14 July 1948.

75. Summaries of the Birmingham events include: "Battle of Birmingham" (Birmingham, AL: Southern Negro Youth Congress, 1948); "Statement of the Southern Negro Youth Congress on the Birmingham Incidents," Papers of the NAACP, microfilm edition, Youth File, General Department File, American Youth for a Free World, 1948–1951, Part 19, Series B, reel 1, frames 14–19.

76. Ben Davis, "Negro Youth Conference Panel Endorses Wagner Health Bill," *Daily Worker*, 1 May 1939.

77. James Dombrowski, "Birmingham Story," *Southern Patriot* 6 (April 1948): 2.

78. Telegram from Louis Burnham to Tom Clark, 30 April 1948, Box 8, Southern Negro Youth Congress Papers.

79. "White Delegates to SNYC Meet Refused Hotel Services," *Birmingham World*, 4 May 1948.

80. Dombrowski, "Birmingham Story," 2.

81. "Birmingham Segregation Laws Face Court Test," *Birmingham World*, 4 May 1948.

82. *Time*, 10 May 1948, page 24.

83. Ibid., 17 May 1948, page 25.

84. "Senator Taylor Convicted on Three Counts," *Birmingham World*, 7 May 1948.

85. "Pastor Asked to Resign," *Birmingham World*, 11 May 1948.

86. "SNYC to Aid Four Arrested at Annual Meet," *Birmingham World*, 7 May 1948; "SNYC Issues Appeal for Legal Funds," *Birmingham World*, 4 June 1948.

87. "Battle of Birmingham," 15.

88. "Youth Congress Speakers Cleared," *Birmingham World*, 15 June 1948.

89. Letter from Glen Taylor to Louis Burnham, 17 May 1948, Box 7, Southern Negro Youth Congress Papers.

90. "Ousted Prof. Quits Southern Negro Youth Congress," *Birmingham World*, 29 June 1948.

91. "Alabama Thought Control,'" *Birmingham World*, 6 July 1948.

92. For more on this idea, see: Timothy Johnson, "'Death to Negro Lynching!' The Communist Party, USA's Position on the African American Question," in *Red Activists and Black Freedom*, edited by Lewis, Nash, and Leab, 84.

93. (Jackson) Strong, "Southern Youth's Proud Heritage," 50.

94. Minutes from Executive Board Meeting, 3 January 1948, Box 1, Southern Negro Youth Congress Papers.

95. Farmer, *Lay Bare the Heart*, 129–31; Diane McWhorter, *Carry Me Home: Birmingham, Alabama, the Climactic Battle of the Civil Rights Revolution* (New York: Touchstone Books, 2001), 60.

96. Singh, *Climbin' Jacob's Ladder*, 203.

97. Angela Davis, "James and Esther Jackson: Connecting the Past to the Present," in *Red Activists and Black Freedom*, edited by Lewis, Nash, and Leab, 103.

98. Du Bois, "Behold the Land," 11.

99. Singh, *Climbin' Jacob's Ladder*, 199.

100. "Anderson-Robeson Lead Fight on African Famine," *People's Voice*, 5 January 1946.

101. "People's Town Hall," *People's Voice*, 2 February 1946.

102. "Robeson, Anderson Pack Aid to Africa Meeting," *People's Voice*, 12 January 1946.

103. "Robeson Asks for Food Aid," *People's Voice*, 23 March 1946.

104. "Robeson Says South Africa Taxes Relief Food Gifts," *PM*, 15 May 1946.

105. *New York Herald Tribune*, 5 June 1946; *PM*, 4 June 1946; *Daily Worker*, 5 June 1946; *New York Times*, 3 June 1946; *New York Post*, 4 June 1946; radio shows listed in council press release, 27 May 1946.

106. Council press release, 25 May 1946, Council on African Affairs Organizational Files, W. A. Hunton Papers.

107. Letter from Robeson to Council supporters, 4 May 1946, Council on African Affairs Organizational Files, W. A. Hunton Papers.

108. Paul Robeson, "Africa—Continent in Bondage," *New York Herald Tribune*, 5 June 1946.

109. Council press release, 8 June 1946, Council on African Affairs Organizational Files, W. A. Hunton Papers.

110. Address by Paul Robeson, 6 June 1946, Paul Robeson Collection, microfilm edition, reel 7, frames 227–29, Schomburg Center for Research in Black Culture, New York Public Library, New York, NY.

111. Letter from Council to members, 28 June 1946, Matt N. and Evelyn Graves Crawford Papers, Manuscript, Archive and Rare Book Library, Emory University, Atlanta, GA.

112. Council press release, 13 July 1946, Council on African Affairs Organizational Files, W. A. Hunton Papers.

113. W. Alphaeus Hunton, "Stop South Africa's Crimes," New York: Council on African Affairs, 1946.

114. *New Africa* 5 (November 1946): 4.

115. Council press release, 21 November 1946, Council on African Affairs Organizational Files, W. A. Hunton Papers.

116. *New Africa* 5 (December 1946): 3.

117. Ibid., 6 (March 1947): 5.

118. Council press release, 17 April 1947, Council on African Affairs Organizational Files, W. A. Hunton Papers.

119. Ibid., 25 April 1947.

120. Ibid., 25 April 1947 (multiple press releases came out that day).

121. Ibid., 26 April 1947.

122. "Churchill Gets No to Next War Buildup," *People's Voice*, 16 March 1946.

123. Letter to Truman from Robeson and Yergan, 8 March 1946, Council on African Affairs Organizational Files, W. A. Hunton Papers.

124. Anthony, *Max Yergan*, 230.

125. Ransby, *Eslanda*, 187–88.

126. Report on February 2nd Meeting, W.E.B. Du Bois Papers, microfilm edition, reel 61, frame 710.

127. "African Affairs Council Fails to Establish Policy," *Birmingham World*, 10 February 1948.

128. Report on March 25th Meeting and Letter from Hunton to Robeson, W.E.B. Du Bois Papers, microfilm edition, reel 61, frames 748–51.

129. "Council on African Affairs Splits over Communist Issue," *Birmingham World*, 16 April 1948; "Yergan Supported in Council Fight," *People's Voice*, 17 April 1948. The resignations are corroborated in the memoir of Vice-Chairman William Jay Schieffelin, who resigned that spring; see Reminiscences of William Jay Schieffelin, Oral History Collection, Butler Library, Columbia University, New York, 76–77.

130. Letter from John Latouche, Mary Church Terrell, and Henry Arthur Callis to Robeson, 15 May 1948, Box 4, Folder 11, Max Yergan Papers, Manuscript Division, Moorland-Spingarn Research Center, Howard University, Washington, DC.

131. *New York Times*, 2, 5, 19, 20, 29 June, 26 August, 24 and 29 September, 1948.

132. Statement by Dr. Max Yergan Regarding His Resignation from the Council on African Affairs, Box 6, Folder 48, Max Yergan Papers.

133. Ransby, *Eslanda*, 188.

134. Letter from Hunton to council members, 7 July 1948, Council on African Affairs Organizational Files, W. A. Hunton Papers.

135. Letter from Hunton and Robeson to council members, 7 October 1948, Box 39, Paul Robeson Papers, Manuscript Division, Moorland-Spingarn Research Center, Howard University, Washington, DC.

136. For example: U.S. Congress, Senate, Subcommittee to Investigate the Administration of the Internal Security Act, of the Committee on the Judiciary, Testimony of Max Yergan, 13 May 1952; "Africa: Next Goal of Communists," *U.S. News and World Report*, 1 May 1953; Max Yergan, "The Communist Threat in Africa," in *Africa Today*, edited by Charles Grove Haines (Baltimore: Johns Hopkins University Press, 1955); "Why There's No Colored Bloc," *U.S. News and World Report*, 3 June 1955. Also, chapter 6 in Anthony, *Max Yergan*, and Gilmore, *Defying Dixie*, 432–49.

137. Paul Robeson Jr. notes that Yergan was an informant for the FBI in Paul Robeson Jr., *The Undiscovered Paul Robeson*, 129.

138. Lynch, *Black American Radicals and the Liberation of Africa*, 53.

139. *New Africa* 8 (October 1949): 4.

140. *New York Times*, 9 April 1949; Associated Negro Press, 11 April 1949 in Claude A. Barnett Papers, Part 3, Series D, reel 5, frame 558.

141. Testimony of W. A. Hunton of the Council on African Affairs in Opposition to the North Atlantic Treaty, 13 May 1949, Council on African Affairs Organizational Files, W. A. Hunton Papers.

142. For more on the Paris conference: Lewis, *W.E.B. Du Bois: The Fight for Equality*, 544–45; Duberman, *Paul Robeson: A Biography*, 341–42.

143. For example: "Robeson as Speaker for Negroes Denied," *New York Times*, 25 April 1949; the Associated Negro Press ran a piece titled "Negroes and Whites Hit Robeson's 'Negro Won't Fight Russia,'" in Claude A. Barnett Papers, Part 3, Series D, reel 5, frames 559–60. That summer, Jackie Robinson was pressured into testifying that Robeson was not a leader in the African American community before the HUAC. See: *New York Times*, 9 and 19 July 1949; *Daily Worker*, 14 and 19 July 1949; Jackie Robinson and Alfred Duckett, *I Never Had It Made* (New York: G. P. Putnam, 1972), 96.

144. "Robeson Speaks for Robeson," *Crisis* 56 (May 1949): 137. See also: "Robeson as Speaker for Negroes Denied," *New York Times*, 25 April 1949; Robert Alan, "Paul Robeson—the Lost Shepard," *Crisis* 58 (November 1951): 569–73.

145. Letter from Hunton to council members, 23 May 1949, Paul Robeson Collection, microfilm edition, reel 7, frame 19.

146. "A Reaction to Robeson," *New York Tribune*, 1 May 1949.

147. "For Freedom and Peace: Address by Paul Robeson" (New York: Council on African Affairs, 1949), 2.

148. Ibid., 14.

149. Council press release containing text of Hunton's speech, 19 June 1949, Council on African Affairs Organizational Files, W. A. Hunton Papers.

150. Council press release containing text of Du Bois's speech, 19 June 1949, Council on African Affairs Organizational Files, W. A. Hunton Papers.

151. "Howard Fast's Eyewitness Account of Fascist Mob's Attack," *Daily Worker*, 30 August 1949. For more on Peekskill, see, for example: Howard Fast, *Peekskill USA: A Personal Experience* (New York: Civil Rights Congress, 1951); "Eyewitness to Peekskill USA" (White Plains, NY: Westchester Committee for a Fair Inquiry into the Peekskill Violence, October 1949); chapter 8 in *The Undiscovered Paul Robeson*, by Paul Robeson Jr. There was ongoing coverage in several newspapers, including the *Peekskill Evening Star*, 22, 27, 29 August 1949; the *New York Times*, 29, 31 August, 4, 6, 11 September 1949; as well as the *Daily Worker*, 28, 29, 30 August, 1, 6 September 1949.

152. Howard Fast, "Peekskill," *Masses and Mainstream* 2 (October 1949): 5.

153. "Two vets in critical condition after raid on Robeson concerts," for Associated Negro Press in Claude A. Barnett Papers, Part 3, Series D, reel 5, frame 573.

154. "Stoning Victims Tell of Violence," *New York Times*, 6 September 1949.

155. "State Police Data on Robeson Drawn," *New York Times*, 11 September 1949.

156. "6,000 Jam Church," for Associated Negro Press in Claude A. Barnett Papers, Part 3, Series D, reel 5, frame 577.

157. "Peekskill and the USA," *New Africa* 8 (October 1949): 1.

158. Claire Nee Nelson, "Louise Thompson Patterson and the Southern Roots

of the Popular Front," in *Women Shaping the South: Creating and Confronting Change*, edited by Angela Boswell and Judith N. McArthur (Columbia: University of Missouri Press, 2006), 209.

159. Louise Patterson, "Southern Terror," *Crisis* 41 (November 1934): 327.

160. Ibid., 328.

161. Nelson, "Louise Thompson Patterson and the Southern Roots of the Popular Front," 228.

162. Louise Thompson Patterson wrote about the tour preparations in an unpublished manuscript titled "Paul Robeson," in the Louise Thompson Patterson Papers, Box 20, Manuscript, Archive, and Rare Book Library, Woodruff Library, Emory University, Atlanta, GA.

163. *New York Times*, 25 January 1948.

Chapter 4. Cold War Consequences

1. Henry Steele Commager, "Who is Loyal to America?" in *Freedom, Loyalty, Dissent* (New York: Oxford University Press, 1954), 140.

2. Ibid., 143.

3. "The United States Objectives and Programs for National Security," 7 April 1950, page 7. This source is available digitally through the Truman Library at http://www.trumanlibrary.org/whistlestop/study_collections/coldwar/documents/pdf/10-1.pdf.

4. Ibid.

5. Cong. Rec., 81st Congress, 2d Session, pt. 2, page 1954.

6. Council press release, 23 July 1950, Council on African Affairs Organizational Files, W. A. Hunton Papers.

7. W.E.B. Du Bois, "African Youth at Prague," *New Africa* 9 (September 1950): 8. See also: W.E.B. Du Bois, *In Battle for Peace* (New York: Masses and Mainstream, 1952).

8. "A Protest and Plea," 11 July 1950, Council on African Affairs Organizational Files, W. A. Hunton Papers.

9. Council press release, 6 September 1950, Council on African Affairs Organizational Files, W. A. Hunton Papers; *New York Times*, 29 August 1950.

10. Council press release, 8 September 1950, Council on African Affairs Organizational Files, W. A. Hunton Papers; *New Africa* 9 (September 1950): 2.

11. Robeson, *Here I Stand*, 64; *Freedom* 2 (April 1952): 5.

12. *New Africa* 9 (September 1950): 3.

13. Alphaeus Hunton, "Africa Fights for Freedom" (New York: New Century, 1950), 10. An excerpt of this pamphlet was reprinted as "Upsurge in Africa," *Masses and Mainstream* 3 (February 1950): 12–21.

14. Ibid., 15.

15. Letter to council members from Robeson, 25 August 1951, Council on African Affairs Organizational Files, W. A. Hunton Papers.

16. Dorothy Hunton, *Alphaeus Hunton*, 84–86; Gerald Horne, *Communist Front? The Civil Rights Congress 1946–1956* (Cranbury, NJ: Associated University Presses, 1988), 241–45.

17. Du Bois, *In Battle for Peace*, 109.

18. *Spotlight on Africa*, 11 (1 February 1952): 1.

19. Dorothy Hunton, *Alphaeus Hunton*, 88.

20. Council press release, 21 March 1952, Council on African Affairs Organizational Files, W. A. Hunton Papers.

21. *Spotlight on Africa* 11 (25 February 1952): 1.

22. Ibid. (14 April 1952): 1.

23. *New York Times*, 7 April 1952.

24. "Resistance Against Fascist Enslavement in South Africa" (New York: New Century, 1953), 49.

25. Ibid., 48.

26. Council press release, 27 March 1952, Council on African Affairs Organizational Files, W. A. Hunton Papers; Letter to Robeson from Walter Sisulu, 9 June 1953, Council on African Affairs Organizational Files, W. A. Hunton Papers. The council also received a message of solidarity from the South African Indian Congress in May 1953, *Spotlight on Africa* 12 (11 June 1953): 1.

27. *Spotlight on Africa* 13 (18 May 1954): 1. See also: Caroline Elkins, *Imperial Reckoning: The Untold Story of Britain's Gulag in Kenya* (New York: Holt, 2005).

28. Resolutions Adopted at Conference in Support of African Liberation, 24 April 1954, Paul Robeson Collection, microfilm edition, reel 7, frames 125–26.

29. Keynote address by Dr. W.E.B. Du Bois, 24 April 1954, Matt N. and Evelyn Graves Crawford Papers.

30. Council press release, 9 April 1954, Council on African Affairs Organizational Files, W. A. Hunton Papers.

31. Council press release, 7 November 1954, Council on African Affairs Organizational Files, W. A. Hunton Papers; *Spotlight on Africa* 12 (11 June 1953): 1; "Here are the Facts, You Be the Judge: The Council Answers Attorney General Brownell," Matt N. and Evelyn Graves Crawford Papers; Herbert Brownell Jr. v. Council on African Affairs in the Subversive Activities Control Board, Docket no. 110–53.

32. Council press release, 24 April 1953, Council on African Affairs Organizational Files, W. A. Hunton Papers.

33. Minutes of meeting of Executive Board, 14 June 1955, Council on African Affairs Organizational Files, W. A. Hunton Papers.

34. Ibid.

35. *Africa Today* 2 (May-June 1955): 2.

36. Richard Wright, *The Color Curtain: A Report of the Bandung Conference* (Jackson, MS: Banner Books, 1994), 12.

37. *Daily Worker*, 19, 20, 21 April 1955; *Afro American*, 30 April 1955; *Spotlight on Africa* 14 (April 1955): 15–16.

38. *Daily Worker*, 21 April 1955.

39. Robeson, *Here I Stand*, 46–47.

40. For example: *New York Tribune*, 18 April 1955; *Afro American*, 30 April and 7 May 1955; *Pittsburgh Courier*, 30 April 1955.

41. *Spotlight on Africa* 14 (May 1955): 21.

42. Ibid., 6 and 22.

43. Francis Njubi Nesbitt, *Race for Sanctions: African Americans against Apartheid, 1946–1994* (Bloomington: Indiana University Press, 2004), 25.

44. Ibid., 9.

45. Chapter 6 in Nesbitt; Randall Robinson, *Defending the Spirit: A Black Life in America* (New York: Plume, 1999), 151–63; *Have You Heard from Johannesburg: Apartheid and the Club of the West*, directed by Connie Fields, Clarity Films, 2006.

46. Odd Arne Westad, *The Global Cold War: Third World Interventions and the Making of Our Times* (Cambridge: Cambridge University Press, 2005), 5 and 7.

47. Robert Dalleck, *The Lost Peace: Leadership in a Time of Horror and Hope, 1945–1953* (New York: Harper Collins, 2010), 7.

48. Ibid., 192.

49. Von Eschen, *Race against Empire*, 186.

50. Gaines, *African Americans in Ghana*, 17.

51. For example: Gaines, *African Americans in Ghana*; Alex Haley, *The Autobiography of Malcolm X* (New York: Ballantine Books, 1999); Stokely Carmichael with Ekwueme Michael Thelwell, *Ready for Revolution: The Life and Struggles of Stokely Carmichael* (New York: Scribner, 2003); Richard Wright, *Black Power* (New York: Harper Perennial, 1995).

52. *Freedom* 1 (March 1951): 2.

53. *Freedom* 2 (May 1952): 6.

54. *Freedom* 2 (April 1952): 6.

55. Robbie Lieberman, "'Another Side of the Story': African American Intellectuals Speak Out for Peace and Freedom during the Early Cold War Years," in *Anticommunism and the African American Freedom Movement*, edited by Lieberman and Lang,, 26. Also: Barbara J. Beeching, "Paul Robeson and the Black Press: The 1950 Passport Controversy," *Journal of African American History* 87 (Summer 2002): 339–54.

56. Lawrence Lamphere, "Paul Robeson, *Freedom* Newspaper, and the Black Press," PhD diss., Boston College, 2003, 6–7; Patrick S. Washburn, *The African American Newspaper: Voice of Freedom* (Evanston, IL: Northwestern University Press, 2006), 5.

57. *Freedom* (November 1950): 4. (This was the introductory issue, and volume 1 started in 1951.)

58. "Minutes of United Freedom Fund Meeting," 12 February 1952, and other related documents, Paul Robeson Collection, microfilm edition, reel 8.

59. Robeson Jr., *The Undiscovered Paul Robeson*, 230.

60. *Freedom* 5 (April 1955): 2.

61. Lorraine Hansberry, *To Be Young, Gifted and Black: An Informal Autobiography of Lorraine Hansberry* (New York: Signet Books, 1970), 99–100. The full piece, written after Burnham's sudden death in 1960, can be found in Box 2, Folder 13, Lorraine Hansberry Papers, Manuscripts, Archives, and Rare Books Division, Schomburg Center for Research in Black Culture, New York Public Library, New York, NY.

62. See, for example: Ransby, *Eslanda*; Gore, *Radicalism at the Crossroads*; Weigand, *Red Feminism*; Gerald Horne, *Race Woman: The Lives of Shirley Graham Du Bois* (New York: New York University Press, 2000); Robert Shaffer, "Out of the Shadows: The Political Writings of Eslanda Goode Robeson," *Pennsylvania History* 66 (Winter 1999): 47–64; Gore, Theoharis, and Woodard, eds., *Want to Start a Revolution?*

63. *Freedom* 2 (January 1952): 4.

64. The columns were later published as: Alice Childress, *Like One of the Family: Conversations from a Domestic's Life* (Boston: Beacon, 1986).

65. Mary Helen Washington, "Alice Childress, Lorraine Hansberry, and Claudia Jones: Black Women Write the Popular Front," in *Left of the Color Line: Race, Radicalism, and Twentieth Century Literature of the United States*, edited by Bill Mullen and James Smethurst (Chapel Hill: University of North Carolina Press, 2003), 189 and 192.

66. Childress, *Like One of the Family*, xxx–xxxi. In her introduction to Childress's collection, Trudier Harris notes that Childress was, at first, not compensated for the columns about Mildred in *Freedom*. When *Freedom* folded, the *Afro-American* picked up the popular series.

67. Hansberry, *To Be Young, Gifted and Black*, 97.

68. Judith E. Smith, *Visions of Belonging: Family Stories, Popular Culture, and Postwar Democracy, 1940–1960* (New York: Columbia University Press, 2004), 288.

69. Hansberry, *To Be Young, Gifted and Black*, 53.

70. Smith, *Visions of Belonging*, 284–88; Michael Anderson, "Lorraine Hansberry's Freedom Family," in *Red Activists and Black Freedom*, edited by Lewis, Nash, and Leab, 93 and 98.

71. Washington, "Alice Childress, Lorraine Hansberry, and Claudia Jones," 193; Smith, *Visions of Belonging*, 307; Anderson, *Eyes Off the Prize*, 95.

72. *Freedom* 1 (October 1951): 6.

73. *Freedom* 2 (April 1952): 3.

74. *Afro-American*, 18 April 1959, page 15.

75. *Freedom* (November 1950): 4.

76. See, for example: Barbara S. Griffith, *The Crisis of American Labor: Operation Dixie and the Defeat of the CIO* (Philadelphia: Temple University Press, 1988). Had this campaign in the South been successful, it would have helped fulfill the vision of a movement uniting labor for civil rights change that was espoused in *Freedom*.

77. See, for example: chapter 6 in George Lipsitz, *Class and Culture in Cold War America: "A Rainbow at Midnight"* (New York: Praeger, 1981); the epilogue of Nelson Lichtenstein, *Labor's War at Home: The CIO in World War II* (Cambridge: Cambridge University Press, 1982).

78. See, for example: Steve Rosswurm, ed., *The CIO's Left-Led Unions* (New Brunswick, NJ: Rutgers University Press, 1992).

79. *Freedom* 5 (March 1955): 5.

80. Lichtenstein, *Labor's War at Home*, 244; Rosswurm, *The CIO's Left-Led Unions*, 14.

81. Lieberman, "Another Side of the Story,'" 26.

82. *Freedom* 3 (October 1953): 6.

83. *Freedom* 1 (December 1951): 6.

84. *Freedom* 3 (September 1953): 3.

85. *Freedom* 1 (December 1951): 6.

86. *Freedom* 1 (March 1951): 4.

87. *Freedom* 3 (October 1953): 6

88. *Freedom* 1 (October 1951): 7.

89. Alex Heard, *The Eyes of Willie McGee: A Tragedy of Race, Sex, and Secrets in the Jim Crow South* (New York: Harper, 2010), 56.

90. *Freedom* 1 (February 1951): 1; *Freedom* 1 (May 1951): 1.

91. *Freedom* 2 (May 1952): 1. The Ingrams were eventually released on parole in 1959. For more on these cases, see, for example: Heard, *The Eyes of Willie McGee*; Horne, *Communist Front?*; Charles H. Martin, "Race, Gender, and Southern Justice: The Rosa Lee Ingram Case," *American Journal of Legal History* 29 (July 1985): 251–68; Eric W. Rise, *The Martinsville Seven: Race, Rape, and Capital Punishment* (Charlottesville: University of Virginia Press, 1995).

92. *Freedom* 4 (February 1954): 1.

93. *Freedom* 2 (July 1952): 2; *Freedom* 5 (July/August 1955): 3.

94. *Freedom* 3 (January 1953): 3.

95. *Freedom* 3 (December 1953): 4.

96. *Freedom* 3 (February 1953): 2.

97. *Freedom* 5 (July/August 1955): 6.

98. Coverage of Robeson's passport case: *Freedom* 1 (November 1951): 8; 2 (April 1952): 5; 2 (June 1952): 1; 5 (July/August 1955): 1.

99. *Freedom* 2 (November 1952): 3.

100. *Freedom* 4 (February 1954): 3.

101. *Freedom* 5 (April 1955): 1; 5 (May/June 1955): 1; 5 (July/August 1955): 1.

102. Louis Burnham, "Behind the Lynching of Emmett Louis Till" (New York: Freedom Associates, 1955), 9.

103. Derrick Bell, *Silent Covenants: Brown v. Board of Education and the Unfulfilled Hopes for Racial Reform* (New York: Oxford University Press, 2004), 4.

Epilogue

1. See: Smethurst, *The Black Arts Movement*, introduction and chapter 1. James Smethurst discusses *Freedomways* as an important forum for publishing African American art and literature during the Black Arts Movement.

2. Esther Cooper Jackson with Constance Pohl, eds., *Freedomways Reader: Prophets in Their Own Country* (Boulder, CO: Westview Press, 2000), xxi.

3. *Freedomways* 1 (Spring 1961): 9.

4. Ibid., 7–8.

5. Singh, *Climbin' Jacob's Ladder*, 8.

6. *Freedomways* 4 (Winter 1964): 5.

7. Audio recording of Southern Negro Youth Congress forum, 6 February 1984, Oral History of the American Left Collection.

8. Ibid., 6.

9. *Freedomways* 5 (Winter 1965): 5.

Sources Consulted

Manuscript Collections

Claude A. Barnett Papers (Associated Negro Press), microfilm edition, Frederick, MD: University Publications of America, 1984.

Doxey Wilkerson Papers, Manuscripts, Archives, and Rare Books Division, Schomburg Center for Research in Black Culture, New York Public Library, New York, NY.

Edward Strong Papers, Manuscript Division, Moorland-Spingarn Research Center, Howard University, Washington, DC.

George Marshall Papers, Manuscripts, Archives, and Rare Books Division, Schomburg Center for Research in Black Culture, New York Public Library, New York, NY.

Hennig Cohen Papers, South Caroliniana Library, University of South Carolina, Columbia, SC.

James E. Jackson and Esther Cooper Jackson Papers, Tamiment Library/Robert F. Wagner Labor Archives, Elmer Holmes Bobst Library, New York University, New York, NY.

John H. McCray Papers, microfilm edition, South Caroliniana Library, University of South Carolina, Columbia, SC.

Lorraine Hansberry Papers, Manuscripts, Archives, and Rare Books Division, Schomburg Center for Research in Black Culture, New York Public Library, New York, NY.

Louis Burnham Newspaper Collection, Manuscripts, Archives, and Rare Books Division, Schomburg Center for Research in Black Culture, New York Public Library, New York, NY.

Louise Thompson Patterson Papers, Manuscript, Archive, and Rare Book Library, Woodruff Library, Emory University, Atlanta, GA.

Mary van Kleeck Papers, Sophia Smith Collection, Smith College, Northampton, MA.

Matt N. and Evelyn Graves Crawford Papers, Manuscript, Archives, and Rare Book Library, Woodruff Library, Emory University, Atlanta, GA.

Max Yergan Papers, Manuscript Division, Moorland-Spingarn Research Center, Howard University, Washington, DC.

Papers of the NAACP, microfilm edition, General Office Files and Youth Files.

Paul and Eslanda Robeson FBI File, Online edition in FBI Electronic Reading Room.

Paul Robeson Collection, microfilm edition, Schomburg Center for Research in Black Culture, New York Public Library, New York, NY.

Paul Robeson Papers, Manuscript Division, Moorland-Spingarn Research Center, Howard University, Washington, DC.

The Reminiscences of William Jay Schieffelen (1949), Oral History Collection, Butler Library, Columbia University, New York, NY.

Southern Negro Youth Congress FBI Files, Tamiment Library/Robert F. Wagner Labor Archives, Elmer Holmes Bobst Library, New York University, New York, NY.

Southern Negro Youth Congress Forum, 6 February 1984, Oral History of the American Left: Radical Histories Collection, Tamiment Library/Robert F. Wagner Labor Archives, Elmer Holmes Bobst Library, New York University.

Southern Negro Youth Congress Papers, Manuscript Division, Moorland-Spingarn Research Center, Howard University, Washington, DC.

W. A. Hunton Papers, microfilm edition, Schomburg Center for Research in Black Culture, New York Public Library, New York, NY.

W.E.B. Du Bois Papers, microfilm edition, Special Collections and University Archives, W.E.B. Du Bois Library, University of Massachusetts, Amherst, MA.

Dissertations, Books, Other Published Materials

Anderson, Carol. *Eyes Off the Prize: The United Nations and the African American Struggle for Human Rights, 1944–1955.* Cambridge: Cambridge University Press, 2003.

Anthony, David Henry. *Max Yergan: Race Man, Internationalist, Cold Warrior.* New York: New York University Press, 2006.

Aptheker, Herbert, ed. *The Correspondence of W.E.B. Du Bois, Volume III: Selections 1944–1963.* Amherst: University of Massachusetts Press, 1978.

Baker, Houston A. *Turning South Again: Re-thinking Modernism/Re-reading Booker T.* Durham: Duke University Press, 2001.

Balaji, Murali. *The Professor and the Pupil: The Politics and Friendship of W.E.B. Du Bois and Paul Robeson.* New York: Nation Books, 2007.

Baldwin, Kate. *Beyond the Color Line and the Iron Curtain: Reading Encounters Between Black and Red 1922–1963.* Durham, NC: Duke University Press, 2002.

"The Battle of Birmingham." Birmingham, AL: Southern Negro Youth Congress, 1948.

Bell, Derrick. *Silent Covenants: Brown v. Board of Education and the Unfulfilled Hopes for Racial Reform*. New York: Oxford University Press, 2004.

Biondi, Martha. *To Stand and Fight: The Struggle for Civil Rights in Postwar New York*. Cambridge: Harvard University Press, 2003.

Borstelmann, Thomas. *The Cold War and the Color Line: American Race Relations in the Global Arena*. Cambridge: Harvard University Press, 2001.

Boyle, Sheila Tully, and Andrew Bunie. *Paul Robeson: The Years of Promise and Achievement*. Amherst, MA: University of Massachusetts Press, 2001.

Brown, Lloyd. "Lift Every Voice for Paul Robeson." New York: Freedom Associates, 1951.

Burnham, Louis. "Behind the Lynching of Emmett Louis Till." New York: Freedom Associates, 1955.

———. "Smash the Chains." New York: American Youth for Democracy, 1946.

Bynum, Thomas L. *NAACP Youth and the Fight for Black Freedom, 1936–1965*. Knoxville: University of Tennessee Press, 2013.

Carew, Joy Gleason. *Blacks, Reds, and Russians: Sojourners in Search of the Soviet Promise*. New Brunswick: Rutgers University Press, 2010.

Carmichael, Stokely. *Stokely Speaks: Black Power to Pan-Africanism*. New York: Random House, 1965.

Castledine, Jacqueline. *Cold War Progressives: Women's Interracial Organizing for Peace and Freedom*. Champaign: University of Illinois Press, 2012.

Cayton, Horace R., and George S. Mitchell. *Black Workers and the New Unions*. Chapel Hill: University of North Carolina Press, 1939.

Childress, Alice. *Like One of the Family: Conversations from a Domestic's Life*. Boston: Beacon, 1986.

Cobb, James C., and William Stueck, eds. *Globalization and the American South*. Athens: University of Georgia Press, 2005.

Cohen, Robert. *When the Old Left Was Young: Student Radicals and America's First Mass Student Movement, 1929–1941*. New York: Oxford University Press, 1993.

Commager, Henry Steele. *Freedom, Loyalty, Dissent*. New York: Oxford University Press, 1954.

Cooper Jackson, Esther. *This Is My Husband: Fighter for His People, Political Refugee*. Brooklyn, NY: National Committee to Defend Negro Leadership, 1953.

Cooper Jackson, Esther, with Constance Pohl, eds. *Freedomways Reader: Prophets in Their Own Country*. Boulder, CO: Westview, 2000.

Council on African Affairs. "Current Data Concerning Economic, Social, and Political Conditions in Certain African Colonial Territories." New York: Council on African Affairs, 1950.

———. For a New Africa: Proceedings of Conference on Africa, April 14, 1944. New York: Council on African Affairs, 1944.

———. "For Freedom and Peace: Address by Paul Robeson." New York: Council on African Affairs, 1949.

———. "The San Francisco Conference and the Colonial Issue." New York: Council on African Affairs, 1945.

———. "Seeing is Believing: Here is the Truth about the Color Bar, Land, Hunger, Poverty and Degradation, the Pass System, Labor Exploitation, Racial Oppression in South Africa." New York: Council on African Affairs, 1947.

Cruse, Harold. The Crisis of the Negro Intellectual from Its Origins to the Present. New York: William Morrow, 1967.

Dallek, Robert. The Lost Peace: Leadership in a Time of Horror and Hope, 1945–1953. New York: Harper Collins, 2010.

Davidson, Basil. The Black Man's Burden: Africa and the Curse of the Nation-State. New York: New York Times Books, 1992.

Denning, Michael. The Cultural Front: The Laboring of American Culture in the Twentieth Century. New York: Verso, 1996.

Dorinson, Joseph, and William Pencak, eds. Paul Robeson: Essays on His Life and Legacy. Jefferson, NC: MacFarland, 2002.

Draper, Theodore. American Communism and Soviet Russia. New York: Viking, 1960.

———. The Roots of American Communism. Chicago: Ivan R. Dee, 1957.

Duberman, Martin B. Paul Robeson: A Biography. New York: Ballantine Books, 1989.

Du Bois, W.E.B. The Autobiography of W.E.B. Du Bois: A Soliloquy on Viewing My Life from the Last Decade of Its First Century. 7th ed. New York: International Publishers, 1968.

———. "Behold the Land." Birmingham, AL: Southern Negro Youth Congress, 1946.

———. Black Reconstruction in America, 1860–1880. New York: Free Press, 1998.

———. Color and Democracy. New York: Harcourt, Brace, 1945.

———. Dark Princess: A Romance. Jackson: University Press of Mississippi, 1995.

———. Dusk of Dawn: An Essay toward an Autobiography of a Race Concept. 7th ed. New Brunswick: Transaction, 1997.

———. In Battle for Peace. New York: Masses and Mainstream, 1952.

———. The World and Africa. 8th ed. New York: International Publishers, 1972.

Dudziak, Mary. Cold War Civil Rights: Race and the Image of American Democracy. Princeton: Princeton University Press, 2000.

Elkins, Caroline. Imperial Reckoning: The Untold Story of Britain's Gulag in Kenya. New York: Holt, 2005.

Esedebe, P. Olisanwuche. *Pan-Africanism: The Idea and the Movement 1776–1991.* 2nd ed. Washington, DC: Howard University Press, 1994.

Farmer, James. *Lay Bare the Heart: An Autobiography of the Civil Rights Movement.* New York: Arbor House, 1985.

Foner, Philip, ed. *Paul Robeson Speaks.* New York: Brunner/Mazel, 1978. Reprint, New York: Citadel Books, 2002.

Foner, Philip, and Herbert Shapiro, eds. *American Communism and Black Americans: A Documentary History, 1930–1934.* Philadelphia: Temple University Press, 1991.

Freedom Archives. *Paul Robeson: Words Like Freedom.* San Francisco, 2008.

Freedomways. *Paul Robeson: The Great Forerunner.* New York: International Publishers, 1998.

Gaines, Kevin K. *African Americans in Ghana: Black Expatriates and the Civil Rights Era.* Chapel Hill: University of North Carolina Press, 2006.

Geiss, Imanuel. *The Pan-African Movement: A History of Pan-Africanism in America, Europe and Africa.* Translated by Ann Keep. New York: Africana Publishing, 1968.

Gellman, Erik S. *Death Blow to Jim Crow: The National Negro Congress and the Rise of Militant Civil Rights.* Chapel Hill: University of North Carolina Press, 2012.

Gilmore, Glenda Elizabeth. *Defying Dixie: The Radical Roots of Civil Rights.* New York: W. W. Norton, 2008.

Gore, Dayo F. *Radicalism at the Crossroads: African American Women Activists in the Cold War.* New York: New York University Press, 2011.

Gore, Dayo F., Jeanne Theoharris, and Komozi Woodard, eds. *Want to Start a Revolution? Radical Women in the Black Freedom Struggle.* New York: New York University Press, 2009.

Griffith, Barbara S. *The Crisis of American Labor: Operation Dixie and the Defeat of the CIO.* Philadelphia: Temple University Press, 1988.

Hansberry, Lorraine. Adapted by Robert Nemiroff. *To Be Young, Gifted and Black: An Informal Autobiography of Lorraine Hansberry.* New York: Signet Books, 1970.

Haywood, Harry. *Black Bolshevik: Autobiography of an Afro-American Communist.* Chicago: Liberator, 1978.

———. *Negro Liberation.* New York: International Publishers, 1948.

Heard, Alex. *The Eyes of Willie McGee: A Tragedy of Race, Sex, and Secrets in the Jim Crow South.* New York: Harper, 2010.

"History of the American Negro People." 2nd ed. New York: Worker's Bookshop, 1941.

Holsaert, Faith S., Martha Prescod Norman Noonan, Judy Richardson, Betty Garman Robinson, Jean Smith Young, and Dorothy M. Zellner, eds., *Hands* on the Freedom Plow: Personal Accounts by Women in SNCC. Champaign: University of Illinois Press, 2010.

Hooker, James R. Black Revolutionary: George Padmore's Path from Communism to Pan-Africanism. New York: Praeger, 1967.

Horne, Gerald. Black and Red: W.E.B. Du Bois and the Afro-American Response to the Cold War 1944–1963. Albany: State University of New York Press, 1986.

———. Communist Front? The Civil Rights Congress, 1946–1956. Cranbury, NJ: Associated University Presses, 1988.

———. Race Woman: The Lives of Shirley Graham Du Bois. New York: New York University Press, 2000.

———. Red Seas: Ferdinand Smith and Radical Black Sailors in the United States and Jamaica. New York: New York University Press, 2005.

Hughes, Cicero Alvin. "Toward a Black United Front: The National Negro Congress." PhD diss., Ohio University, 1982.

Hughes, Langston. I Wonder As I Wander. New York: Hill and Wang, 1993.

Hunton, Dorothy. Alphaeus Hunton: The Unsung Valiant. Privately published, 1986.

Hunton, W. Alphaeus. "Africa Fights for Freedom." New York: New Century, 1950.

———. Decision in Africa. New York: International Publishers, 1957.

———. "Resistance against Fascist Enslavement in South Africa." New York: New Century, 1953.

———. "Stop South Africa's Crimes." New York: Council on African Affairs, 1946.

Isserman, Maurice. Which Side Were You On? The American Communist Party during the Second World War. Middletown, CT: Wesleyan University Press, 1982.

Jackson, James E. "Mission to Mobile: An Investigation of Race Relations in the Shipyards of the Alabama Dry Dock and Shipbuilding Company." Birmingham, AL: Southern Negro Youth Congress, 1942.

———. "Our Battle for the Ballot." Birmingham, AL: Southern Negro Youth Congress, 1940.

James, C.L.R. A History of Pan-African Revolt. Washington, DC: Drum and Spear, 1969.

Kelley, Robin D. G. Freedom Dreams: The Black Radical Imagination. Boston: Beacon, 2002.

———. Hammer and Hoe: Alabama Communists during the Great Depression. Chapel Hill: University of North Carolina Press, 1990.

Klehr, Harvey, and John Earl Haynes. The American Communist Movement: Storming Heaven Itself. New York: Twayne, 1992.

Korstad, Robert Rodgers. Civil Rights Unionism: Tobacco Workers and the Struggle for Democracy in the Mid-Twentieth-Century South. Chapel Hill: University of North Carolina Press, 2003.

Lamphere, Lawrence. "Paul Robeson, *Freedom* Newspaper, and the Black Press." PhD diss., Boston College, 2003.

Layton, Azza Salama. *International Politics and Civil Rights in the United States, 1941–1960.* Cambridge: Cambridge University Press, 2000.

Lewis, David L. *W.E.B. Du Bois: Biography of a Race, 1868–1919.* New York: Henry Holt, 1993.

———. *W.E.B. Du Bois: The Fight for Equality and the American Century, 1919–1963.* New York: Henry Holt, 2000.

———, ed. *W.E.B. Du Bois: A Reader.* New York: Henry Holt, 1995.

Lewis, David L., Michael H. Nash, and Daniel J. Leab, eds. *Red Activists and Black Freedom: James and Esther Jackson and the Long Civil Rights Revolution.* New York: Routledge, 2010.

Lichtenstein, Nelson. *Labor's War at Home: The CIO in World War II.* Cambridge: Cambridge University Press, 1982.

Lieberman, Robbie, and Clarence Lang, eds. *Anticommunism and the African American Freedom Movement.* New York: Palgrave Macmillan, 2009.

Lipsitz, George. *Class and Culture in Cold War America: "A Rainbow at Midnight."* New York: Praeger, 1981.

Logan, Rayford W., ed. *What the Negro Wants.* Chapel Hill: University of North Carolina Press, 1944.

Lynch, Hollis R. *Black American Radicals and the Liberation of Africa: The Council on African Affairs, 1937–1955.* Ithaca, NY: Cornell University Africana Studies Research Center, 1978.

McWhorter, Diane. *Carry Me Home: Birmingham, Alabama, the Climactic Battle of the Civil Rights Revolution.* New York: Touchstone Books, 2001.

Meriwether, James H. *Proudly We Can Be Africans: Black Americans and Africa, 1935–1961.* Chapel Hill: University of North Carolina Press, 2002.

Mulzac, Hugh. *A Star to Steer By.* New York: International Publishers, 1963.

Myrdal, Gunnar. *An American Dilemma.* New York: Harper and Row, 1944. Reprint, New York: McGraw-Hill, 1964.

Naison, Mark. *Communists in Harlem during the Depression.* New York: Grove, 1983.

Naxos Audio Books. *Voices of Black America: Historical Recordings of Poetry, Humor, and Drama, 1908–1947.* Franklin, TN: Naxos Audio Books, 2002.

Nelson, Claire Nee. "Louise Thompson Patterson and the Southern Roots of the Popular Front." In *Women Shaping the South: Creating and Confronting Change.* Edited by Angela Boswell and Judith N. McArthur. Columbia: University of Missouri Press, 2006.

Nesbitt, Francis Njubi. *Race for Sanctions: African Americans against Apartheid, 1946–1994.* Bloomington: Indiana University Press, 2004.

New York State Communist Party. "The Negro Question: Outline and Study Guide." New York: New York State Communist Party, 1949.

Nkrumah, Kwame. *The Autobiography of Kwame Nkrumah.* 2nd ed. New York: International Publishers, 1972.

O'Reilly, Kenneth. *Black Americans: The F.B.I. Files.* New York: Carroll and Graf, 1994.

———. *Hoover and the Un-Americans.* Philadelphia: Temple University Press, 1983.

———. *Racial Matters.* New York: Free Press, 1989.

Ottanelli, Fraser M. *The Communist Party of the United States from the Depression to World War II.* New Brunswick, NJ: Rutgers University Press, 1991.

Padmore, George. *Africa and World Peace.* 1937. 2nd ed. London: Frank Cass, 1972.

———. *Pan-Africanism or Communism?* New York: Doubleday, 1971.

Painter, Nell Irvin. *The Narrative of Hosea Hudson: His Life as a Negro Communist.* Cambridge: Harvard University Press, 1979.

Patterson, William. *We Charge Genocide: The Crime of Government against the Negro People.* 2nd ed. New York: International Publishers, 1970.

———. *The Man Who Cried Genocide.* New York: International Publishers, 1971.

Perucci, Anthony Thomas. "Tonal Treason: Paul Robeson and the Politics of the Cold War." PhD diss., New York University, 2004.

Perucci, Tony. *Paul Robeson and the Cold War Performance Complex: Race, Madness, Activism.* Ann Arbor: University of Michigan Press, 2012.

Plummer, Brenda Gayle. *Rising Wind: Black Americans and U.S. Foreign Affairs 1935–1960.* Chapel Hill: University of North Carolina Press, 1996.

Rampersand, Arnold, ed. *The Collected Poems of Langston Hughes.* New York: Vintage Books, 1994.

Ransby, Barbara. *Eslanda: The Large and Unconventional Life of Mrs. Paul Robeson.* New Haven: Yale University Press, 2013.

Record, Wilson. *The Negro and the Communist Party.* Chapel Hill: University of North Carolina Press, 1951.

Richards, Johnetta G. "The Southern Negro Youth Congress: A History." PhD diss., University of Cincinnati, 1987.

Ring, Natalie J. *The Problem South: Region, Empire, and the New Liberal State, 1880–1930.* Athens: University of Georgia Press, 2012.

Rise, Eric W. *The Martinsville Seven: Race, Rape, and Capital Punishment.* Charlottesville: University of Virginia Press, 1995.

Robeson, Eslanda. *African Journey.* New York: John Day, 1945.

———. *Paul Robeson, Negro.* New York: Harper, 1930.

———. "What do the People of Africa Want?" New York: Council on African Affairs, 1945.

Robeson, Paul. *Here I Stand*. Boston: Beacon, 1988.

———."The Negro People and the Soviet Union." New York: New Century, 1950.

Robeson, Paul, Jr. *The Undiscovered Paul Robeson: An Artist's Journey, 1898–1939*. New York: John Wiley, 2001.

———. *The Undiscovered Paul Robeson: Quest for Freedom, 1939–1976*. New York: John Wiley, 2010.

Robeson, Susan. *The Whole World in His Hands: A Pictorial Biography of Paul Robeson*. Secaucus, NJ: Citadel, 1981.

Robinson, Cedric J. *Black Marxism: The Making of the Black Radical Tradition*. London: Zed, 1983.

Robinson, Jackie, with Alfred Duckett. *I Never Had It Made*. New York: G. P. Putnam, 1972.

Robinson, Randall. *Defending the Spirit: A Black Life in America*. New York: Plume, 1998.

Rolinson, Mary G. *Grassroots Garveyism: The Universal Negro Improvement Association in the Rural South, 1920–1927*. Chapel Hill: University of North Carolina Press, 2007.

Roman, Meredith L. *Opposing Jim Crow: African Americans and the Soviet Indictment of U.S. Racism, 1928–1937*. Lincoln: University of Nebraska Press, 2012.

Rosenman, Samuel I. *The Public Papers and Addresses of Franklin D. Roosevelt*. Vol. 10. New York: Harper, 1950.

Rosswurm, Steve, ed. *The CIO's Left-Led Unions*. New Brunswick, NJ: Rutgers University Press, 1992.

Saunders, Francis Stonor. *The Cultural Cold War: The CIA and the World of Arts and Letters*. New York: The New Press, 1999.

Scales, Junius Irving, and Richard Nickson. *Cause at Heart: A Former Communist Remembers*. Athens: University of Georgia Press, 1987.

Self, Robert O. *American Babylon: Race and the Struggle for Postwar Oakland*. Princeton: Princeton University Press, 2003.

Sherwood, Marika. *Claudia Jones: A Life in Exile*. London: Lawrence and Wishart Limited, 1999.

Singh, Nikhil Pal. *Black Is a Country: Race and the Unfinished Struggle for Democracy*. Cambridge: Harvard University Press, 2004.

———, ed. *Climbin' Jacob's Ladder: The Black Freedom Movement Writings of Jack O'Dell*. Berkeley: University of California Press, 2010.

Smethurst, James Edward. *The Black Arts Movement: Literary Nationalism in the 1960s and 1970s*. Chapel Hill: University of North Carolina Press, 2005.

Smith, Jon, and Deborah Cohn, eds. *Look Away: The U.S. South in New World Studies*. Durham: Duke University Press, 2004.

230 · Sources Consulted

Smith, Judith E. *Visions of Belonging: Family Stories, Popular Culture, and Postwar Democracy, 1940–1960*. New York: Columbia University Press, 2004.

Solomon, Mark. *The Cry Was Unity: Communists and African Americans, 1917–1936*. Jackson: University of Mississippi Press, 1998.

Stephens, Michelle Ann. *Black Empire: The Masculine Global Imaginary of Caribbean Intellectuals in the United States, 1914–1962*. Durham: Duke University Press, 2005.

Stewart, Jeffrey C., ed. *Paul Robeson: Artist and Citizen*. New Brunswick: Rutgers University Press, 1998.

Storrs, Landon. *The Second Red Scare and the Unmaking of the New Deal Left*. Princeton, NJ: Princeton University Press, 2012.

Streater, John Baxter. "The National Negro Congress: 1936–1947." PhD diss., University of Cincinnati, 1981.

Sugrue, Thomas J. *Sweet Land of Liberty: The Forgotten Struggle for Civil Rights in the North*. New York: Random House, 2008.

Swindall, Lindsey R. *The Politics of Paul Robeson's Othello*. Jackson: University Press of Mississippi, 2011.

Theoharris, Jeanne, and Komozi Woodard, eds. *Freedom North: Black Freedom Struggles Outside the South, 1940–1980*. New York: Palgrave Macmillan, 2003.

———, eds. *Groundwork: Local Black Freedom Movements in America*. New York: New York University Press, 2005.

Voices of Black America: Historical Recordings of Poetry, Humor and Drama, 1908–1947. Franklin, TN: Naxos Audio Books, 2002.

Von Eschen, Penny M. *Race against Empire: Black Americans and Anticolonialism, 1937–1957*. Ithaca, NY: Cornell University Press, 1997.

Wald, Alan M. *Trinity of Passion: The Literary Left and the Antifascist Crusade*. Chapel Hill: University of North Carolina Press, 2007.

Walters, Ron W. *Pan Africanism in the African Diaspora*. Detroit: Wayne State University Press, 1993.

Washburn, Patrick S. *The African American Newspaper: Voice of Freedom*. Evanston, IL: Northwestern University Press, 2006.

Washington, Mary Helen. "Alice Childress, Lorraine Hansberry, and Claudia Jones: Black Women Write the Popular Front." In *Left of the Color Line: Race, Radicalism and Twentieth-Century Literature of the United States*. Edited by Bill V. Mullen and James Smethurst. Chapel Hill: University of North Carolina Press, 2003.

Weigand, Kate. *Red Feminism: American Communism and the Making of Women's Liberation*. Baltimore: Johns Hopkins University Press, 2001.

Welch, Rebeccah. "Black Art and Activism in Postwar New York 1950–1965." PhD diss., New York University, 2002.

Westad, Odd Arne. *The Global Cold War: Third World Interventions and the Making of Our Times*. Cambridge: Cambridge University Press, 2005.

Woods, Jeff. *Black Struggle, Red Scare: Segregation and Anti-Communism in the South 1948–1968*. Baton Rouge: Louisiana State University Press, 2004.

Wright, Richard. *Black Power*. New York: Harper Perennial, 1995.

———. *The Color Curtain: A Report of the Bandung Conference*. New York: World Publishing, 1956. Reprint, Jackson, MS: Banner Books, 1994.

Yergan, Max. "Africa in the War." New York: Council on African Affairs, 1942.

———. "America's Stake in Colonial Freedom." In *Trust and Non Self Governing Territories, Papers and Proceedings of the Tenth Annual Conference of the Division of Social Sciences, the Graduate School, Howard University*. Edited by Merze Tate. Washington, DC: Howard University Press, 1948.

———. "The Communist Threat in Africa." In *Africa Today*. Edited by Charles Grove Haines. Baltimore: Johns Hopkins University Press, 1955.

———. "Democracy and the Negro People Today." Washington, DC: National Negro Congress, 1940.

———. "Gold and Poverty in South Africa." New York: International Industrial Relations Institute, 1938.

———. "A Petition to the United Nations on Behalf of 13 Million Oppressed Negro Citizens of the United States." New York: National Negro Congress, 1946.

Yergan, Max, and Paul Robeson. "The Negro and Justice." New York: The Citizens' Committee to Free Earl Browder, 1941.

Zieger, Robert H., ed. *Life and Labor in the New New South*. Gainesville: University Press of Florida, 2012.

Zinn, Howard. *A People's History of the United States, 1492–Present*. New York: Harper Collins, 2003.

Index

The letter *i* following a page number denotes an illustration.

Lindsey R. Swindall is teaching assistant professor at Stevens Institute of Technology in Hoboken, New Jersey. She is the author of *The Politics of Paul Robeson's Othello* and *Paul Robeson: A Life of Activism and Art*. Swindall works with actor Grant Cooper to dramatize themes from her biography of Paul Robeson for students, and she cofacilitates public discussions on race in America through the New Jersey Council for the Humanities' Public Scholars Project.

NEW PERSPECTIVES ON THE HISTORY OF THE SOUTH
Edited by John David Smith

"In the Country of the Enemy": The Civil War Reports of a Massachusetts Corporal, edited by William C. Harris (1999)

The Wild East: A Biography of the Great Smoky Mountains, by Margaret L. Brown (2000; first paperback edition, 2001)

Crime, Sexual Violence, and Clemency: Florida's Pardon Board and Penal System in the Progressive Era, by Vivien M. L. Miller (2000)

The New South's New Frontier: A Social History of Economic Development in Southwestern North Carolina, by Stephen Wallace Taylor (2001)

Redefining the Color Line: Black Activism in Little Rock, Arkansas, 1940–1970, by John A. Kirk (2002)

The Southern Dream of a Caribbean Empire, 1854–1861, by Robert E. May (2002)

Forging a Common Bond: Labor and Environmental Activism during the BASF Lockout, by Timothy J. Minchin (2003)

Dixie's Daughters: The United Daughters of the Confederacy and the Preservation of Confederate Culture, by Karen L. Cox (2003; first paperback edition, 2006; second paperback edition, 2018)

The Other War of 1812: The Patriot War and the American Invasion of Spanish East Florida, by James G. Cusick (2003)

"Lives Full of Struggle and Triumph": Southern Women, Their Institutions, and Their Communities, edited by Bruce L. Clayton and John A. Salmond (2003)

German-Speaking Officers in the U.S. Colored Troops, 1863–1867, by Martin W. Öfele (2004)

Southern Struggles: The Southern Labor Movement and the Civil Rights Struggle, by John A. Salmond (2004)

Radio and the Struggle for Civil Rights in the South, by Brian Ward (2004; first paperback edition, 2006)

Luther P. Jackson and a Life for Civil Rights, by Michael Dennis (2004)

Southern Ladies, New Women: Race, Region, and Clubwomen in South Carolina, 1890–1930, by Joan Marie Johnson (2004)

Fighting Against the Odds: A History of Southern Labor since World War II, by Timothy J. Minchin (2005; first paperback edition, 2006)

"Don't Sleep with Stevens!": The J. P. Stevens Campaign and the Struggle to Organize the South, 1963–80, by Timothy J. Minchin (2005)

"The Ticket to Freedom": The NAACP and the Struggle for Black Political Integration, by Manfred Berg (2005; first paperback edition, 2007)

"War Governor of the South": North Carolina's Zeb Vance in the Confederacy, by Joe A. Mobley (2005)

Planters' Progress: Modernizing Confederate Georgia, by Chad Morgan (2005)

The Officers of the CSS Shenandoah, by Angus Curry (2006)

The Rosenwald Schools of the American South, by Mary S. Hoffschwelle (2006; first paperback edition, 2014)

CPSIA information can be obtained
at www.ICGtesting.com
Printed in the USA
LVHW051730160919
631217LV00004B/282/P

9 780813 056340